GRANDMOTHER'S GARDEN

GRANDMOTHER'S GARDEN

The Old-Fashioned American Garden
1865–1915

MAY BRAWLEY HILL

HARRY N. ABRAMS, INC., PUBLISHERS

FOR B.

"Every botanizing old maid, male or female, knows plant names.
Every good nurseryman knows the plants. Only the artist and the genius
know how to blend these materials into pictures of abiding beauty."

Frank Waugh, *The Landscape Beautiful* (1910)

EDITOR: RUTH A. PELTASON

COPY EDITOR: ELLYN CHILDS ALLISON

DESIGNER: ANA ROGERS

RIGHTS AND REPRODUCTIONS: ROXANA MARCOCI

Page 2: Anne Millay Bremer. AN OLD FASHIONED GARDEN.
Oil on canvas, 20 x 24 in. Mills College Art Gallery, Oakland

Page 3: Kate Sanborn at "Breezy Meadows," Metcalf, Massachusetts.
In this photograph from Sanborn's Memories and Anecdotes *(1915), the writer wears*
a colonial-style dress for greeting visitors to her vine-covered eighteenth-century home.

Library of Congress Cataloging-in-Publication Data

Hill, May Brawley.
Grandmother's garden : the old-fashioned American garden,
1865–1915/May Brawley Hill.
p. cm.
Includes bibliographical references and index.
ISBN 0–8109–3389–6
1. Gardens, American—History. 2. Cottage gardens, American—History.
3. Landscape gardening—United States—History.
I. Title.
SB457.53.H55   1995
712'.0973'09034—dc20   94-49447
                                             CIP

Published in 1995 by Harry N. Abrams, Incorporated, New York
A Times Mirror Company

Printed and bound in Japan

CONTENTS

ACKNOWLEDGMENTS   6

INTRODUCTION   8

THE ROOTS OF GRANDMOTHER'S GARDEN   10

GRANDMOTHER'S GARDEN REDISCOVERED   26

AMERICAN SCENES AND COTTAGE GARDENS   42

RESCUING THE OLD PLACE   58

THE COLONIAL REVIVAL AND THE OLD-FASHIONED GARDEN   76

PAINTING GRANDMOTHER'S GARDEN   92

TWO AMERICAN COTTAGE GARDENS   110

THE ARTS AND CRAFTS MOVEMENT AND THE AMERICAN COTTAGE GARDEN   124

COTTAGE GARDENS FOR LABORERS AND SUBURBANITES   142

GRANDMOTHER'S GARDEN IN THE MIDDLE ATLANTIC AND SOUTH   162

GRANDMOTHER'S GARDEN ON THE FRONTIER   178

GRANDMOTHER'S GARDEN ON THE PACIFIC COAST   196

NOTES   214

SELECTED BIBLIOGRAPHY   220

INDEX   232

PHOTOGRAPH CREDITS   240

ACKNOWLEDGMENTS

In writing this book I found myself treading in the footsteps of William H. Gerdts who touched on the subject in *Down Garden Paths: The Floral Environment in American Art* (1983). Although Bill disclaims any floral expertise and prefers city streets to garden paths, I am indebted to him and his splendid library for documentation of many artists' gardens. More recently, Virginia Tuttle Clayton in "Reminiscence and Revival: the Old-Fashioned Garden 1890–1910" (*Antiques,* April 1990) focused on turn-of-the-century paintings of these gardens. Mac Griswold and Eleanor Weller in their staggering documentation of estate gardens from 1890 to 1940, *The Golden Age of American Gardens* (1992), included a few personal, old-fashioned gardens.

As a novice in the field of garden history, I owe a tremendous debt to those more knowledgeable who have shared their expertise personally or through their books and articles listed in the bibliography. Everyone in the museums, libraries, and historical societies across the country whom I contacted, both in person and by letter and telephone, was unfailingly helpful. Many went out of their way to suggest other possibilities for documentation when their own collections had nothing appropriate. Finally, I would like to thank all those who gave suggestions, leads, and encouragement, in particular my very patient family, my agent, Helen Pratt, and my editor, Ruth Peltason.

For Francine who is my idea of what a writer ought to be

with affection

Mac

Matilda Browne. IN VORHEES' GARDEN. 1914. Oil on canvas, 18 x 14 in. The Fine Arts Collection of
the Hartford Steam Boiler Inspection and Insurance Company, Connecticut
Browne was one of the few women artists to settle in Old Lyme.

INTRODUCTION

An immensely appealing garden, small in scale but generous in its planting, frequently appears in American paintings of the late nineteenth century with titles such as *Old Garden, The Old Fashioned Garden,* or *Grandmother's Garden.* As a historian of American art and a fledgling gardener eager to know more about "Grandmother's Garden," I looked into general surveys of garden history and drew a blank. In these histories, high Victorian bedding-out schemes of ribbon borders or carpet beds derived from English prototypes are succeeded at century's end by an eclectic assortment of "Italian," "French," or "English" style gardens. Garden historian William Howard Adams in *Nature Perfected* (1991), for example, writes that America lacked "an indigenous national gardening tradition or even a regional one" and detects in American gardens of the late nineteenth century only the influences of English writers William Robinson and Gertrude Jekyll and the English Arts and Crafts Movement. Since the painted gardens seemed nothing like English ones, I turned to American gardening books published after the Civil War, many written by women, and discovered that most either mention or describe at length the sort of garden I had seen in the paintings. Clearly, here was an American style of gardening waiting to be discovered.

In the world of American gardening, the fifty years between the Civil War and World War I were a time of tremendous ferment. Seed companies, nurseries, and horticultural professionals proliferated. Garden manuals were published by the score, horticultural societies abounded, and popular magazines, as well as specialized gardening ones, devoted space to gardens and garden design. Hundreds of new plants introduced from the Orient, Africa, and Central and South America, particularly tender annuals with brilliantly colored bloom and spectacular foliage, inspired new methods of laying out grounds and arranging flower beds.

America's approaching centennial of 1876 aroused keen interest in the nation's past, including early gardens. General-interest publications as well as gardening manuals and magazines began to promote an old-fashioned garden of hardy perennials, self-sown annuals, and native American plants based on imagined colonial gardens. The motives behind this patriotic alternative to labor-intensive bedding-out schemes and the newly introduced, foreign annuals they required paralleled a nativist inclination on the part of many writers and artists that reached its height in the 1890s.

By the 1890s, this old-style American garden—grandmother's garden—had been embraced by critics, novelists, popular historians, garden writers, and civic reformers who saw in the values, virtues, and gardens of pre-Revolutionary and Federal America a refuge from the social and economic upheavals of rampant industrialization, labor unrest, and massive immigration. Even professional horticulturists were not immune to nostalgia and its evocative power. Just as did the amateur gardeners, they used homey common names for the old-fashioned flowers, among them Johnny-jump-up, heartsease, and gillyflower, rather than their botanically correct ones, in their descriptions. By all accounts, grandmother's garden was usually arranged in rectangular beds bordered by planks, stones, or some low-growing plant, preferably dwarf box. The arrangement of the flowers within the beds was informal and exuberant, seemingly haphazard but often with a painterly feel for harmonies and contrasts of color, shape, and texture.

Women who made this informal, American garden saw there an escape not just from rigid ideas about gardening, but from the confines of their lives; their gardens became places where they could discover their own voices, create their own identities. Many went on to successful careers as garden writers, painters, photographers, and landscape designers. Others used these gardens as a focus of everyday activities, making them an integral part of a consciously crafted domestic life. For all of them, grandmother's garden offered a palpable connection both to their family's and the country's past that enriched the present.

Grandmother's garden was eagerly adopted by creative amateurs across the country, including many artists and crafts workers, taken as much with the aesthetic possibilities of an exuberant and informally planted garden of hardy flowers that could be maintained by one person as by its links to America's past. Early on, these links were based as much on collective memory and traditions as on solid research and documentation. By the 1890s, as the Revolution became part of a more distant past, seventeenth- and eighteenth-century garden manuals and plant lists began to be consulted, and photos and plans of early gardens published. Even so, a romantic haze as well as a cloud of fragrance hovered over grandmother's garden well into the twentieth century.

Like the gardens of England's coetaneous cottage gardening movement, these American gardens were for the most part creations of an upwardly mobile middle class seeking to affirm gentility. They were usually tucked into the restricted spaces of new suburbs and rural villages colonized by former city dwellers. In appearance and intent, they were distinct from both professionally designed estate gardens and gardens on working farms.

As the creations of the owners who planned, planted, and maintained them, these gardens form part of the vernacular garden heritage of the United States, which is just beginning to be studied. Like all such gardens, they were influenced as much by do-it-yourself manuals, nursery catalogues, magazine articles, novels, short stories, poetry, illustrations, and other manifestations of popular culture as by any serious study of garden literature on the part of their makers. Although the gardens themselves were ephemeral, many of the horticultural and aesthetic ideas embodied in grandmother's garden, as well as its potent associations with the past, linger still.

Beardsley Limner. MRS. HEZEKIAH BEARDSLEY. c. 1790. Oil on linen, 45 x 43 in. Yale University Art Gallery,
New Haven, Connecticut. Gift of Mrs. E. A. Giddings, great-great-great niece of the Beardsleys. (1952. 46. 2)
*Both the possibilities and limits of Mrs. Beardsley's life are defined in this portrait. The well-kept interior, the faithful dog,
and the basket of fruit attest to Mrs. Beardsley's sexually determined role as wife and homemaker. The limit of her sphere is
defined by the picket fence, which encloses the front dooryard garden with its central path and primly bordered flower beds.*

THE ROOTS OF
GRANDMOTHER'S GARDEN

All sorts of roots and herbes in gardens grow,

Parsnips, carrots, turnips, or what you'll sow,

Onions, melons, cucumbers, radishes,

Skirrets, beets, coleworts, and fair cabbages.

Here grow fine flowers many and mongst those,

The fair white lily and sweet fragrant rose.

William Bradford, "Descriptive and Historical
Account of New England in Verse"

EARLY AMERICAN GARDENS America's rich and varied garden heritage has grown from the resourceful accommodation of foreign ideas and exotic plants to American culture and native soil over four centuries. From the time of the earliest settlements, the history of our gardens can be read as a succession of glowing expectations foundering under the weight of climate, geography, and economic necessity to be reborn in new and particularly American gardening traditions.

The first settlers of Plymouth Colony in Massachusetts brought with them high hopes and English seeds. After the starving winter of 1620–21 when half the small company perished, native corn, pumpkins, and squash proved to be the colonists' salvation, for their initial planting of English wheat, barley, and peas had failed. A generation later, however, Governor William Bradford could write of the thriving gardens in verse that mentions flowers as well as food crops.

By 1672, when John Josselyn's *New England's Rarities* was published, flourishing gardens were filled not only with English vegetables and flowering herbs but with scores of American natives. Main-crop vegetables—corn, peas, pumpkins, and squash—were grown in the field, but the housewife was in sole charge of the garden next to the house, fenced to keep out wandering livestock. Here under her watchful eye and easily accessible were the plants she needed for making medicine, freshening air, repelling vermin and insects, brewing and baking, preparing and dyeing cloth, or flavoring foods and cordials. Here also she grew the savory vegetables and salad herbs that accompanied meals and those precious flowers that may have been planted simply for their beauty and fragrance.

These gardens had to be large enough to contain nearly a hundred plants commonly grown, with room for walks but otherwise no wasted space. For greatest efficiency they were probably laid out in rectangular beds bordered with planks, the plants being crowded in haphazardly as convenient, those harvested whole separated from those yielding blossoms or leaves. An edging of some low plant such as box, hyssop, pinks, or thrift would give finish to the beds and serve to keep the soil in place. Such gardens would have been simplified versions of those described in gardening manuals of the time such as William Lawson's *Contrie Housewife's Garden* (1617; reprinted together with his *A New Orchard and Garden* in several editions until 1683).[1]

This sort of garden combining herbs, vegetables, and flowers continued to be made well into the eighteenth century. Anne Grant (1755–1838), a Scotswoman who as a child lived with the Schuyler family in Upstate New York, described such gardens in Albany in her *Memoirs of an American Lady* (1808).

> Everyone in town and country had a garden, but all the more hardy plants grew in the field in rows. . . . Kidney beans, asparagus, celery, great variety of salads and sweet herbs, cucumbers, etc. were only admitted into the garden into which no foot of man intruded. . . . A woman in very easy circumstances, and abundantly gentle in form and manners, would sow and plant, and rake incessantly. These fair gardeners, too, were great florists: their emulation and solicitude in this pleasing employment did indeed produce "flowers worthy of Paradise." These though not set in "curious knots," were ranged in beds, the varieties of each kind by themselves; that, if not varied and elegant, was at least rich and gay.[2]

By the middle of the eighteenth century, kitchen gardens of herbs and tender vegetables were beginning to be separated from the pleasure garden reserved for flowers. In modest New England farmhouses the flower garden occupied the traditional position directly in front of the house under the parlor windows, enclosed by a fence and divided by a central walk leading from the door to the road. In more affluent establishments North and South, the flower garden might be placed to one side or perhaps occupy a series of terraces behind the house, with extensive kitchen gardens located farther away. It was still usual to arrange the flower garden symmetrically with paths dividing balanced beds.

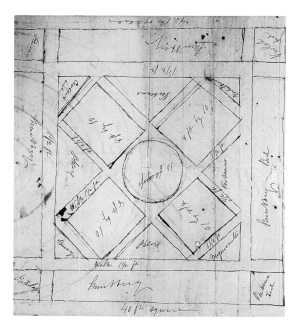

Plan of an ornamental flower bed after Lady Jean
Skipwith. n.d. Earl Gregg Swem Library, College
of William and Mary, Williamsburg, Virginia
*Lady Skipwith centered her plan for a 40-foot-square flower
garden on a circular bed flanked by rectangular and triangular ones,
all enclosed with flowering shrubs.*

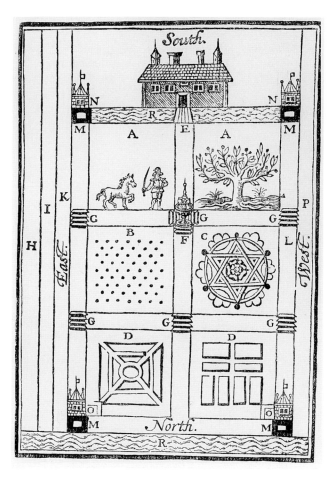

Plan of an orchard and garden from William Lawson,
A New Orchard and Garden (1618)
*Lawson's kitchen garden (D on his plan) was arranged in the geometric
beds that characterized American colonial gardens. Bordered beds like these,
filled with many of the fragrant herbs and flowers known to Lawson,
would reappear in grandmother's garden.*

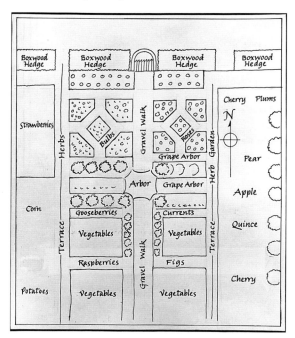

Plan of Benjamin Waller's garden in Williamsburg (after a
drawing by Luty Blow). c. 1807. Colonial Williamsburg
Foundation, Williamsburg, Virginia
*Gardens on large town lots often combined symmetrical, ornamental
flower beds with plots for vegetables and soft fruits. An arbor, a box
hedge, or a change in level would serve to separate them.*

An adventurous gardener in Mecklenburg County, Virginia, left a record of the flowers that might have been planted in such gardens. Jean Miller (1748–1826) married at forty Sir Peyton Skipwith and moved with him to a new plantation house, "Prestwould," where she pursued her great interest in native flowers and shrubs. Her surviving garden records from about 1790 to 1805 include plant lists, propagating instructions, and notes of bloom times taken from her own observations of indigenous and cultivated plants, among them those perennials and American natives that would appear in nineteenth-century cottage gardens.

Her list of "wild flowers in the garden" mentions dogtooth violet, bloodroot, celandine, fumitory, monkshood, moccasin flower, Claytonia, Solomon's seal, trillium, spiderwort, hound's-tongue, asters, violets, phlox, Dodecatheon, Ornithogalum, columbine, hepatica, and wild senna among others. On other lists appear fraxinella, candytuft, statice, anemone, hyacinth, narcissus, snowdrop, daffodil, lily of the valley, iris (four kinds), yellow and tawny day lilies, white lily, wallflower, sweet William, double and single pinks, hollyhocks, mallow, sunflowers, lupines, mignonette, stock, blackberry lily, hibiscus, rocket, perennial pea, sweet scabious, Martagon lily, rose (double and single yellow roses, marbled rose, and cabbage rose), purple and white lilac, white and yellow jasmines, honeysuckle, mock orange, double and common altheas, and Calycanthus. These were the proven flowers, shrubs, and vines. On another list she noted ruefully, "I once had a tolerable collection of annual and other flowers but the neglect of a few years had lost the greater part of them and only the most hardy and such as sow themselves now remain."[3]

The eighteenth-century pleasure garden reached its apogee in the southern plantations and northern country estates: "Middleton Place" near Charleston, South Carolina, with its formal parterres and elegant butterfly-shaped lake, begun in the 1740s; William Hamilton's estate of the 1780s near Philadelphia; and of course in Virginia, Thomas Jefferson's "Monticello" and George Washington's "Mount Vernon," the best-known landscape gardens in America where English naturalistic landscaping ideas found early expression. These splendid gardens, while venerated by those enamored of America's Revolutionary past, were too grand and too English to serve as models for most Americans. Even John Adams, who accompanied Jefferson on his 1786 tour of English estates, confided to his diary, "It will be long, I hope, before Ridings, Parks, Pleasure Grounds, Gardens and ornamented Farms grow so much in fashion in America."[4]

PRE–CIVIL WAR GARDENS By the end of the century, however, English ideas about landscape gardening and arrangement of flower beds did begin to influence even modest American gardens. Bernard McMahon's *The American Gardener's Calendar* (1806), the

Ralph Earle. HOUSES FRONTING NEW MILFORD GREEN. c. 1795. Oil on canvas, 48 x 54 1/8 in.
Wadsworth Atheneum, Hartford, Connecticut
In wealthy households like these in New Milford, the fenced flower garden was placed to the side or in the back
of the house and often included a pergola, arbor, or other ornamental structure.

first comprehensive book on horticulture for American climate and soil, followed the noted English landscape designer Humphrey Repton's principles in laying out grounds. Discarding formal beds and straight walks, McMahon advocated curved expanses of lawn bordered with flowers in beds of irregular shape with artfully placed clumps of trees through which the distant landscape could be viewed.

In England, John Claudius Loudon had adapted such landscape gardening ideas to smaller properties with the emphasis on gardening rather than on landscape. His "gardenesque" designs employing arabesque flower beds with shrubs and trees in irregular groupings became well known in America through his *Encyclopedia of Gardening* (1822) and the *Gardener's Magazine*. His American follower Andrew Jackson Downing's own immensely influential *A Treatise on the Theory and Practice*

Residence of Mrs. Cutting, Windham, New Hampshire. Photograph by Baldwin Coolidge, September 17, 1918
Even after 1900, conservative New England farmers maintained the enclosed front dooryard garden as a gesture of gentility on an otherwise utilitarian property.

Opposite: Andrew Warren. LONG ISLAND HOMESTEAD, STUDY FROM NATURE. 1859. Oil on wood, 12½ x 23⅞ in. National Museum of American Art, Smithsonian Institution, Washington, D.C.
On working farms like this, hollyhocks and sunflowers frequently shared space with cabbages in the vegetable patch.

of *Landscape Gardening Adapted to North America* (1841) and his magazine *The Horticulturist* (begun in 1845) were read with great attention by a burgeoning population with the means to build country residences and the desire to ornament them tastefully.

In his publications, Downing advocated curving paths and irregular groupings of trees and shrubs. The ornamental flower beds adjoining the house were to be dependent on intensive use of annuals and constant grooming, the aim being brilliance of effect. Downing advised those with modest cottages to use only lawn and trees.

Few publications addressed the needs of the gardener with limited space or income. The exception at mid-century was Walter Elder's *The Cottage Garden of America* (1848). Elder, assuming his audience to be the "intelligent cottager" who rented or owned his small home on less than an acre of land, was more concerned with the disposition of fruit trees and vegetables than flowers, although he advised placing a fenced flower garden behind the house.[5] At mid-century a "cottage" for Downing and other writers was a modest house in a rural or suburban location whose occupants, owners not tenants, were solidly middle class: farmers, businessmen, and professionals of various sorts.

By about 1850, Downing's ideas had become widespread throughout the affluent middle class, particularly in the new suburbs. At the same time, the enclosed front garden, which the well-to-do abandoned, had been adopted by farmers and village dwellers across the country. This arrangement could be seen not only in older houses on the East Coast such as that of John Blair in Brooklyn, New York, still very rural in the 1860s, but also in the Midwest and on the western frontier. When

Ernst Wagener, an original settler of Atlanta in San Joaquin County, California, was prosperous enough in 1860 to build himself a house, he designed a frame structure with its picket fence enclosing a dooryard garden.[6]

PAINTERS AND WRITERS CELEBRATE OUR NATIVE LAND A series of essays in *The Magazine of Horticulture* in the late 1850s had urged the use of native American plants and trees to ornament residences.[7] A similar patriotic interest led educated Americans to champion native literature and painting. At mid-century, artists and writers, consciously engaged in establishing an American culture and aesthetic distinct from that of Europe, turned to the American landscape and the wilderness experience for subjects.

In the spring of 1825, young artist Thomas Cole (1801–1848) had made a trip up the Hudson River; on his return, he exhibited three landscape paintings romantically portraying the wilderness he had visited that precipitated him into public notice. Through his example, landscape painting in America came to assume an importance and moral weight previously accorded only to history painting. Cole's untimely death at the age of forty-seven enshrined him as the father of America's distinctive landscape school. His house at Catskill, New York, with its exuberant cottage garden, became a place of pilgrimage for the next generation.

In 1843, John Ruskin had published in England the first volume of his *Modern Painters*, a book that had a profound effect on Cole's followers, the painters of the Hudson River School. Ruskin's requirement of specific natural fact, rather than the rules of art, as the basis for landscape painting was adopted wholeheartedly by all but the most conventional. Close views of nature—flowering branches against the sky, ferns in a forest glade, wild flowers seen from a worm's-eye view—began to appear in exhibitions. A group of radical young artists and writers organized themselves in 1863 into the Society for the Advancement of Truth in Art, a short-lived Pre-Raphaelite group dedicated to a Ruskinian vision of the American landscape. One of these, Charles Herbert Moore, settled in Catskill, where he painted a view of Thomas Cole's house and garden in 1868.

Writers also found compelling metaphors in the American wilderness and native plants. The wilderness became a protagonist in James Fenimore Cooper's series of Leatherstocking tales set in northern New York State and on the western prairies. William Cullen Bryant's most effective lyrics dealt with the vast landscape and native flowers of America. Henry Wadsworth Longfellow in his

Opposite: Charles Herbert Moore. THOMAS
COLE'S HOUSE. 1868. Oil on canvas,
6 x 9 ¼ in. Collection Edith Cole
Silberstein
*The residences of American writers and painters
such as Thomas Cole, the founder of the Hudson
River School, became pilgrimage spots and were
recorded in hundreds of sketches and paintings
by both amateurs and professionals. The Cole
family's informal perennial garden exemplifies
what was beginning to be called grandmother's
garden or the old-fashioned garden.*

William Cullen Bryant's garden, Cedar
Mere, Long Island. n.d. Glass slide.
Smithsonian Institution, Archives of
American Gardens, Washington, D.C.,
Garden Club of America Collection
*Bryant, like Longfellow, was a much-revered
writer whose house and garden became a shrine.
Mementos, in the form of plants, cuttings, or
seeds, of a visit to such a residence were cherished.*

verse narratives *The Song of Hiawatha* (1855), *The Courtship of Miles Standish* (1858), and *Paul Revere's Ride* (1861) gave heroic form to the American past. Longfellow himself lived in an eighteenth-century house in Cambridge, Massachusetts, that had been George Washington's headquarters during the winter of 1775. This house and traditional flower garden, arranged in box-bordered beds, became a pilgrimage site visited by thousands, even before Longfellow's death in 1882.

Ralph Waldo Emerson's first book was titled *Nature* (1836). For Emerson, the American landscape spoke directly to the intellect; divinity could be found in each natural fact. In his clarion call for independence, "The American Scholar" (1837), he exhorted, "We have listened too long to the courtly muses of Europe. . . . We will walk on our own feet, we will work with our own hands, we will speak our own minds."[8]

Poet Emily Dickinson (1830–1886) in her father's house in Amherst, Massachusetts, heeded Emerson's call. Emerson's beliefs that the great persons of the past were different only in degree rather than in kind from common humanity and that each person's conscious experience of the world had

J. B. Smith. THE RESIDENCE AND PROPERTY OF MR. JOHN BLAIR, "ROSE-DALE." 1865.
Watercolor on paper, 11 x 15 in. Collection David A. Schorsch Company, New York
*In Brooklyn, as elsewhere at mid-century, gentlemen's residences began to reflect the landscaping
ideas of Andrew Jackson Downing with lawns and artfully grouped trees, although the
flower garden still needed a fence to keep out free-ranging livestock.*

RESIDENCE OF ERNST WAGENER, ESQ., SAN JOAQUIN, CALIFORNIA. 1861. Watercolor,
pencil and ink on paper, 11 x 15 in. Collection Jeffrey H. Pressman, M.D.
*Wagener, a pioneer settler of San Joaquin County, California, stands proudly in front of
his frame house set off by a picket fence and flanked by an ornamental flower garden
that would have been heavily dependent on the windmill for water.*

universal application encouraged Dickinson in her solitary pursuit of poetry. Dickinson consciously refused a woman's role as that of a wife and deliberately contracted her already circumscribed domestic sphere; by doing so, however, she enlarged the circumference of her inner life to encompass the universal.

Emerson's idea that true poetry shapes its own form, growing organically from individual expression, legitimized Dickinson's radical transformation of syntax and language. She determined to "see—New Englandly," and her poetic voice is direct, often colloquial, with deceptively simple images drawn from the world immediately around her as well as from her wide reading in history, natural science, and theology. Emerson's comment in his essay "The Poet" that "the air should suffice for his inspiration, and he should be tipsy with water," prompted Dickinson's rejoinder, the poem "I taste a liquor never brewed":

Inebriate of Air—am I—
And debauchee of Dew—
Reeling through endless summer days—
From inns of Molten Blue—
When "Landlords" turn the drunken Bee
Out of the Foxglove's door—
When Butterflies—renounce their "drams"—
I shall but drink the more! [9]

EMILY DICKINSON'S FLOWERS AND GARDEN Dickinson used flower imagery frequently in her poems; roses are named most often; next the old-fashioned blossoms—primroses, gillyflowers, mignonette, sweet alyssum, peonies, sweet Williams, sweet peas, foxgloves, asters, lilies, Canterbury bells, pansies, and morning glories. More modest wild flowers appear in close-focus vignettes recalling paintings of the time. Arbutus and gentians received Dickinson's intense scrutiny as signposts of the seasons and for reflection on resurrection and death. The daisy often stood in for Dickinson herself.

As her surrogates, flowers from her garden and greenhouse frequently accompanied notes to friends. She greeted her mentor Thomas Wentworth Higginson with a stalk of day lilies when he first visited this unknown poet who had sent her enigmatic verses to his attention at the offices of the *Atlantic Monthly*. In the only known photograph of Dickinson, she holds a bunch of pansies (heartsease), the subject of an early poem.

Henry Wadsworth Longfellow's garden, Cambridge, Massachusetts. Photograph by Mabel Osgood Wright, n.d.
Longfellow's garden, dating from the 1840s, arranged in geometric, box-bordered beds, was included in Mabel Osgood Wright's The Garden, You and I *(1906) as an example of the old-fashioned garden.*

Below: Gardener Charles Frier in the garden at "Olana." Photograph by John Eberle, 1906
Landscape painter Frederic Church's grand home, "Olana," had equally grand landscaping in the natural style. There was, however, an informal perennial garden not unlike that found at the home of Cole, who had been Church's teacher.

Emily Dickinson. Daguerreotype, 1847 or 1848.
Robert Frost Library, Amherst College,
Massachusetts
In this, the only known photograph of Dickinson, the poet
holds the pansies or heartsease that she had addressed in an
early poem as "Dear, Old fashioned, little flower!"

Dear, Old fashioned, little flower!

Eden is old fashioned, too!

Birds are antiquated fellows!

Heaven does not change her blue.

Nor will I, little Heart's Ease—

Ever be induced to do! [10]

The Dickinson homestead, built in 1813 and still standing on Main Street in Amherst, in Dickinson's lifetime occupied fourteen acres enclosed by picket fence and hemlock hedge. The property included a vegetable garden, apple orchard and other fruit and ornamental trees, a barn for livestock, and open meadows. In 1855, Dickinson's father expanded the house to include a conservatory, Dickinson's special charge, as was the flower garden to the east of the house.

Although the dimensions and exact arrangement of her garden are uncertain, it is evident that it occupied an important place in her life and thoughts. She took pride in its lushness and span of bloom from March, when she began to count peony "noses," until the black frosts of November cut down the last of her gillyflowers. She seems to have been adventurous both in what she grew, including many wild flowers, and in her color combinations, delighting in yellow and the "imperial" purple. Judging from her niece's description of the garden as it was in the 1870s, it was informal in its planting with a profusion of scented, old-fashioned flowers—roses and honeysuckle on two arbors, self-sown flowers among the peonies and spring bulbs, humble annuals mixed with formal perennials, all "a meandering mass of bloom."[11]

THE HOME AND GARDEN OF HARRIET BEECHER STOWE If Emily Dickinson contracted her domestic sphere in order to live an intense interior life, Harriet Beecher Stowe (1811–1896) determined to expand the values of the home into public and political life. Her immensely influential novel *Uncle Tom's Cabin* (1852) was a powerful indictment of slavery, demonstrating its destruction of the home and family. She brought vivid descriptive powers to scenes of domestic life where home environment became as revealing of character as physiognomy or manner. Uncle Tom's cabin, kept neat as a pin by his wife, Chloe, a consummate cook, was draped with native vines and multiflora roses. Not surprisingly, it boasted an old-style dooryard garden, "where every summer strawberries, raspberries and a variety of fruits and vegetables flourished under careful tending. . . . Here also, in summer, various brilliant annuals such as marigolds, petunias, four-o'clocks, were the delight and pride of Aunt Chloe's heart."[12]

By mid-century, the home had become the focus of efforts to preserve the values of an earlier agricultural society rapidly disappearing in the face of industrialization and the growth of cities. In 1820, only 7 percent of the population lived in cities; by 1870 one quarter and by 1920 nearly half.[13] For Stowe and many other writers the home was vitally important as a moral guide; a simple cottage wreathed in vines surrounded by a well-kept garden and centered on a hearth presided over by the mother was as effective a moral force as a noble mansion.

Believing "the chief cause of women's disabilities and sufferings" to be that "women are not trained, as men are, for their particular duties," Stowe wrote with her sister Catherine Beecher *The American Woman's Home; or, Principles of Domestic Science* (1869), covering every branch of useful knowledge applicable to the home. In the chapter devoted to the "Care of Yards and Gardens," they followed Downing in recommending groups of trees with flower beds cut into the lawn, "made into the shape of cresents, ovals or other fanciful forms."[14]

Stowe herself gardened enthusiastically as a welcome escape from the constant need to publish to support her husband and seven children. When she wrote in 1865 that "architecture and landscape-gardening are arts every way suited to the genius of women," she had already explored both fields herself. In 1862, revenue from early best sellers enabled her to plan and build her ideal

Harriet Beecher Stowe seated in front of her Forest Street home, Hartford, Connecticut. Photograph, August 18, 1886
Visible in this photograph of Stowe's last home in the Nook Farm suburb are the flower borders beside the house
where sunflowers tower and the vines that were encouraged to drape the porch.

house in the suburban "Nook Farm" development in Hartford, Connecticut. Here she supervised construction and planned her garden, writing to a friend, "You should see the joy with which I gaze on manure heaps in which the eye of faith sees Delaware grapes and D'Angoulême pears, and all sorts of roses and posies."[15]

The house, with two-story conservatory, fountain, and Downingesque garden, proved ruinously expensive, but made her something of an expert on greenhouses. Samuel Clemens (Mark Twain), a later arrival at "Nook Farm," credited his semicircular conservatory to "a pattern invented by Miss Harriet Beecher Stowe, and adopted in most of the houses of her kindly neighbors."[16]

In 1873, the Stowes moved within "Nook Farm" to a modest gambrel-roof cottage, now open to the public. Here Stowe made an old-fashioned garden with trellised porches covered in vines and roses. Flower beds on either side of the path to the door were filled with a mix of annuals and perennials, including petunias, marigolds, zinnias, gillyflowers, sweet peas, lobelias, veronicas, and asters. A Wardian case of ferns occupied her bedroom, while her drawing room had windows hung with ivy instead of curtains.[17]

Hamilton Hamilton. GIRL WITH HOLLYHOCKS. c. 1885. Oil on canvas,
20 x 12 in. Private collection
Not only do the flesh tones of the young woman and the color of the hollyhocks correspond,
but the shape of the blossoms is echoed in the bell of her bonnet. This equivalence of woman
and flower was repeated endlessly in paintings of the 1880s and 1890s.

Grandmother's Garden Rediscovered

I've been back to grandmother's garden

Where the dear old flowers grow,

That she planted there and tended,

In the summers long ago—

The sweet, old-fashioned flowers

That used to delight her so.

Eben E. Rexford,
"Grandmother's Garden"

LADIES IN THE GARDEN In a series of "House and Home Papers" for *Atlantic Monthly* in 1864, Harriet Beecher Stowe urged women to relinquish their dependence on hired immigrant help for household chores. One article was bluntly titled, "The Lady Who Does Her Own Work." In the 1860s, feminists had begun to promulgate the radical idea that women were not by nature weak or delicate and ought to enjoy the physical health and abundant exercise that were expected of men.[1] The home and garden were culturally approved places for a woman to begin a physically active life.

Although there had been a succession of gardening manuals for women since the American reprinting of two English works, Louisa Johnson's *Every Lady Her Own Flower Gardener* (1832) and Mrs. Loudon's *Gardening for Ladies* (together with her *Ladies' Companion to the Flower Garden*, 1843), none had encouraged women to do the work themselves. Even Mrs. S. O. Johnson, who titled her manual *Every Woman Her Own Flower Gardener* (1871), assumed the aid of a "Pat O'Shovelem." For this writer, gardening was seen as an indication of gentility since "a beautiful garden, tastefully laid out, and well kept, is a certain evidence of taste, refinement and culture." Mrs. Johnson, who wrote under the pen name of Daisy Eyebright, recommended beds cut into the lawn and extolled the new,

Anna Bartlett Warner at the door of her home on Constitution Island, New York. Photograph c. 1890, Constitution Island Association, West Point, New York
Warner wrote what must be the most endearing, and is certainly the first, book devoted completely to the old-fashioned American garden, Gardening by Myself *(1872).*

brilliantly colored annuals as "the chief ornament of the flower garden." She did admit, however, to "a great fondness for the older annuals and hardy perennials which are now too often despised and neglected."[2]

Mrs. Johnson's manual was followed within a year by Anna Bartlett Warner's *Gardening by Myself* (1872), written for those like herself who did their own gardening. Warner's book fit comfortably within the long American tradition of testimonial self-help publications, such as Charles Barnard's *My Handkerchief Garden, Size 20 x 60 Feet; Results: A Garden, Fresh Vegetables, Exercise, Health and $20.49* (1869). Warner herself wrote a book of this sort, *Miss Tiller's Vegetable Garden and the Money She Made by It* (1873), reflecting her experience of running her garden as a business.

Anna Warner (1824–1915) and her older sister, Susan, had been forced to earn their own living when their widowed father lost his fortune in the Panic of 1837. They settled with him in the family's summer cottage on Constitution Island in the Hudson River, near Cold Spring, New York.

Susan became a popular author of inspirational books. Her first novel, *The Wide, Wide World* (1850), was surpassed only by *Uncle Tom's Cabin* as a best seller at home and abroad. Anna Warner wrote some two dozen novels, several biographies, and religious works, including the children's hymn "Jesus Loves Me," but it was her solitary experience gardening in the rocky and inhospitable soil of Constitution Island that led to her passionate advocacy of grandmother's garden in *Gardening by Myself.*

Anna Bartlett Warner's Old-Fashioned Garden

For dedicated, if impecunious, gardeners, Warner recommended the old-fashioned garden, "much talked against, much laughed at, by most people who have facilities. Yet for those who have not, it is after all often the best." Not only was an old-fashioned garden of informally planted hardy flowers easier to maintain than geometric beds and ribbon borders of annuals—and certainly more suited to an exacting climate—its subtle, sensual delights were also far superior. As Warner put it, "not trim shapes, and inlaid figures, and gorgeous masses of colour; but rich, soft mingled bloom, and tender tints, and wafts of nameless sweetness. . . ." For Warner, the informality of such a garden was a great part of its appeal:

> Fair, rich confusion is all the aim of an old-fashioned flower garden, and the greater the confusion, the richer. You want to come upon mignonette in unexpected places, and to find sprays of heliotrope in close consultation with your roses. . . . Sweet peas bow to phloxes here, and the gladiolus straightens itself with harmless pride among its more pliant companions, and the little white sweet alyssum goes visiting all the day. There is the most exquisite propriety and good fellowship, with utter absence of "deportment"; and the perennials that pass out of flower are kindly hid and merged by their blooming neighbors. . . . No stiffness, no ceremony—flowers, and not a garden—this is the beauty of the old style.

Such a garden was not without order. Warner advised, "Scatter your colours broadcast indeed, and yet with a certain thought and method; have plenty of tufts of pure green."[3]

Warner's own mixed beds of perennials and hardy annuals were arranged in clumps and drifts of harmonious colors, shapes, and textures for succession of bloom. She cautioned her readers:

> Keep always in mind the general effect as well as the individual display. . . . Notice even the style of leaf and growth, as well as the colour of the flower, in your arrange-

ment; let the soft feathery kinds have room to toss and wave their tresses, and the sturdier ones shew all the beauty of their strength in a tall background; and skillfully scatter those plants which bloom but once among those which are always in bloom, so that there may be no bare, flowerless places in your beds at any time.

In such a garden, variety and the charm of the unexpected played an important role. She cautioned, "Let the combinations be different. Do not have everything everywhere except, indeed, those few rare things, like roses, without which no combination is quite complete. But let there be a natural system of surprises in your garden."[4]

Warner's advice, drawn from thirty years of experience, was always practical since she believed that "in all gardening matters one must use plenty of common sense." Her planting was based firmly on cultural requirements as well as on aesthetic considerations. She advised her readers to do as she had done: "Try experiments with part of your flowers—experiments in grouping and bedding; proving their capabilities, and what suits your soil and climate and above all what suits *you;* and then keep a record of your experience." Above all, she urged her readers, "have all the old-fashioned beauties you can get and find room for."[5]

Most of Warner's flowers were the old-fashioned ones resonant with associations, chosen "for the scent of present fragrance and the perfume of olden times." She started many of her plants from seed or from cuttings; others were transplants from the wild or gifts from friends. That her readers might be equally independent of the nurseryman, she gave instructions for preparing seed beds and starting many different sorts of seeds, both indoors and out; for making cuttings and striking them; and for budding, grafting, and layering. Warner took great delight in using her Yankee ingenuity to improvise gardening tools, containers for seedlings and flowers, and garden ornaments, for she felt lack of means was a positive advantage: "If you have not the money to buy cheap statues— poor plaster figures of men and beasts—to set about your grounds, be thankful." The one purchased tool she depended on was a good, light spade, for she did her own digging and urged her readers to do the same.[6]

Years after the publication of *Gardening by Myself,* Warner still cultivated her garden. She reported proudly to a friend in 1896, "Even now, this 28th day of November, there are exquisite buds just opening out, in my flower borders . . . all through the summer I have had such lovely old fashioned bloom: Sweet Sultan, and scabious, and larkspur, and corn flowers; along with the more brilliant geraniums and other foreign beauties."[7]

Winslow Homer. IN THE GARDEN. 1874. Watercolor on paper, 9 1/6 x 6 11/16 in. Private collection
In the 1870s Homer frequently painted farm girls in the garden and fields, occasionally dressed in eighteenth-century costume.

THE AESTHETIC MOVEMENT AND GRANDMOTHER'S GARDEN Warner's reasons for preferring the old-fashioned garden of hardy flowers were aesthetic as well as practical. Such gardens provided an alternative to the bright, harsh colors and rigid shapes that had characterized aspects of decoration other than gardens in mid-century and still lingered in popular taste. Her "rich, soft, mingled bloom, and tender tints" and her informal arrangements would have been at home in the "Aesthetic" interior newly popular in both England and America.

International expositions, in London (1862), Paris (1867), and Philadelphia (the Centennial Exposition of 1876), had made the general public aware both of the new Aesthetic objects and of the Japanese decorative arts that were an important influence on them. It began to be conceded that objects in an interior did not have to match or even be in the same style, that arrangements of objects ought to be asymmetrical and informal, and that simplicity in decoration was not a bad thing, nor was a certain amount of controlled disorder. The sunflower and the lily, prominent in the old-fashioned garden, were adopted as emblems by the Aesthetic Movement on both sides of the Atlantic.

The change in taste occasioned by the Aesthetic Movement, together with the fascination with all things colonial generated by the centennial celebrations, combined in creating a new appreciation for native forms in both furniture and gardens. The influential critic Clarence Cook, whose articles on decoration for *Scribner's Monthly* were published as *The House Beautiful* (1878), felt that the increasing demand for colonial furniture was "one of the best signs of returning good taste in a community that has long been the victim to the whims and impositions of foreign fashions. . . . Things we come upon in our own country are soon at home in our houses, because they were used by our ancestors. . . . They neither look affected, nor strange, nor pretentious, but native and natural."[8]

The new idea that the home should express the owner's personality as much as his or her status or wealth found a reflection in the notion of the garden as an individual's aesthetic creation, rather than the work of a gardener following a predictable plan. Books advising individuals on both home decoration and gardening were much in demand. Ella Rodman Church (b. 1831), who wrote on both, revealed in *The Home Garden* (1881) a decided preference for the informal planting of flower beds. "The patterns usually given in works on horticulture are often more suitable for embroidery or mosaic-work. . . . A garden made in these principles has a bare, dreary look to the lover of nature, who longs for the old-fashioned arbors and arches covered with roses or clematis, honeysuckle and Virginia creeper." Church articulated the sentiments of many other sophisticated gardeners in the years following the Civil War when she wrote, "The old gardens stir within us a feeling which modern ones, with their stiff massing and 'blaze of color,' fail to excite."[9] Members of the educated middle class, early converts to the Aesthetic interior, were understandably receptive to the charms of the

Jeremiah Hardy. THE ARTIST'S ROSE GARDEN. 1855. Oil on canvas, 30 x 20 in. Colby College Art Museum, Waterville, Maine
Mrs. Hardy waters a patch of heartsease under an impossibly tall arbor covered with climbing roses in the Bangor, Maine, garden. This is the sort of genteel activity that ladies were expected to perform in the garden at mid-century.

old-fashioned garden. Artists, already attuned to the sources from which the Aesthetic Movement evolved, saw in the old-fashioned garden a new and appealing setting for figure painting.

THE GARDEN AS OUTDOOR PARLOR The spread of refinement in America downward from the mansions of the eighteenth century to modest village houses and rural cottages by the middle of the nineteenth century was manifest not only in the growing use of parlors set aside for formal entertainment but also in the importance of flower gardens as settings for leisure activity. The cult of gentility was embraced both by the affluent middle class and by those for whom real leisure was fleeting at best, such as the young farm women in Winslow Homer's watercolors of the 1870s. The wife of painter Jeremiah Hardy (1800–1888), shown watering pansies in her garden in Maine, was more typical of the well-dressed women who ornamented their outdoor

Fidelia Bridges. DAISY, LARKSPUR AND NASTURTIUM. c. 1880. Watercolor on paper, 12 x 9 in. Private collection
This watercolor of a tangle of blossoms depicted as they grow is typical both of the old-fashioned flowers in Bridges's garden and of her close-focus studies of the natural world.

Opposite: William Trost Richards. A SUMMER AFTERNOON IN A GARDEN IN PHILADELPHIA. 1859. Oil on canvas, 11½ x 14¾ in. Private collection
Nasturtiums climb the grape arbor beside hollyhocks in what may be the Richards's own garden.

parlors in hundreds of paintings and photographs from the 1860s onward.[10] In these years when a significant number of women began to forge careers for themselves outside the home, some still chose to be seen as ladies of leisure in the parlor and garden.

Painter and illustrator Fidelia Bridges (1834–1923), who cultivated by herself an extensive old-fashioned garden in Canaan, Connecticut (reportedly, she bent elegantly from the waist rather than kneel while weeding), appears in photographs of her garden dressed to receive guests. Bridges, like Warner brought up as a lady, had been forced on her own resources after the early death of her father, a sea captain from Salem, Massachusetts. Her first opportunity for serious study of painting occurred only in 1860, following six years as an unpaid helper for a cousin, in Brooklyn, New York. That year she traveled to the Pennsylvania Academy of the Fine Arts in Philadelphia for a series of

lectures given by landscape painter William Trost Richards (1833–1905). Richards, only a year older than Bridges, became her mentor; adopted as "Aunt Fidgy" by Richards's young family, she remained in Philadelphia for three years' study.

While still in Brooklyn, Bridges had become acquainted with contemporary art, including the English Pre-Raphaelite works featured in the 1857 "American Exhibition of British Art." Her reading of Ruskin's *Modern Painters* was reinforced by study with Richards, himself a follower of Ruskin's dictum to paint directly from nature, "rejecting nothing, selecting nothing and scorning nothing." Bridges's own early paintings were unconventional close-focus views of ferns or wild flowers painted in a high key with imperceptible brushwork.

At mid-century the restrictions encountered by a young woman who attempted to become

Fidelia Bridges. Carte de visite, c. 1865. Collection
George C. Lay
*Bridges posed in a photographer's studio for this portrait of herself
equipped for out-of-door landscape painting; she wears a shortened
skirt, bloomers, and sturdy boots.*

a professional artist were well-nigh insurmountable. As late as 1900, the consensus was still that,
"China painting and decorative art in general are the speciality of woman, who excels in the minor,
personal artistic impulses and in this way gives vent to her restricted life."[11] Unable to sell enough of
her exhibited paintings to support herself, in the 1870s Bridges turned to illustration, producing watercolors for cards, calendars, and gift books. In the 1880s, she became one of Louis Prang and Company's
permanent designers. Her new financial security allowed her to settle permanently in Canaan,
Connecticut.

ARTISTS' GARDENS OF   The garden Bridges created behind her cottage on the
THE 1870S AND 1880S   banks of the Blackberry River in Canaan was an uncon-
ventional one filled to overflowing with the hardy plants, both wild and cultivated, that she loved.
According to a visitor in 1901, "Never was a home more truly the projection of a personality. . . .

Rustic arbor in Fidelia Bridge's garden, Canaan, Connecticut. Photograph, c. 1900. Collection George C. Lay
The path to the seat under the apple tree is lined with irises and phlox and bordered with stones.

Below: Fidelia Bridges in her garden, Canaan, Connecticut. Photograph, c. 1900. Collection George C. Lay
The gardener is dwarfed by her very healthy phlox. There are hollyhocks in the left foreground and an arch formed of bent saplings surmounted by a birdhouse at the end of the path.

George Cochran Lambdin. AMONG THE ROSES. 1877. Oil on canvas, 20 x 14 in.
Collection Mr. and Mrs. John Hoerner
Lambdin believed that a young woman's flesh tones had exact equivalents in the hues of roses and he loved to juxtapose the two.
The Lambdin family's garden in Germantown, famous for its roses, served as the setting for many of his paintings.

George Cochran Lambdin. ROSES ON A WALL. 1874. Oil on canvas, 20¼ x 16½ in. Private collection
*Lambdin, like Fidelia Bridges, had studied with William Trost Richards. His out-of-door studies
evidence a close observation of flowers as they grow.*

Looking about upon its wealth of books and pictures, its rare old furniture and treasures from beyond the seas, one can understand in part the influences which have shaped Miss Bridges . . . but only in part, for not until you have followed her down the terrace back of her house and into her garden can you measure them in full."[12] Phlox and larkspur in great drifts were especially noted by this visitor. Iris was another favorite, ranging from bearded German ones to native blue flag and the *Iris Pseudacorus* which Bridges depicted in a watercolor of 1880, her first year in Canaan.

The garden was approached by a flight of wooden steps down from the terrace into a sea of flowers, backed by apple trees on one side and the river on the other. Meandering paths bisected the garden; one ended in a rustic seat, another in a trellis of interlaced poles meant for climbers, surmounted by a birdhouse. Other birdhouses were placed in trees to accommodate the models for many of Bridges's illustrations. A path through a wild-flower meadow along the river afforded a distant view of Canaan Mountain and was a favorite painting spot.

Fidelia Bridges's garden was as much an original vision as were her lovely watercolors; underlying both were a sensitivity to Japanese design and a passionate engagement with the natural world. Bridges's use of a worm's-eye view in her paintings made possible the viewer's intimate acquaintance with each plant. In her garden the narrow paths, the towering plants (she loved snakeroot and other aggressive natives), the seats and other viewing spots, encouraged a similar intimacy.

For other artists in the 1870s and 1880s, an interest in the newly fashionable Aesthetic interior as well as historic gardens often went hand in hand with the cultivation of an old-fashioned garden. Among these was George Cochran Lambdin (1830–1896) who, after study in Europe, returned to his family's home in Germantown, Pennsylvania. Here he established a reputation as a genre painter specializing in sentimental images of women and children. A visitor to his studio in Philadelphia's Baker Building remarked on its decor, which included Chinese and Japanese carvings, china, a Greek torso, ancient weapons, and old furniture. His opinion in matters of taste was highly regarded, and in 1885 he decorated the dining room of art patron Fairman Rogers's townhouse in properly Aesthetic style.[13]

Germantown was well known for its historic gardens and was a center for rose culture, particularly of the new hybrid tea roses that were all the rage in the early 1870s. The Lambdin family had a notable garden there that included many rose varieties, and on these George Lambdin became something of an expert. He was a founding member of the Germantown Horticultural Society and became its first secretary in 1873. In his article "The Charm of the Rose" for the *Art-Union Magazine* in 1884, Lambdin revealed his favorite rose to be 'La France,' chosen not just for its color but for its old-fashioned fragrance, "the very breath of summer."[14]

Lambdin's love of roses and his gardening experiences seem to have drawn him away from

Julia McEntee Dillon. THE ARTIST'S HOME AND STUDIO. n.d. Oil on board, 18 x 24 in.
Collection Jenkinstown Antiques, New Paltz, New York
Like many others who had old-fashioned gardens, Dillon was proud of her descent from early English and Dutch settlers.

figure painting to a concentration on the flowers themselves. His many paintings of roses include such Ruskinian images as *Roses on a Wall* (1874), executed in his garden, as well as more conventional arrangements of cut flowers.

Another flower painter, Julia McEntee Dillon (1834–1919), helped establish a garden club in her hometown of Kingston, New York. Her interest in gardens was antiquarian as well as painterly and horticultural. She wrote a pamphlet for the garden club, *Old Gardens of Kingston* (1915), that offered a nostalgic glimpse of Dutch and Huguenot gardens of the eighteenth century, including that of her own great-grandfather Christopher Tappen. The garden surrounding her old stone house was naturally an old-fashioned one, befitting a mainstay of the Kingston Daughters of the American Revolution.[15]

Worthington Whittredge. In the Garden. After 1880. Oil on canvas, 16¾ x 22 in. Private collection
Whittredge painted his two daughters in what may be the garden at his home in Summit, New Jersey.

American Scenes
and Cottage Gardens

Romance beside his unstrung lute

Lies stricken mute.

The old-time fire, the antique grace,

You will not find them anywhere.

Today we breathe a commonplace,

Polemic, scientific air:

We strip illusion of her veil;

We vivisect the nightingale

To probe the secret of his note.

Thomas Bailey Aldrich, "Realism"

PICTURESQUE VILLAGES AND LOCAL COLOR By the 1870s, the romantic taste for the sublime and untamed American wilderness painted by Thomas Cole, Frederic Edwin Church (1826–1900), and others of the Hudson River School had given way to a longing for the picturesque, for intimate landscapes that were domesticated and approachable, neither wild nor urban. Such views could be found in the two-volume *Picturesque America* (1874), edited by William Cullen Bryant, where cities were seen from a comfortable suburban distance. Increasing numbers of city dwellers moved out to such spots when railways and trolley lines made easy commutes to work possible.

Many books began to be written about former city folks in such locales, some of them comic, like Frederick S. Cozzens's *The Sparrowgrass Papers; or, Living in the Country* (1856). In a more reflective vein, prominent clergyman Henry Ward Beecher, brother of Harriet Beecher Stowe, in *Plain and Pleasant Talk about Fruits, Flowers, and Farming* (1859), inveighed against urban evils and praised the healthfulness of rural life. Anna Sophia Stephens's *The Old Homestead* (1855) was not unique in pointing

Thomas Bailey Aldrich's house and garden. Photograph by Talbot Aldrich, 1908. Patch Collection, Strawbery Banke, Portsmouth, New Hampshire
The colonial-style garden seen here, planted with the old-fashioned flowers mentioned in his poems, was made as a memorial to Aldrich.

Opposite: Eastman Johnson. OLD MOUNT VERNON. 1857. Oil on canvas, 12 ½ x 19 ½ in. Collection Fraunces Tavern Museum, New York
One of Johnson's first painting forays after his return from study in Europe was to "Mount Vernon," where he found Washington's home and gardens in disrepair. Their restoration by the Mount Vernon Ladies' Association began in 1859.

out the other side of the story—the destructive forces of city wealth and industrial growth on the rural economy, with agricultural laborers forced into factory work and once productive farms bought up as summer homes.

By the 1870s, villages near major cities were no longer rural, their inhabitants subject to many of the stresses of contemporary urban life, both physical and psychological. Charles Dudley Warner, who gardened in the "Nook Farm" suburb of Hartford, cast one of these quandaries in amusing vegetable terms in his *My Summer in the Garden* (1870). "Oh for the good old days when a strawberry was a strawberry and there was no perplexity about it. There are more berries now than churches and no one knows what to believe. . . . May heaven keep me to the old roots and herbs of my forefathers!"[1]

Among the writers who began to consider their own roots was poet Thomas Bailey Aldrich (1836–1907). Born in his grandfather's house in Portsmouth, New Hampshire, he returned there with his widowed mother to live in 1849. He wrote lovingly of eighteenth-century Portsmouth in *An Old Town by the Sea* (1874), in which he blamed the coming of the railroad for the erosion of old customs and the dilution of the New England character, and lamented that all over New England traces of the past were fading away. Aldrich's concern with the disappearance of old values and traditions had a less benign side. He blamed unregulated immigration both for labor unrest and loss of political power by old New England families. One of his best-known poems, "Unguarded Gates"

(1892), was written in support of government-established quotas for immigrants from southern and eastern Europe. In a letter at the time, he described it as a poem of "protest against America becoming the cesspool of Europe" and concluded, "I believe in America for the Americans."[2]

Aldrich's immensely popular *The Story of a Bad Boy* (1870) gave a realistic account of his school days in Portsmouth, when "certain bits of local color, certain half obsolete customs and scraps of the past" still lingered. The centerpiece of the story was his grandfather's late-eighteenth-century house, "a low-studded structure with a wide hall running through the middle . . . [and] large rooms wainscotted and rich in woodcarvings about mantlepieces and cornices." There was, of course, a garden covering a quarter of an acre between house and stables, with plum trees and gooseberry bushes that were, as Aldrich put it, "old settlers."[3] After his death, the house was preserved as a memorial to him. The garden was replanted using the old-fashioned flowers mentioned in his poems in an appropriately ancient design of four symmetrical beds flanking a central path backed by an arbor.

Many an artist, too, began looking back in nostalgia to an earlier, less complicated, and certainly more picturesque time, and began to seek out locales where earlier, typically American, ways of life as well as ancient houses survived. For a lover of such places, as an essay in *Picturesque America* pointed out, "the glare of the new enters like iron into his soul. But a fine bit of dilapidation, . . . old chimneys and old roofs, the dark grays and browns that form into such rich pictures in an old town, these things would be sure to catch his eye and delight his fancy."[4]

PAINTERS OF AMERICAN SCENES AND OLD-FASHIONED GARDENS

Following the Civil War, American artists had flocked to the ateliers and art schools of Europe. They returned not only with academic fluency of technique, but with a taste for European motifs. Their foreign ways were not kindly received in the nativist climate of the 1870s and 1880s, and most quickly adopted more typically American subject matter. Thomas Worthington Whittredge (1820–1910) spent ten years in Europe. On his return in 1859, he realized, "If I was to succeed I must produce something new which might claim to be inspired by my home surroundings." As well as traveling to the West seeking American subjects, he spent several summers in Newport, Rhode Island, drawn there because, as he put it, "it was the home of my forefathers."[5] In Newport he painted many of the old houses, including several with informal cottage gardens combining vegetables and flowers. His own house in Summit, New Jersey, to which he retired in 1880, seems to have had a similar old-fashioned garden.

Whittredge's good friend, genre painter Eastman Johnson (1824–1906), studied in both Düsseldorf and Paris. Back in America, he established his reputation with a succession of paintings showing rural families engaged in such quintessentially American tasks as cornhusking, maple sugaring, or cranberry gathering. One of the first paintings he executed on his return was of the neglected house and grounds of George Washington's "Mount Vernon," soon to be taken in hand by the Mount Vernon Ladies' Association.

Johnson began spending summers on Nantucket Island, Massachusetts, following his marriage in 1870. Fellow painter Will Low, who visited Nantucket in 1879, agreed with Johnson that "to be of one's time, to express a native sentiment in art, one should live in a characteristic native town in close touch with its life."[6] On Nantucket, both Low and Johnson found the American faces and unchanging rural activities they sought as subjects for their genre paintings. Here, Johnson also found an old walled garden filled with hollyhocks that was the setting for *Catching the Bee* (1873) and *Hollyhocks* (1876). These two paintings, together with several Nantucket interiors, depicted ladies at leisure, not as in other paintings of Johnson's, farm women engaged in rewarding work. The setting of an old-fashioned garden or middle-class parlor still demanded both genteel dress and deportment in paintings, as in photographs.

Eastman Johnson. HOLLYHOCKS. 1876. Oil on canvas, 25 x 31 in. New Britain Museum of American Art, Connecticut
The two girls wearing working clothes in the shadowy background of this painting look on in amusement at the posturings of the elegantly clad young women.

Thomas Moran in the garden, East Hampton. Photograph, c. 1915. The Guild Hall Museum, East Hampton, New York

Opposite: Theodore Wores. THOMAS MORAN'S HOUSE, EAST HAMPTON, LONG ISLAND. c. 1894. Oil on board, 9 x 12 in. Collection Drs. Ben and A. Jess Shenson
A wonderful variety of blossoms spills over and through the fence around Moran's garden, among them nasturtiums, meadowsweet, phlox, Maltese Cross, coneflower and hollyhocks. His Queen Anne—style house is wreathed in Virginia creeper and other vines.

East Hampton on Long Island, New York,— an ancient offshoot of the Massachusetts Bay Colony—was equally attractive to painters. As Elizabeth Champney (1850–1922), wife of painter James Wells Champney, wrote, "Nowhere on our coast can be found quainter houses and people. . . . Here are associations and legends, old manuscripts and romances for the antiquary, with Chippendale sideboards, blue China, and colonial spinning wheels for the collector."[7] In 1879, painter Thomas Moran (1837–1926) and his wife, Mary Nimmo Moran, an etcher, began to summer in East Hampton. In 1884 they built a house and studio in the Queen Anne Revival style with an old-fashioned garden, where riotous blossoms spilled over a picket fence.

Old-fashioned costume as well as old-fashioned gardens could indicate an affiliation with the values and virtues of a genteel past. Francis David Millet (1846–1912), a Harvard graduate whose family traced its roots back to 1633 in Massachusetts, exhibited in the Philadelphia Centennial Exposition his *Portrait of a Lady in a Costume of 1840.* Millet, like other artists of the 1870s, had been impressed by the colonial objects featured at the exposition, in particular the reconstruction of a "New England Farmer's Home and Kitchen," which demonstrated life in 1776.[8] Millet's studio in East Bridgewater, near Boston, incorporated an accurately reconstructed kitchen taken from a seventeenth-century house nearby that served as a background for his figure paintings of life in past times.

A number of painters began to make a speciality of such costume pieces. Among the earli-

est was George Henry Boughton, whose *Pilgrims Going to Church* of 1867 was often reproduced. The best known of these painters was Edward Lamson Henry (1841–1919), who specialized in both historical and contemporary genre paintings with rural settings. This sort of painting not only pleased the general public but was viewed with approbation by critics. As one wrote in 1895, "This is an art of which we cannot have too much, for nothing so strengthens national life, so nourishes patriotism as the revival in the popular imagination of these historic periods." Will Low inadvertently disclosed the xenophobia underlying such paintings in his memorial tribute to Henry: "There are few American artists who have better served their country in preserving for the future the quaint and provincial aspects of a life which has all but disappeared since we have become a melting pot for other races than our own."[9]

In the 1860s, while living and working in New York, Henry became friendly with illustrator Eliza Pratt Greatorex (1820–1897), an early collector of American antiques. Greatorex had begun to record in drawings neglected early Manhattan houses and their gardens, an invaluable historical resource that would be published in 1875 as *Old New York from the Bowery to Bloomingdale.* Under her

Sarah Orne Jewett in the garden.
Photograph, c. 1870
*Jewett's childhood home in South Berwick, Maine,
was next door to her grandfather's house and
old-fashioned garden. Such gardens would play
an important role in many of her stories.*

Opposite: Emily Tyson and Sarah Orne
Jewett at "Hamilton House." Photograph
by Elise Tyson Vaughan, 1905
*Jewett persuaded her friend Emily Tyson to buy
and restore the eighteenth-century "Hamilton
House" in South Berwick.*

tutelage, Henry became an equally avid antiquer. His collections of early clothing, furniture, cooking utensils, and farm implements served as models for the meticulously recorded details of his paintings.

Greatorex in 1881 bought an eighteenth-century farmhouse in the Shawangunk Mountains near Ellenville, New York, where she created a noted old-fashioned garden. Henry had first visited Cragsmoor, as the settlement came to be called, a few years earlier. He and his wife built a house there in 1883, incorporating architectural details salvaged from some of the early buildings recorded by Greatorex.

The area around Cragsmoor, the farms, country roads, and picturesque inhabitants, increasingly furnished the subject matter for Henry's immensely popular paintings. Typical is *News of the War of 1812* (1913), appealing not just as a nostalgic evocation of bygone times but as a beautifully painted study of garden flowers—some in the informal border along the house front and others nodding in the enclosed bed surrounding the wellhead in the background. Henry occasionally depicted his own house and sprawling, old-fashioned garden, mostly in small oil studies. These reveal a lilac walk, a tidy vegetable garden behind the house protected by hedge and arbor, and exuberantly planted flower beds lining a walk between the house and barn.

SARAH ORNE JEWETT'S GARDENS IN FICTION AND FACT After the Civil War, there was a marked change in what were considered appropriate subjects for literature as for art. Emerson and Dickinson had written of a higher reality, a transcendent realm behind the mundane. New authors of the 1870s and 1880s were preoccupied with the everyday experience of ordinary men and women, a shift from the sublime to the domestic, paralleling that in painting.

Both William Dean Howells, who followed Higginson as editor of the influential *Atlantic Monthly,* and Thomas Bailey Aldrich, his successor in the 1880s, sought realistic stories enlivened with local color and descriptions of vanishing folkways. Among their frequent contributors was Sarah Orne Jewett (1849–1909), who was born in her grandfather's handsome Georgian house in South Berwick, Maine, but who wrote about the fishermen, farmers, and villagers living in preindustrial backwaters along the Maine coast. It was as nostalgic chronicles of a rich and vanishing heritage that Aldrich chiefly valued her stories:

The few old-fashioned men and women—quaint, shrewd, and racy of the soil—
who linger in little, silvery-gray old homesteads strung along the New England roads
and by-ways will shortly cease to exist as a class, save in the record of . . . Sarah
Jewett or Mary Wilkins, on whose sympathetic page they have already taken to
themselves a remote air, an atmosphere of long-kept lavender and pennyroyal.[10]

Jewett's first book was a collection of stories reworked into a continuous narrative, *Deephaven*
(1877). In her next collection, *Country By-ways* (1881), appeared her often-quoted remark about old-
fashioned dooryard gardens.

People do not know what they lose when they make away with the reserve, the sep-
arateness, the sanctity of the front yard of their grandmothers. It is like writing down
the family secrets for anyone to read; it is like having your house in the middle of
the road. . . .[11]

Edward Lamson Henry. GARDEN AT CRAGSMOOR. After 1883. Oil on canvas, 9³/₄ x 13³/₄ in.
New York State Museum, Albany
*The vegetable garden behind Henry's house also included flowers, among them sunflowers and nasturtiums,
with goldenrod encouraged along the path to the barn.*

Opposite: Edward Lamson Henry painting Mrs. Henry. Photograph by Jessie Tarbox Beale, 1908.
Collection Kaycee Benton
*Henry's house incorporated details from eighteenth-century buildings, including the finial perched on the roof. Among
the garden ornaments were an elaborate birdhouse and the truncated stone column topped by a potted plant.*

Her masterwork, *The Country of the Pointed Firs* (1896), a novel, expands the parameters of local color narrative into an exploration of the profound connections possible between women and of a mythic order rooted in the same rocky New England coast that engendered Winslow Homer's powerful Prout's Neck, Maine, paintings. The novel is the deceptively simple account of a woman writer's summer spent in a Maine fishing village where she boards with a widow, Mrs. Todd, who initiates her into the domestic life of her family and friends and the larger rhythms of nature that underlay them. Many of these transactions take place in the guise of rituals associated with gardening or housekeeping.

Mrs. Todd is both monumental and deeply human, an herb woman linked to a mythic past through her dooryard garden where the flowers, "two or three gay hollyhocks and some London-pride," are relegated to the house wall. This is a working garden with:

> growths of a rustic pharmacopoeia, great treasure and rarities among the common-
> er herbs. There were some strange and pungent odors that roused a dim sense and
> remembrance of something in the forgotten past. Some of these might once have
> belonged to sacred and mystic rites.[12]

In the *Atlantic Monthly* (July 1869), Thomas Wentworth Higginson had published an article of his own on the Greek Goddesses, where he recognized in his own time a keen desire for the excluded feminine qualities in the sacred and poignantly concluded, "We toil among the dust and the rubbish waiting for the goddess and the shrine."[13] Jewett's response was to reveal the numinous in the person of Mrs. Todd and in the rhythms and ceremonies of domestic life in house and garden.

An old-fashioned garden was for Jewett a sign of continuity with the human past and of the possibility for deep human connection with others and with the natural world. In the short story "Martha's Lady," a garden of the 1840s could serve as setting and catalyst for a moment of profound understanding between the main characters. Martha's worth is revealed through her work in the garden, just as the soul of the garden is manifest in its color and fragrance:

> the large sunshiny garden, where the last of the red and white peonies and the gold-
> en lilies, and the first of the tall blue larkspurs lent their colors in generous fashion.
> The straight box borders were all in fresh and shining green of their new leaves, and
> there was a fragrance of the old garden's innermost life and soul blowing from the
> honeysuckle blossoms on a long trellis.[14]

"The old-fashioned gardens, Westboro, Massachusetts." Photograph to illustrate Mary E. Wilkins, *Evelina's Garden* (1898)
By 1900, everyone knew what was meant by the old-fashioned garden or grandmother's garden, thanks to popular writers
such as Mary Wilkins, as well as numerous articles in gardening and general-interest magazines.

Jewett grew up with such an old-fashioned garden, the front dooryard of her grandfather's house, described by an early biographer:

> It was a miracle in the spring when the yellow and white daffodils came into bloom. And later came the larkspur and the honeysuckle, Canterbury bells and London pride. A good many ladies' delights always grew under the bushes and sprang up anywhere in the chinks of the walk or the doorstep, and a little green sprig called ambrosia was a famous stray-away.

Significantly Jewett's first composition at age six was written on the old-fashioned roses growing there.[15]

When Jewett moved with her sister into her grandfather's house in 1887, they set about remaking the garden along self-consciously old-fashioned lines. According to residents' recollections:

> The trellised arborway leading from the back door was covered with honeysuckle
> blossoms; and the garden circumscribed by box. Mignonette and petunias, larkspur,
> snowberry bushes, hollyhocks, roses, peonies, and asters abounded.[16]

Jewett wrote an artist friend of the pictorial possibilities, "The garden is so nice—old-fashioned indeed
with pink hollyhocks and tall blue larkspurs. You might make a sketch with but slight trouble, with
figures of old ladies wearing caps in the long walks."[17]

Jewett's contemporary, writer Mary E. Wilkins (1852–1930), also centered several of her stories around old-fashioned flowers and grandmother's garden. In her collection *Understudies* (1901),
the personalities of the main characters of stories titled "Bouncing Bet," "Morning Glory," "Peony,"
and "Prince's Feather" echoed attributes associated with the flowers. In *Evalina's Garden* (1899), a
long story subsequently published as a book, the protagonist was a spectacular old-fashioned flower
garden cultivated over a period of fifty years by a lonely old maid. The garden was inherited by her
equally lonely niece who was forced to destroy the garden in order to achieve the wedded happiness
her aunt had been denied.

Although Jewett had regretted the disappearance of the traditional dooryard garden, she
welcomed the change in women's status implied by the dropping of such boundaries.

> The disappearance of many of the village front yards may come to be typical of the
> altered position of women. . . . She used to be shut off from the wide acres of the
> farm, and had no voice in the world's politics; she must stay in the house, or only
> hold sway out of doors in this prim corner of land where she was queen. The whole
> world is their front yard nowadays![18]

Jewett was perhaps overly optimistic in her assessment of women's improved position. As
late as 1892, books such as Emma Hewett's *Queen of the Home: Her Reign from Infancy to Age, from Attic
to Cellar,* advocating woman's continued confinement to the domestic sphere still appeared. In this
year Charlotte Perkins Gilman's autobiographical story of a woman's mental collapse as a result of
such confinement, "The Yellow Wallpaper," was published. Gilman saw in the "colonial mansion"
and its ancient garden with "those mysterious deepshaded arbors, the riotous old-fashioned flowers,
and bushes and gnarly trees" that provided the setting for the story, a telling metaphor for the very
real entrapment suffered by the heroine.[19]

Edward Lamson Henry. NEWS OF THE WAR OF 1812. 1913. Oil on canvas, 25½ x 42½ in. J. N. Bartfield Galleries, New York

Henry specialized in painting these nostalgic re-creations of life in the early nineteenth century. The enclosed garden seen beyond the house would have been recognized as grandmother's garden.

John Henry Hill. SUNNYSIDE WITH PICKNICKERS. 1878. Watercolor on paper, 19 ½ x 29 in.
Collection Historic Hudson Valley, Tarrytown, New York
The vernacular architecture of Washington Irving's picturesque home overlooking the Hudson River appealed to the same taste that appreciated grandmother's garden.

RESCUING THE OLD PLACE

The walks are hedged with dusky green of box,
That once enclosed long borders, trim and neat;
Within them stood great clumps of snowy phlox,
But now the phlox wild morning-glories seek . . .

The pale sweet-william, ringed with pink and white,
Grows yet within the damp shade of the wall;
And there the primrose stands, that as the night
Begins to gather, and the dews to fall,
Flings wide to circling moths her twisted buds,
And all the air her heavy fragrance floods . . .
A wedge of vivid blue the larkspur shines
From out the thorny heart of the sweetbriar,
And at its side are velvet brandy-wines,
Shadowed by honeysuckle's fringe of fire.
On the long grass, where still the drops of dew
Are threaded like a necklace for the dawn,
The flaming poppies their soft petals strew. . . .

Margaret Deland, "The Old Garden"

NOSTALGIA FOR THE PAST Those who had written about and cultivated old-fashioned gardens in the 1870s and 1880s could base their plantings and layouts on actual gardens remembered or still existing, often those of their own grandmothers. But by the 1890s, when all things colonial had become immensely popular, many of those who wanted to re-create an old-fashioned garden had to rely on published descriptions. Although more than two hundred arti-

George Ellwanger with Chinese peonies, Rochester, New York. Photograph, 1899. Ellwanger and Barry Collection,
Department of Rare Books and Special Collections, University of Rochester
*Ellwanger owned a noted nursery in Rochester and began his own garden there in 1867 with old-fashioned perennials,
an apple orchard underplanted with spring bulbs and beds of specimen plants.*

cles on colonial buildings were published in American magazines between 1876 and 1895, the first
full-length pieces on old-fashioned gardens did not begin to appear until the 1890s in the wake of
the 1893 World's Columbian Exposition in Chicago, where both colonial buildings and old-fashioned
gardens were featured. There had, however, been tantalizing glimpses in earlier gardening books.

George H. Ellwanger (1816–1906), a nurseryman who had established the Mount Hope
Botanic and Pomological Gardens in Rochester, New York, in 1840, wrote *The Garden's Story* (1889)
to give eager amateurs the benefit of his experience. Here he argued against both the stiff formal garden and carpet, or ribbon, beds, and was pleased to note that "the objectionable forms of gardening
are being superseded by a more natural style—a revival of the old-fashioned hardy flower borders,
masses of stately perennials." In such a garden, he felt, one should avoid "stiffness and rigidity of outline" and aim for "continuity of bloom—a luxuriance of blossom from early spring to late autumn."
He urged, "Plant permanently, mass boldly!"[1]

In a chapter, "The Summer Flowers," Ellwanger catalogued the sensual riches of an old-fashioned garden enclosed by its "prim box hedge":

I push open the wooden gate, to be greeted by the first snow-drops, the daffodils, the yellow crown-imperials, the grape hyacinths. I see the blue irises, the larkspurs, the bell-flowers, the bachelor-buttons, the monk's-hood. I note the big double white poppies, the clumps of sweet-clover, the drifts of snow-pinks, the white phloxes. I see the *Dielytras [Dicentra spectabilis]*, the sweet-williams, the tall, yellow tulips, the sword-grass and ribbon-grass and *Tradescantia*. I smell the sweet peas, the valerian, the madonna-lilies, the white and purple stocks. I inhale the breath of the lilies of the valley, the brier-rose, the white day-lily, and the purple wisteria twining about the porch. I see, too, the double-flowering rockets, the spotted tiger-lilies, the dahlias, the rows of hollyhocks and the phalanx of sunflowers.[2]

Ellwanger's own garden, begun in 1867 in Rochester, had something of this flavor, although as a nurseryman he could not resist a spectacular specimen plant strategically placed in the midst of the lawn.

Another notable horticulturist, Samuel Parsons, Jr. (1844–1923), Superintendent of Parks for New York City, sounded a clarion call for grandmother's garden in his *Landscape Gardening* (1891). Here he advocated a flower garden removed from the lawn, "a distinct and comfortable abode for flowers . . . and an old-fashioned one, if you choose to call it, of hardy perennials." He saw in the renewed demand for simple, single forms of common flowers rather than the "glittering novelties of the modern horticultural world" a promising sign of a change in gardening taste.[3]

Parsons devoted an entire chapter called "Grandmother's Garden" to a loving evocation of his own grandmother's garden in an old New England town. He felt that such a garden had great distinction. "The old garden behind grandmother's house . . . was, I confess, a somewhat formal and prim affair; but there was nothing commonplace or vulgar about it, as in the baser sort of what is now called ribbon gardening. On the contrary, there was a distinct flavor of individuality in the character of its appearance. . . . Unlike modern gardens created for external show alone, it was a real storehouse of color and odor." Abundance and informality of planting had characterized her garden: "The paths were laid out with entire regularity, and marked with long rows or borders of dwarf box; but there the regularity and sameness ceased." There were masses of the expected old-fashioned flowers—old roses, pinks, sweet Williams, phlox, larkspur, peonies, sweet peas, and hollyhocks along with spring bulbs—that "all stood together just as they happened to come behind the borders of box." There were also "nookeries of the pleasantest sort," such as "an old arbor festooned with grape-vine, honeysuckle and trumpet creeper."[4]

Parsons would have agreed with Anna Warner that lack of means was no disadvantage in making such a garden, declaring, "We can, I think, do it all the better if we are poor and have only

"Grandmother's Garden."
Photograph by T. C. Sandson,
c. 1900. Collection Rudy J.
Favretti
This properly riotous old-fashioned
garden includes a gardener in dress of the
1820s, but the fence that would have
enclosed both house and garden at that
time is missing.

half an acre." Washington Irving's Dutch Colonial cottage in Tarrytown, New York, was held up by Parsons as exemplary: "The repose, the dignity, the quaint simplicity and unconscious self-restraint of Sunnyside is my ideal of what a small place should be with grandmother's garden behind it." Size and extent were of no importance; what counted was an artist's eye in the arrangement of plants "in the most effective, harmonious, and pleasing way."[5]

GRANDMOTHER'S GARDEN FOR EARLY AMERICAN HOUSES

In the 1890s, influential publications such as the weekly *Garden and Forest* began to feature articles on old-fashioned gardens and old houses. In 1891, a series "How We Renewed an Old Place" by Mary Caroline Robbins (1842–1912) was run; the next year it was published as *The Rescue of an Old Place*. The Robbinses had chosen to settle in Hingham, Massachusetts, because they felt that in such a village traditional American values were preserved. As Robbins put it,

> The place to study the characteristics of a people is not among the very rich, but among those in moderate circumstances, . . . those who occupy its longer settled regions, and best represent its individual and continuous modes of thought. . . . Here can be found the American race at its best, unadulterated by foreign admixture, or perverted from its instincts by the pressure of conventions; a people that has lived on the soil for two hundred and fifty years and has had time to develop its characteristics.[6]

Cushing house, Hingham, Massachusetts. Photograph, before 1887
This is the ancient house bought by Mary Caroline Robbins and her husband, who were proud of being its first owners outside of the original family. Nonetheless, the Robbinses tore down the house while restoring and enlarging what remained of the garden.

The ancient house and garden they bought were in ruinous condition but had been in the same family from the beginning. Robbins made much of the fact that "we hold the first deed and paid the first money that was ever given for it," and confessed that "in this new country of ours, we yearn for stability, for tradition, for something to link us with the past."[7] Even so, the Robbinses elected to tear down the old house and build on a hill farther from the road.

Their gardening was equally pragmatic. Robbins wrote that by making use of native plants wherever possible, "our object has been partly to see what can be done without much money and with only a moderate amount of help." They transplanted trees and shrubs from the wild, then turned their attention to the waste of the garden where the old house had stood. Plants were freed of encroaching weeds and preserved for their links with the past as much as for their beauty. Although Robbins considered the flowers to be "simple and homely," she admitted that "their quaint familiar faces are more appealing than the far showier and splendid blooms of today. They must have family records of interest, these ladylike old blossoms."[8]

Among the plants Robbins mentioned were "dignified Narcissus," a "sweet June Honey-suckle" with "an old-time fragrance," a pink bridal rose that had "the very tint of soft color one sees in the cheek of an ancient maiden," clematis, prince's-feathers, lady's-delights, single hollyhocks, English violets, tulips, stars-of-Bethlehem, and crocuses. Other surviving roses were old-fashioned white and

blush-pink ones, damask rose, "a luxuriant 'Baltimore Belle'," and a single-flowered red rose. The
garden of course had box, its central feature: "the fine old Box arbor, which has grown up from a garden border until its stout trees are now six inches in diameter, and nearly ten feet high. . . . Here we
sit and look out upon the meadow and growing plants, and feel linked with the past by this memen-
to of those who loved this garden spot."[9]

Emboldened by such articles in garden and home periodicals, encouraged by fiction and self-
help books, many adventurous city dwellers began to buy and restore old homes and surround them
with appropriately old-fashioned gardens. Many of these sought out country as opposed to suburban locations. The young hero of J. P. Mowbray's *The Making of a Country Home* (1901) realized that
"there was a distinction, sharp and clear, between rural and rustic. Rural meaning country life that
does not relinquish the city, and rustic meaning country life that is independent of it, and doesn't
care much." This young man sought out the rustic where houses were "half hidden by old trees and
wearing heavy veils of Virginia creeper and wild trumpet-honeysuckle. Nearly always they were
enclosed by old gardens in which phlox and lady's slippers and tansy were conspicuously mixed."
The house he finally chose and laboriously restored had such a garden that included native flowers
and shrubs "picked up in the woods."[10]

Multitudes of abandoned New England farms tempted the impecunious with rustic allure.

One of whom, lecturer and journalist Kate Sanborn (1839–1917), in *Adopting an Abandoned Farm* (1891) and its sequel, *Abandoning an Adopted Farm* (1894), recounted her adventures with a rented place in rural Massachusetts. Sanborn's determination to "plant nothing but a few hardy flowers of the old-fashioned kind" soon gave way before the temptations of gardening. She admitted that "several long flower beds were one brilliant mass of bloom, while sun-flowers reared their golden heads the entire length of the farm." To the unprepossessing farmhouse, she added an ornamental piazza "gay with hanging baskets, vines . . . lanterns of all hues." Her attempts to spruce up the place were not understood by the less aesthetically sophisticated locals, who exclaimed on seeing the well-furnished porch, "It's a saloon!"[11]

The sequel amusingly recounted Sanborn's attempts to make the farm pay for itself by raising hens. The project and the farm were abandoned when Sanborn purchased an early-nineteenth-century house on seventy acres in Metcalf, Massachusetts. At "Breezy Meadows" she was content to wreathe the house in vines and let abundant wild flowers provide color. She did, however, become a serious farmer and could state in 1898, "My happiest hours are now those devoted to . . . agricultural enterprises—no longer a blue-stocking, but a full-fledged farmer!"[12]

THE OLD-FASHIONED GARDEN AS AN AMERICAN ART

American critics were beginning to recognize that gardening could be as much an art as painting or architecture—indeed, that it had a great deal in common with both those disciplines. In the 1890s, the aesthetics of the old-fashioned garden became as important as its antiquity and patriotic associations; aesthetic tastemakers as well as horticulturists and popular writers began to sing its praises.

Mariana Griswold Van Rensselaer (1851–1934), best known as an art critic and champion of the American renaissance in painting and the decorative arts, wrote on gardening in *Art Out-of-Doors: Hints on Good Taste in Gardening* (1893). Here she argued that gardening shared principles of "composition, color, lights and darks, and light and shadow" with landscape painting. Like Samuel Parsons, she felt the harmonious association of the plants was of first importance, but she gave equal weight to the accord of the garden with the site and the natural landscape. She concluded, "To be harmonious, and therefore beautiful, grounds over which we see the Berkshire Hills or the Valley of the Hudson must evidently be American gardens."

Van Rensselaer's insistence on national character—"We want American gardens, American landscapes, American parks and pleasuregrounds, not the features of those of a dozen different coun-

New York State garden, World's Columbian Exposition. Construction photograph, c. 1893 *This plot behind the Horticultural Building was planted by New York State as an example of an old-fashioned New York garden.*

tries huddled together"—led her to champion native plants. She was not entirely opposed to foreign introductions, admitting those "from lands with climates akin to our own," but felt that "to secure this local character, local plants are essential as a foundation." She admonished, "Did we appreciate the half of our treasury, we should see how little we really need Europe or Asia or Africa to help us furnish forth our works of landscape-art." Not surprisingly, Van Rensselaer viewed grandmother's garden as appropriately American. Although she felt a lawn was of first importance in laying out grounds, she advised those with limited space to give up a lawn and "arrange in front of the house an old-fashioned garden with as many beds and walks and box hedges as the space will allow."[13]

Van Rensselaer's book had been prompted in part by the extraordinary landscaping for the 1893 World's Columbian Exposition in Chicago. Designed by architect Daniel Burnham, the layout featured monumental buildings, wide boulevards, and profuse plantings originally planned by Frederick Law Olmsted, Jr. To the west of the Horticulture Building, New York State planted a 2,500-square-foot garden designed as "a model of an old-fashioned New York garden," with many plants brought from old gardens in the state. The *Report of the Board of General Managers* enthused, "Seldom, if ever, has there been such a collection of 'old-time' flowers seen together in so small a space." The description of the garden in the report is worth quoting in full.

Mignonette and marigolds nestled together; hollyhock and foxglove reared their rival spires of many colored blossoms over the monkshood and snapdragons, as they were wont to do against the old cottage door. Phloxes, larkspur and Jacob's ladder were there too with dusty miller, Joseph's coat and heartsease. The brilliant glow of zinnias, the old fuchsias and geraniums, the petunias, the verbenas, the sweet breath of heliotropes, reminded many a gray-haired visitor of other days. Columbines and Canterbury Bells too, were there. Old Fleur-de-lis guarded by bayonet-like foliage laughed at the nodding lilies, the day lily, tiger lily, St. Bruno's lily, plantain lily and lily-of-the-valley. Sweet William, wall flowers, polyanthus, primroses and auriculas [were] all cherished acquaintances of a floral past. There were sunflowers and poppies and sea pink. Indian pinks and old clove carnations vied with each other as of old. There were other old favorite garden flowers, some of them unknown to the present generation. This galaxy of every hue and color of delicious sweetness, garlanded as it were by climbing roses and golden honeysuckles, by clematis and nasturtiums, made a picture long to be remembered by the hundreds and thousands who saw and admired it.[14]

The Massachusetts State Building, a re-creation at the exposition of the demolished eighteenth-century Hancock house in Boston, was also given an old-fashioned garden praised by many visitors. A description of the Massachusetts building noted, "As in the old house, a raised terrace, with old-fashioned fence and well-stocked flower beds, added more than any one feature to the look of dignified repose that characterized the building."[15] The Chicago exposition not only popularized the colonial in architecture and the decorative arts, but transformed the old-fashioned garden from a New England phenomenon to a national one. Landscape architect Frank Waugh reflected years later on its lasting influence. "In spite of its short life, it was viewed by hundreds of thousands of people. . . . These men and women went home inspired with new ideas of beautiful things and a determination to make their own homes more orderly and artistic, their own grounds more beautiful."[16]

Charles Sprague Sargent could announce in *Garden and Forest* on July 17, 1895, "the taste for old-fashioned gardens is revived. There is a fresh call for the perennials and annuals which enlivened the borders of long ago, and those who are fortunate enough to still possess one of these old-time gardens show with pride the long-treasured plants which have bloomed for so many years." Sargent pointed out that there was perhaps more variety of plant material in old gardens than modern ones and followed with a lyrical description of many of the old-fashioned flowers. He felt that "the charm of those old gardens was in their wealth and tangle of bloom. . . . Stiff in outline they might be, but the rampant growth of well-tended shrubs and perennials hid all straight lines and carpeted the paths with falling petals." Above all, Sargent valued the distinctiveness of the old-fashioned garden, the personality revealed in its planting: "It is not one of many copies, but an expression, and

that is what the finest gardens must ever be. In them one should read something of the characteristics of the guiding intelligence which shaped them into being and lifted them from mere conventional toys into works of art."[17]

PAINTERS OF COLONIAL ARCHITECTURE AND OLD-FASHIONED GARDENS

The aesthetic appeal of the gardens, their range of color, variations in silhouette and mass, and abundance of foliage and blossom made them compelling motifs for American painters, particularly those who also appreciated colonial architecture. Some, like Abbott Fuller Graves (1859–1936), made a speciality of painting such houses and gardens. Early in his career in Boston, Graves had been a painter of floral still lifes. In 1895, after returning from Europe, he bought an eighteenth-century house in Kennebunkport, Maine, where

Abbott Fuller Graves. IN A KENNEBUNKPORT GARDEN. c. 1895. Oil on canvas, 24 x 30 in. Private collection
Graves made a speciality of painting ancient New England houses and their cottage gardens.

Opposite: Abbott Fuller Graves. GRANDMOTHER'S DOORWAY. c. 1900. Oil on canvas, 40⅛ x 50 in.
Strong Museum, Rochester, New York

he owned and restored dozens of others and was one of the founders of the Village Improvement Society.[18]

The architecture and inhabitants of the old town fascinated Graves and insinuated themselves into his paintings—at first, genre scenes of local gathering places, the post office or country store, and later views of colonial houses and old-fashioned gardens. Graves became identified with paintings of Georgian doorways wreathed in vines, or more modest Cape-Cod cottages with dooryard gardens. His *In a Kennebunkport Garden* (c.1895), with its brilliant Impressionist palette, captures the luxuriance of color and texture of the old-fashioned cottage garden and includes most of the elements that made these gardens so appealing—a profusion of flowers and flowering shrubs enclosed by a picket fence, its gate standing open in welcome, and the presence of the gardener actively at work.

Among the Kennebunkport residents whose gardens Graves is known to have painted was

Opposite: John Henry Twachtman. ON THE TERRACE. c. 1890–1900. Oil on canvas, 25 1/4 x 30 1/8 in. National Museum of American Art, Smithsonian Institution, Washington, D.C. Gift of John Gellatly
A path lined with phlox and terminating in a rose arch formed the main axis of Twachtman's old-fashioned garden on his farm near Greenwich, Connecticut.

Dorothy Weir in the garden. Photograph c. 1915
The Weir family's garden, entered through rustic gates wreathed in clematis and honeysuckle, included phlox, lilies, and other old-fashioned flowers.

poet and popular novelist Margaret Deland (1857–1945). Her first book had been a collection of poems named after the longest one, "The Old Garden," quoted in part at the beginning of this chapter. The book was published in 1886 and by 1890 it had gone through ten editions. The title poem may describe the garden of an eighteenth-century house in the Boston suburbs that Deland and her husband once rented, where "ancient box borders and ragged cinnamon rose bushes . . . outlined what was once a flower garden."[19]

Deland's serious gardening did not begin, however, until 1889, when she and her husband bought a cottage in Kennebunkport. The nondescript riverside Cape Cod was transformed by discreet piazzas and lookouts, and wreathed in Virginia creeper and honeysuckle. The garden, featured in *Country Life in America* (March 1909), relied on hardy flowers such as poppies, larkspur, and sweet alyssum, as Deland put it, "just those plants that will give me the greatest results with the least care." Her roses were "the old-time favorites" chosen for "fragrance and profusion of bloom." The seven

John Henry Twachtman. THE CABBAGE PATCH. 1894–95. Oil on canvas, 25 x 25 in. Private collection
Turk's-cap lilies and other flowers provide a dash of hot color in this brilliant study of green.

Childe Hassam. OLD HOUSE AND GARDEN, EAST HAMPTON. 1898. Oil on canvas, 24 x 30 in.
Collection Henry Art Gallery, Seattle, Washington
Hassam was one of many American painters attracted to the old houses and gardens of unspoiled villages like East Hampton.

narrow flower beds radiated from an inverted bell that formed an impromptu fountain and were backed by a rustic pergola covered in vines.[20]

Childe Hassam (1859–1935), a close friend of Graves's, likewise admired colonial architecture and summered in New England towns associated with the country's Revolutionary past, spending the summer of 1891 in Lexington and Concord, Massachusetts. Many of Hassam's paintings of the 1890s are of colonial houses occasionally enlivened with figures in period dress or with old-fashioned gardens. His fascination with the colonial past extended to his own ancestry; he called attention so often to his old New England family that he was given the nickname "Puritan."[21]

Hassam frequently visited his good friends John Henry Twachtman (1853–1902) and Julian Alden Weir (1852–1919) at their farms in Connecticut where they had found the intimate rural landscapes that they sought for their paintings. Twachtman's seventeen-acre farm near Greenwich, with its garden full of old-fashioned flowers, appeared in many of his paintings of the 1890s. Twachtman favored natives such as asters, goldenrod, and azaleas as well as the more expected perennials massed informally. His kitchen garden also included Turk's-cap lilies and other flowers seen in his oil painting *The Cabbage Patch* (1897–98).

The flower garden flanking Weir's studio on his Branchville farm, now open to the public, was begun in 1886 by his wife, Anna. Photographs of about 1915 show a fence-enclosed space entered through two rustic arbors covered in vines. Here were beds of peonies, phlox, iris, and other old-fashioned flowers separated by grass paths with a fountain circled by a box. The flower garden seldom appeared in Weir's work. He preferred to paint the pastoral landscape and farm buildings, adding floral accents as required whether existing in fact or not, a process he called "hollyhocking."[22]

Weir was not the only painter to indulge in "hollyhocking." A group of Boston Impressionists and avid gardeners, John Leslie Breck (1860–1899), Ross Turner (1847–1915), and Dwight Blaney (1865–1944), often painted old-fashioned gardens, frequently their own. Breck painted Blaney's house and garden on Ironbound Island, Maine, on a visit probably in 1896, filling the whole dooryard of the cottage with an unlikely profusion of giant poppies. Blaney himself used a photograph of his wife and a friend standing in front of the house, no flowers in evidence, as the basis for a painting where masses of phlox and towering hollyhocks loom behind the figures.[23]

John Leslie Breck. GARDEN, IRONBOUND ISLAND, MAINE. 1896. Oil on canvas, 18⅛ x 21⅞ in. Collection Daniel J. Terra
This lush garden belonged to painter and antique collector Dwight Blaney, a friend of Breck's.

Wallace Nutting's garden, Framingham, Massachusetts. n.d. Glass slide.
Smithsonian Institution, Archives of American Gardens, Washington, D.C.
Garden Club of America Collection
Nutting's own garden was the subject of more than one hundred of his hand-colored photographs offered for sale, including "An Old Fashioned Garden," "Colonial Primness," and "An Outdoor Parlor."

THE COLONIAL REVIVAL AND THE OLD-FASHIONED GARDEN

The pensile Lilacs still their favors throw.

The Star of lilies, plenteous long ago,

Waits on the summer dusk, and faileth not.

The legions of the grass in vain would blot

The spicy Box that marks the garden row.

Edith Thomas, (title unknown)

ALICE MORSE EARLE POPULARIZES THE OLD-FASHIONED GARDEN Historian Alice Morse Earle (1851–1911), whose career was made possible by the burgeoning Colonial Revival of the 1890s, effectively popularized all things colonial, including old-fashioned gardens and their flowers. Her first articles on colonial life appeared in 1891, the last in 1904, and in the interval she wrote sixteen books and more than thirty articles on colonial times and American antiques. Earle's passionate interest in what is now called material culture was fueled in part by a longing for continuity and status in an increasingly fluid and fragmented society.

Earle viewed social customs, household objects, and even ancient plants as carriers of values from an earlier time and as potent symbols of a way of life that was in danger of disappearing. Her preoccupation with the ancestry of plants as well as of people was a way of maintaining firm connections with an orderly and decorous past, when there was "the true dignity which comes from simplicity of living, simplicity in dress, in home furnishing, in hospitality, in all social and domestic relations."[1]

Earle's paean to grandmother's garden, "Old Time Flower Gardens," published in *Scribner's Magazine* (August 1896), was illustrated with her own drawings of surviving early gardens and their flowers. The article began with an enchanting description of a neighbor's garden in Worcester, Massachusetts, Earle's childhood home, "a garden which had been tended for over half a century." For Earle, one of the most appealing characteristics of such a garden was "the crowding abundance, the over-fullness of leaf, bud and blossom . . . the dull earth was covered with a tangle of ready-growing, self-sowing, lowly flowers, that filled every space left unoccupied by the statelier garden favorites." For Earle, "old-time gardens" were not just those of her grandparents' generation, but much earlier ones dating from before the Revolution. She consulted seventeenth- and eighteenth-century sources for her discussion of plants grown in early gardens and cited a 1760 Boston seed advertisement for its list of old-fashioned flowers revered because, as she put it, "we have no older inhabitants than these garden plants, they are old settlers."[2]

"Old Time Flower Gardens" was reprinted as the last chapter of Earle's vastly popular *Home Life in Colonial Days* (1898) which crossed the Atlantic, as did so many other American best sellers, to influence no less a personage than Gertrude Jekyll. In a letter of May 4, 1904, to one of her editors, Earle reported that "a letter today from Miss Gertrude Jekyll tells me she has sent to me her latest (a very new) book—Old Surrey Life—It is modelled—she writes me—upon my Home Life in Colonial Days. She is a cordial friend—and I may say in delighted vanity—my admirer. In that it is mutual. She writes me that the book has illustrations, many of which are precisely like mine."[3]

Earle had probably read Jekyll's first two books, *Wood and Garden* (1899) and *Home and Garden* (1900), when she began to write her comprehensive *Old Time Gardens* (1901), for she refers to Jekyll several times, twice to agree with her abhorrence of magenta. It was not the color of flowers, however, but their antiquity and familial associations that interested Earle. She rhapsodized, "When I see one of the old English flowers grown of those days, blooming now in my garden, from an unbroken chain of blossom to seed of nearly three centuries, I thank the flower for all that its forebears did to comfort my forebears, and I cherish it with added tenderness."[4]

Old Time Gardens was illustrated with 204 photographs of nearly sixty individual gardens, most in New England and the Middle Atlantic states, and an equal number of individual plants. Some of the photographs were taken by Earle's sister, Frances Clary Morse. Very few of the gardens illustrated dated to colonial times, but many belonged to the early nineteenth century, when box borders and geometric beds were beginning to be common; others were more recent creations, self-consciously old-fashioned. As Earle admitted, "Sylvester Manor" on Shelter Island and Van Cortlandt Manor, Croton-on-Hudson, New York, were among the few gardens in America that could really be called colonial.

Prominent in many of the garden photographs were borders of box, which for Earle indicated not only a garden's antiquity but the colonial lineage of the garden's owner: "The unique aroma

The garden of Edwin A. Fawcett, Worcester, Massachusetts. Photograph by Frances Clary Morse from Alice Morse Earle, *Old Time Gardens* (1901)
According to Alice Morse Earle, the garden's box-bordered beds were filled with Canterbury bells, lady's-delight, pinks, sweet William, phlox, stock, dame's rocket, evening primrose, and other fragrant flowers.

Left: The garden of Frances Clary Morse, Worcester, Massachusetts. Photograph by Frances Clary Morse, c. 1900. Collection Donald John Post, Jr.
Alice Morse Earle's sister, Frances Morse, lived in the family house and cultivated the old garden there. The photograph is inscribed, "The door leads down to the path through the old fashioned garden."

"Van Cortlandt Manor," bordered flower beds near the house. Photograph, c. 1910. Collection Historic Hudson Valley, Tarrytown, New York
These turf-bordered beds, laid out by Pierre Van Cortlandt III in the 1840s, were meant to be enjoyed from the porch.

Opposite: "Van Cortlandt Manor," rose walk and sundial. Photograph, c. 1910
The "Van Cortlandt" garden was begun in the mid-1700s when the long walk, seen here planted with roses, was laid out. The rustic garden house and sundial were nineteenth-century additions.

of the Box . . . is a hereditary memory half-known by many, but fixed in its intensity by those of New England birth and descent, true children of the Puritans." Another such horticultural class-marker was the peony: "Fine peony plants in an old garden are a pretty good indication of the residence of what Dr. [Oliver Wendell] Holmes called New England brahmins. . . ." In fact, for Earle, the persistence of old-fashioned flowers testified not only to their own long pedigree, but to that of the gardens and their owners; they were "true representatives of old families."[5]

In all of the gardens Earle discussed, hardy perennials were the mainstays, as they were in the garden Earle's parents had established in Worcester. Here there were no disturbing immigrants. "In our garden the same flowers shoulder each other comfortably and crowd each other a little year after year. They look, my sister says, like long-established neighbors, like old family friends, not as if they had just 'moved in' and didn't know each other's names and faces." The garden's plan was that of so many others made in the years before the Civil War: a path leading from house to barn or stable flanked by flower beds, with beds for especially fragrant or valued flowers next to the house, and fruit trees along the back boundary. There was a hierarchy among the garden spaces and the flowers contained in them, just as there was in the rooms of the house. Pride of place was given to the parlor and the parlor flower garden, whether it was located directly in front of or to the side of the house. Flowers of doubtful lineage, annuals, and "sunflowers and other plants of no social position" were relegated to the area of the barn![6]

Earle's own garden at her Brooklyn, New York, brownstone had a few of the old favorites,

but she felt that in a limited garden space "grass room under our feet, with flowering vines on the surrounding walls are better than many crowded flower borders." She confessed that she once made the mistake of planting portulaca, "not a flower of colonial days; I am glad to learn that our great-grandmothers were not pestered with it."[7]

OLD GARDENS PRESERVED AND RESTORED By 1900, many old gardens, whether pre-Revolutionary or merely pre–Civil War, were beginning to be known and published in popular magazines. Two years before *Old Time Gardens* came out, landscape architect Arthur A. Shurtleff's article "Some Old New England Gardens" appeared in *New England Magazine.* As did Earle, Shurtleff equated the ancestry of the gardens with that of the owners. "In some of the quiet towns of New England which were once the homes of persons of comfortable means, there are . . . families who cling to old things because they like them." One of the three unnamed gardens he discussed was the "Osgood-Brockway House" garden in Newburyport,

The Verplank garden at "Mount Gulian," Fishkill, New York. *Virginia Verplank described the early-nineteenth-century garden that had been her charge since 1885 and included this photograph in* A Year in My Garden *(1909). The garden was bisected by a walk with box-edged beds of fraxinella, lemon lilies, old roses, and spring bulbs on one side and a long peony border on the other.*

Massachusetts, identifiable through its plan. He considered it "a type of the old-fashioned garden" containing "old-fashioned flowers of all kinds" with the obligatory box edgings and an arbor.[8] This garden, like so many others that served as exemplars of the old-fashioned garden, in plan dated to the early nineteenth century.

A Newburyport garden of similar date and plan was described in the March 1907 issue of *Country Life in America,* which was devoted entirely to "Old-Fashioned Gardens." The garden of "Lorenzo" in Cazenovia, New York, dating to about 1810, had been published in the November 1902 issue. The "John Cotton Smith House" garden in Sharon, Connecticut—its layout dating to just after the Revolution—was described in *Century Magazine* (May 1906).[9]

The increasing awareness of America's garden heritage facilitated the public acquisition and preservation of some of these old gardens. In 1891, naturalist John Bartram's early-eighteenth-century garden in Philadelphia, the oldest botanical garden in America, was bought and preserved by the city. The "Moffatt-Ladd House" garden, Portsmouth, New Hampshire—in its present form dating to the 1840s—was acquired by the National Society of the Colonial Dames in 1912. Other gardens were privately preserved by descendants of the original owners as was the early-nineteenth-century garden at "Mount Gulian," Fishkill, New York.

America's historic-preservation movement, begun in mid-century and given a boost by the centennial celebrations, had gathered considerable momentum by 1900. Enthusiastic amateurs who restored, documented, and maintained their own early houses and gardens and who used their new expertise in work on more public projects were in the forefront of the movement. The preservation of historic homes and gardens was seen as an endeavor particularly appropriate for women, at least until the professionalization that characterized so many other fields at the time overtook historic preservation as well and university-trained men assumed a leading role.

Early New England towns that had been the locus of artists' pilgrimages, tourist itineraries, and summer homes became sites of preservation efforts. York, Maine, settled in 1652, attracted two New York women, Mrs. Newton Perkins and her daughter Elizabeth (1879–1952), who bought the oldest house there in 1898. They expanded the simple four-room structure into a Colonial Revival showplace and reestablished a flower garden of native and old-fashioned flowers.

Mrs. Perkins was estranged from her husband and Elizabeth never married. The restoration and furnishing of their house, the creation of an appropriate garden, and leadership in restoration efforts were central in their lives. Elizabeth Perkins's documentation of the house and garden involved not only research into their history but also the creation of a photographic record of them. Their house and garden in order, the Perkinses turned their attention to the preservation of York's colonial past. Mrs. Perkins led the drive to acquire the Old Gaol as a museum in 1899 and Elizabeth became a charter member of the York Historical and Improvement Society and, a year later, its director.[10]

The restoration of the 1787 "Hamilton House" in nearby South Berwick, Maine, was instigated by Sarah Orne Jewett, who persuaded two Boston friends, Mrs. George Tyson and her stepdaughter Elizabeth, to purchase it in 1898 as a summer home. Jewett had always loved the house, which she used as the setting for a romance set in Revolutionary times, *The Tory Lover* (1901), and probably advised on its restoration. The Tysons added two wings to the house and designed an appropriate old-fashioned garden, which acquired an Italian accent following their tour of Italy in 1905 and further evolved over the years of Elizabeth Tyson Vaughn's ownership.

In 1910, when garden writer Hildegard Hawthorne visited there, the main garden was complete. Hawthorne's article for *Century Magazine*, "A Garden of Romance," began with a description of the formal garden to the east of the house, enclosed on three sides by vine-covered arbors and divided into four beds centered on a sundial. "Most romantic is the outlook over the enclosed garden from which rises a perfume of flowers. . . . Narrow grass paths separate the long beds crowded with flowers, the brilliant colors of which seem unstudied, and the arrangement so easy and withall so sure . . . with iris, rose, delphinium, country pinks, Canterbury bells, spotted lilies, heliotrope, sweet alyssum, pansies, tall hollyhocks." Beyond lay a smaller garden for cut flowers and the garden cottage built of architectural elements salvaged from an abandoned early house. Its dooryard garden enclosed by a fence Hawthorne considered to be "the quaintest and most charming of cottage gardens," its rectangular beds bordered in dwarf box and "crowded with old-fashioned flowers."[11]

The Tysons, like the Perkinses, made their house and garden the focus of their summer lives. Living rooms opened on the garden and bedrooms overlooked it. Tea was taken in a trellised garden house covered in vines. As Hawthorne described it, their way of life was itself an aesthetic creation:

"Hamilton House" cottage garden. n.d. Glass slide. Smithsonian Institution, Archives of American Gardens, Washington, D.C., Garden Club of America Collection

Opposite, above: Garden of Elizabeth Perkins, York, Maine. n.d. Glass slide. Smithsonian Institution, Archives of American Gardens, Washington, D.C., Garden Club of America Collection
Planks edged this border of hollyhocks, phlox, lilies, and wild flowers, backed with roses on rustic arches.

Opposite, below: "Sylvester Manor," Shelter Island. n.d. Glass slide. Smithsonian Institution Archives of American Gardens, Washington, D.C., Garden Club of America Collection
The garden of "Sylvester Manor," in cultivation since the mid-1600s, was given old-fashioned bordered flower beds at the turn of the century by its tenth-generation owner, Cornelia Horsford.

"The same art that made the garden and reclaimed the house, the half-whimsical, half-loving sympathy that is everywhere felt are also applied to life itself, and the guests of the house respond to their power and charm as do the flowers."[12]

GRANDMOTHER'S GARDEN PHOTOGRAPHED Elizabeth Tyson Vaughn, a dedicated amateur photographer, documented both "Hamilton House" and its garden between 1901 and 1905 in scores of beautifully composed images. Also included in her photograph albums were studies of colonial artifacts and architectural features as well as portraits of friends. Her hobby, one taken up by many women in the 1880s and 1890s, had been facilitated by the availability of dry glass plates that were relatively easy to use and could be developed at leisure.

Photography was seen as a suitable pastime for women. In 1884, the first exhibition of pho-

Opposite: "Hamilton House" garden, South Berwick, Maine. Photograph by Elise Tyson Vaughn, August 13, 1901
Emily Tyson and her stepdaughter Elise began an old-fashioned garden centered on a sundial as part of their restoration of "Hamilton House" in 1898. This view shows the rose-covered arch marking the entrance through a privet hedge from the cutting garden.

Right: "Marguerite Childs in the Garden." Photograph by Frances and Mary Allen, c. 1900
Marguerite Childs was the sister-in-law of Frank Boyden, headmaster of Deerfield Academy. Dressed in a costume of the 1840s, she stands in the Allens's own garden.

Below: "Champney's House." Photograph by Frances and Mary Allen, c. 1900
Painter James Wells Champney married into a Deerfield family and made a sprawling old-fashioned garden beside the family home, which he embellished with gambrel roof ell, pedimented window trim, and an entrance taken from Alexander Hamilton's New York home.

tographs taken by nonprofessionals was held by the Boston Society of Amateur Photographers. The aim of such exhibitions and the proliferating camera clubs was to encourage amateurs to produce artistic photographs rather than mere snapshots. Many middle-class women took up photography and were accepted as full members in the camera clubs.[13]

Some women photographers with an original vision and skilled craftsmanship were able to become self-supporting professionals, among them Emma Louise Coleman (1853–1942), who had studied art in Paris in the 1860s and who took up photography on her return. Coleman brought to her photography a sensibility shaped both by French Barbizon painting and its reflection in the landscapes of Boston painter William Morris Hunt. In the 1890s, Coleman, together with C. Alice Baker (1833–1909), a historian who ran a girls' school near Boston, vacationed together in York, Maine. Here Coleman photographed inhabitants and suitably costumed friends engaged in traditional crafts. Many of these photographs were orchestrated by Sarah Orne Jewett for use in an illustrated edition of *Deephaven* (1885).

Coleman and Baker subsequently summered in the seventeenth-century village of Deerfield, Massachusetts, where they found many congenial spirits interested in the preservation of old houses, gardens, and crafts. Baker's cousin, historian George Sheldon, who had founded the Pocumtuck Valley Memorial Association for the preservation of colonial artifacts there, advised Baker on her restoration of the 1635 "Frary House," bought as a summer home in 1890. Baker and her friends made the house a focus for Deerfield summer social and cultural activities. In 1892, Baker gave an annual ball that was a re-creation of an eighteenth-century one, complete with appropriate costumes and refreshments.[14]

Baker's near neighbors Ellen Miller (1854–1929) and Margaret Whiting (1860–1946), who together had written and illustrated with their own drawings *Wild Flowers of the Northeastern States* (1895), in 1898 established the Deerfield Blue and White Society, a cottage industry for the reproduction of eighteenth-century crewel embroidery. Margaret Whiting's garden, a suitably old-fashioned one, was hidden from the street by a hedge. It was still being tended by Whiting in 1930 when a new neighbor visited. She later recalled that she was given "foxglove plants, southernwood, and none-so-pretties for my garden. . . . We were invited to see the white trillium and the yellow lady slippers . . . and the little 'primavera' [spring] garden under the south windows."[15]

Whiting's garden and many others in Deerfield were recorded in photographs taken by two sisters who in 1896 had come to live in their family home in the old town. Frances Allen (1854–1941) and Mary Allen (1858–1941) had taken up photography when increasing deafness prevented them from teaching school. Frances seems to have specialized in portraits of children, Mary in gardens and other Deerfield views, wild flowers, landscapes, and interiors. Their photographs of Deerfield inhab-

James Wells Champney. POPPIES AND HOLLYHOCKS. c. 1900. Gouache on paper, 15¼ x 10¾ in.
Private collection
Champney's home may have been pretentious, but his garden flowers were not.

itants posed in colonial garb and of the pastoral surroundings of the village were in great demand as tourists' souvenirs as well as for book and magazine illustrations. (A number of the illustrations in Earle's *Home Life in Colonial Days* were photographed by the Allens.) Their *Old Fashioned Garden* appeared as the frontispiece of the March 1906 *Country Life in America.*

The particularly American flavor of the Allens's photographs as well as their evident skill in pictorial composition and the techniques of printing explains much of their success. In 1901, noted professional photographer Frances Benjamin Johnston wrote of the Allens in a *Ladies' Home Journal* series, "The Foremost Women Photographers in America": "They have put character, dignity and artistic feeling into their pictures, and they stand unrivaled in their line of work."[16]

Painter James Wells Champney (1843–1903), neighbor of the Allens and an amateur photographer, moved with his wife, Elizabeth Williams Champney, into the Williams family house in 1876, adding a studio and expanding the garden. Here they lived fulltime until Champney gave up his teaching position at nearby Smith College to become a fashionable pastel portraitist in New York. Their modest Deerfield house became a summer home, "improved" into a Colonial Revival showplace, as was the garden.

Both Champney and his wife, a writer of children's books set in colonial times, were active in Deerfield preservation efforts. Elizabeth Champney, in an article for *Century Magazine,* summed up the village's attractions: "The historic associations of Deerfield carry the imagination back across two centuries. Hatchets and spinning-wheels, looms and fool-stones, and all the obsolete and prehistoric paraphernalia of the olden time abound in the village—the paradise of the antiquary as well as of the artist."[17]

Many photographers followed Coleman and the Allen sisters in romantic re-creations of colonial interiors and pastoral New England scenes. The most widely known of these specialists, Wallace Nutting (1861–1941), was a one-man Colonial Revival industry, his reproductions of colonial furniture becoming nearly as popular as his hand-colored photographs.

Believing that "a thorough acquaintance with the life of earlier generations is only another name for culture," Nutting immersed himself in the American past in his homes as in his photographs. He moved from his first eighteenth-century house in Southbury, Connecticut, to another in Framingham, Massachusetts, in 1912, and owned other historic houses which he used as settings for his photographs. Although his own garden was the subject of nearly a hundred hand-colored photographs offered for sale, his wife was the flower gardener of the family. The old-fashioned garden at their house in Framingham, entered through a "little arch of heavenly blue morning glories," was her creation, as were many of the interiors seen in other photographs.[18]

"Watering the Beds." Photograph by Frances and Mary Allen, c. 1900
*The Allens often posed their suitably costumed friends in Deerfield gardens. The 1903 catalogue of their
photographs listed "Watering the Beds" among the more than three hundred views available.*

John Leslie Breck. IN MONET'S GARDEN. c. 1887. Oil on canvas, 18⅛ x 21⅞ in. Terra Museum of American Art, Chicago.
Daniel J. Terra Collection
Breck was the first of the American artists to be given entree to Monet's splendid cottage garden in Giverny. Such lush, informal gardens
became a favorite motif of American Impressionist painters.

Painting
Grandmother's Garden

Give me sunlight, cupped in a paint brush

And smear the red of peonies

Splash blue upon it,

The hard blue of Canterbury bells,

Paling through larkspur

Into heliotrope,

To wash away among forget-me-nots.

Dip red again to mix a purple,

And lay on pointed flares of lilacs against bright green.

Streak yellow for nasturtiums and marsh marigolds

And flame it up to orange for my lilies . . .

Fill up with cobalt and dash in a sky

As hot and heavy as you can make it,

Then tree-green pulled up into that

Gives a fine jolt of colour . . .

Toss on some Chinese white to flash the clouds,

And trust the sunlight you've got in your paint.

Amy Lowell, "Impressionist Picture of a Garden"

AMERICAN PAINTERS AND FRENCH COTTAGE GARDENS By 1890, an American interested in either paintings or gardens need not have gone to France to be aware of Impressionism or Impressionist paintings of exuberant, informal gardens. One of Claude Monet's garden paintings had been shown as early as 1883 in the foreign section of the important "Foreign Exhibition," Boston Mechanic's Hall. Three years later, a comprehensive exhibition of Impressionist paintings, including forty-eight Monets and organized by French

dealer Paul Durand-Ruel, was shown in New York and Boston. The show received a great deal of attention, especially Monet's paintings of poppy fields and gardens.

The first of the horde of American painters who were attracted to the village of Giverny, where Monet made his home, arrived in the summer of 1887. One of them, John Leslie Breck, sent back to Boston paintings in the advanced Impressionist style, among them studies of Monet's garden. Tourists as well as painters began to make Giverny a destination. Monet's garden became widely known in America through many published accounts. For example, a contributor to the *Boston Evening Transcript* in 1898 described the garden as "one huge, gorgeous mass of color" that "well deserved its fame which has spread abroad."[1]

French cottage gardens (of which Monet's was a palatial example) and fields of poppies were painted by Americans elsewhere in France. Robert Vonnoh and Edward Hamilton, for example, painted charming ones in 1890 at Grez-sur-Loing, an artists' colony near Barbizon. On their return to the United States, these French-trained artists sought out rural villages offering native versions of such gardens and rural landscapes to paint in their newly acquired Impressionist style.

Some of these painters had previously lived and gardened in Giverny itself—for example, Mariquita Gill, from 1892 until 1897. In her garden, according to her biographer, poppies, lilies, and roses filled the pathway border and "stiff, proud hollyhocks made a decorative pattern against the pink stucco wall," furnishing "an inexhaustible supply of subjects."[2] When Gill settled in Salem, Massachusetts, such a garden seemed right at home among the enclosed old-fashioned dooryard gardens there.

THE OLD-FASHIONED GARDEN IN AMERICAN ARTISTS' COLONIES

Many painters who had studied in France were drawn to already existing artists' colonies such as the one in East Hampton, Long Island. In 1891, William Merritt Chase's popular school for plein-air Impressionist painting, the Shinnecock Hills Summer School of Art, which attracted many aspiring women artists, was established in nearby Southampton. Lydia Emmet (1866–1952), one of the students and later a portrait painter, produced two paintings there in the early 1890s of old-fashioned gardens titled *The Deserted Garden* and *Grandmother's Garden*.

Gaines Ruger Donoho (1857–1916), who had studied in Paris and painted at both Grez-sur-Loing and Giverny, bought and restored an eighteenth-century house in East Hampton in 1891. He began his garden immediately and painted it almost exclusively in the mid-1890s, perhaps inspired by his friend Childe Hassam's garden paintings. Though there were much grander artists' gardens on Long Island, for example, those of Alfred and Adele Herter in East Hampton or Louis Comfort Tiffany's in Oyster Bay, none were so central to the artist's work.

In Donoho's garden, old favorites together with modern beauties like Japanese iris, anemones, and lilies were generously massed in box-bordered beds. In Donoho's paintings, both lush modern blooms and single-flowered, old-fashioned ones appeared in vistas and close-up views as rich in color and texture as the garden itself must have been.

In 1898, Childe Hassam visited Donoho and painted his garden, lit by Japanese lanterns, in *July Night*. Hassam was charmed by the wealth of old shingled houses he found in East Hampton and eventually bought an eighteenth-century one that Donoho had restored next door to his own. Before settling there, however, Hassam was attracted in 1903 to another colonial village, Old Lyme, Connecticut, already established as an artists' colony.[3]

Soon after Hassam arrived in Old Lyme, the colony changed allegiance from a Barbizon-influenced aesthetic to Impressionism. His presence in the colony attracted several fellow Impressionists, including Willard Metcalf (1858–1925), who spent part of the same summer there and returned in 1905. Metcalf probably painted *Purple, White and Gold* (1903) at Old Lyme, perhaps in the garden of Clark Vorhees (1871–1933), whose 1740 gambrel-roof cottage had an appropriate old-fashioned garden. The garden was well known and frequently painted by Vorhees himself and other resident artists.

Vorhees had stayed in Florence Griswold's boardinghouse on his initial visit in 1896. The Griswold family were among the early settlers of Old Lyme, and Griswold's garden was as old-fashioned as her grand colonial house. Many of the artists who stayed with Griswold and subsequently bought homes in the area followed her lead in gardening. According to an article on Old Lyme in *Country Life in America,* the personal interest Griswold continued to take in the artists she had boarded extended to their gardens, "in which she has endeavored to infuse the air of yesteryear through the medium of the good old-fashioned flowers." The gardens modeled after hers had in common not just their plantings but also their informal arrangements in box-edged beds, "old-style . . . with stone retaining walls and an utter absence of formality." Remains of earlier gardens lingered around some of the houses. One old house had a "quaint little front door-yard overflowing with what was once a garden. A damask rose to the left of the front door and a white one at the right are delightful reminders of a planting custom of other days."[4]

Robert Vonnoh (1858–1933), who also made an old-fashioned garden there, came to Old Lyme only when World War I made further trips to his beloved Grez-sur-Loing impossible. Earlier, he had gardened ardently at his cottage on Rockland Lake, New York. On trips away for portrait commissions, Vonnoh wrote daily to his wife, sculptor Bessie Potter, often enclosing blossoms; after a visit to "Mount Vernon," he sent a sprig of flowering almond "plucked surreptitiously from George Washington's garden." There he had admired the effect of the box borders, "the richest imaginable," and the "mass of lilacs, paenoias and flowering almonds with their fragrance." He added, "I want my paradise filled in bewildering profusion with these beauties. To love them and to paint them is my ideal."[5]

Vonnoh missed being away from his garden and filled his letters with plaintive inquiries about nursery orders or the eagerly awaited blossoming of favorite plants. A group of letters written in May 1901 were typical. In one he exclaimed, "I do hope the tulips and the little purple plum will hold out until Sunday" and added, "I have seen lots of beautiful Magnolias but none more fragrant or beautiful than those we have." He asked about the arrival of a 'Clara Barton' rose and requested that it be planted in the big rose bed where its delicate amber pink would set off the reds. Other letters suggest planting plans. He wrote, "I'm glad you got the Lilies and hope you see massing them. That will be my aim in [the] future. I notice how beautiful some of these things are in masses." A

Childe Hassam. JULY NIGHT. 1898. Oil on canvas, 37 x 31 in. Private collection
Hassam painted his wife, Maud, at a July 4th celebration in Donoho's garden illuminated with Japanese lanterns.
The setting provided Hassam an opportunity for a flattened, decorative treatment and nearly pointillist technique.

Edmund Greacen. THE OLD GARDEN. c. 1912. Oil on canvas, 30¼ x 30¼ in. Florence Griswold Museum,
Old Lyme, Connecticut
Greacen painted a series of views of Florence Griswold's garden between 1910 and 1913, the first titled Old Fashioned Garden.

Opposite: William Chadwick. ON THE PORCH. c. 1908. Oil on canvas, 24 x 30 in. Florence Griswold Museum,
Old Lyme, Connecticut
*Chadwick painted his wife on the porch of Florence Griswold's grand colonial house overlooking the old-fashioned
garden that served as a model for many other gardens in Old Lyme.*

Norway-spruce hedge was being put in while he was away, and he wrote, understandably, "I shall be anxious about that until I see it for myself." The titles of two unlocated paintings, *Salvia, Petunia, Ageratum* (1903) and *Dahlia, Salvia, Petunia* (1905), suggest that annuals as well as perennials were included in Vonnoh's garden, although the old-fashioned flowers and flowering shrubs remained his favorites.[6]

For all these painters, the brilliance and spontaneity of Impressionist painting found an equivalent in the lush informality of grandmother's garden. A writer on colonial houses, in describing an example belonging to "our most noted Impressionist painter" (probably Hassam), noted that his garden was as "thoroughly New England" as his house, "so entirely does the informal formality echo our early gardens." Landscape architect Beatrix Jones Farrand, who felt that "a garden large or small must be treated in the impressionist manner," ruefully pointed out that the Impressionist painter had an advantage over the gardener.

Willard Metcalf. PURPLE, WHITE AND GOLD. 1903. Oil on canvas, 26 x 18 in. Private collection
This may have been painted in Clark Vorhees's noted garden in Old Lyme, Connecticut.

Opposite: Lydia Emmet. GRANDMOTHER'S GARDEN. c. 1912. Oil on canvas, 32 x 43 in.
National Academy of Design, New York
Emmet was one of scores of women painters who studied plein air painting with
William Merritt Chase on Long Island and elsewhere.

The two arts of painting and garden design are closely related, except that the landscape gardener paints with actual color, line and perspective to make a composition . . . while the painter has but a flat surface on which to create his illusion; he has, however, the incalculable advantage that no sane person would think of going behind a picture to see if it were equally interesting from that point of view.[7]

ARTISTS' GARDENS IN CORNISH, NEW HAMPSHIRE The village of Cornish, New Hampshire, first settled in 1763, became an artists' colony after sculptor Augustus Saint-Gaudens and his family began summering there in 1885. The following year, they were joined by painters Thomas Wilmer Dewing (1851–1938) and his wife, Maria Oakey Dewing (1845–1927), the first among scores of artists and writers who settled

Robert Vonnoh painting in the garden. Photograph, c. 1901. Collection Mrs. Robert Rowe Thompson
Vonnoh's garden at Rockland Lake, New York, was the setting for a painting of his second wife, sculptor Bessie Potter, titled Hydrangeas.

there for a season or full time. Cornish was never an Impressionist colony like Old Lyme, but its gardens were central to the community there and proved far-reaching in their influence.

The site of Cornish, which recalled the hills of Tuscany to the European-trained artists there, suggested garden designs owing something to Italian gardens as well as to colonial ones, just as the piazzas and pergolas of the predominately Colonial Revival houses at Cornish gave them an appealing Italian accent. Cornish gardens were personal, each with a distinctive flavor. Rose Standish Nichols, a niece of Saint-Gaudens who began her career as a landscape designer with her own Cornish garden, later wrote of them, "Charming gardens were created by struggling artists who hardly knew the

Gaines Ruger Donoho's garden,
East Hampton, Long Island.
n.d. Glass slide. Smithsonian
Institution, Archives of American
Gardens, Washington, D.C.,
Garden Club of America
Collection
*Donoho's garden, begun in 1891, was a
grand old-fashioned one of oblong box-
bordered beds separated by grass paths.*

Below: Albert and Adele Herter's
garden, East Hampton,
Long Island. n.d. Glass slide.
Smithsonian Institution,
Archives of American Gardens,
Washington, D.C., Garden Club
of America Collection
*In 1899, the Herters built a house
flanked by pergolas and fronted with
a formal garden. More informally
planted beds of old-fashioned flowers
led toward the water.*

Gaines Ruger Donoho. AURATUM LILIES. 1907. Oil on canvas, 24 x 20 in. Private collection

Donoho painted his garden in East Hampton, Long Island, almost exclusively in the last twenty years of his life. His close views of flowers there are dense tapestries of color and sinuous forms.

commonest flowers by name, but who were thoroughly conversant with the principles of design. Every householder was his own head gardener and landscape architect."[8]

Charles Adams Platt (1861–1933), whose career as an architect and landscape designer also began in Cornish, was a painter when he arrived there in 1890. His garden of rectangular flower beds quartered by intersecting paths was modified after an 1892 trip to Italy to study Italian gardens. (His influential *Italian Gardens* was published in 1894.) Platt's subsequent house and landscape designs perhaps owed as much to the Colonial Revival as to Italy, while his own garden relied on the hardy flowers and shrubs that the Dewings had previously put to the test in their garden.[9]

The Dewings's garden had been created expressly for Maria Dewing, a plein-air painter of flowers with a keen interest in her family's long New England history. The Dewings's endeavors to find plants that were reliably hardy in New Hampshire's exacting climate, according to an early account, resulted in "a garden expressly grown with flowers of the old-fashioned sort—dahlias, phlox and sweet william." Some favorite combinations appear in Maria Dewing's paintings, as in her *Rose Garden* (1901), where morning glories are depicted climbing through Souvenir de la Malmaison and Gloire de Dijon roses. Maria Dewing wrote to a collector that the Shirley poppies of the unlocated *Poppies and Italian Mignonette* were "in a large bed mixed with a tall white mignonette that grows wild in Italy."[10]

Maria Dewing was interested in interior design, having written a book on household decoration, *Beauty in the Household* (1882), but she left the planning of their flower garden to her husband. The aesthetic refinement of Thomas Dewing's paintings of aristocratic New England women in classicized colonial dress probably had a counterpart in his garden design, in which the colonial was viewed as an indigenous variant of the classical. Dewing seemed to have been the arbiter of taste for the entire Cornish community—as resident sculptor Frances Grimes wrote, "Everyone was . . . in awe of his artistic judgement." Frances Duncan, in an article on Cornish gardens published several years after the Dewings had left, detected his lingering influence there. "Mr. Dewing's garden-craft and the rare quality of his artistic instinct are plain to see in many a Cornish garden."[11]

The Dewings moved to remote Green Hills, New Hampshire, in 1903 because they felt Cornish was losing its exclusivity and its commitment to Puritan "plain living and high thinking." Here they began another garden that also featured "a great bed of poppies" as well as an old-fashioned arrangement of "brick walks, and bordered beds where larkspur and yellow lilies, irises and peonies and other perennials grow."[12]

Exclusivity was offered by extreme aestheticism as by affiliation with America's colonial past, and in Cornish the two went hand in hand. A visitor in 1907 reported that artists had come to Cornish "to form there an aristocracy of brains and to keep out that element which displays its gray mat-

Garden of Stephen Parrish, Cornish, New Hampshire. Photograph by Maxfield Parrish, 1906.
Dartmouth College Library, Hanover
A lily pool marked the end of one axial path from the house and the beginning of another to the orchard.
A second pool provided an anchor for a walk toward the workshop and studio.

ter by an expenditure of money in undesirable ways." The visitor noted further that "there is little that is ostentatious about these homes . . . displaying the good taste and effort at simplicity that every one of the inhabitants has sought. It is in the gardens that effects have been reached without apparently having to be striven after."[13]

Landscape painter Stephen Parrish (1846–1938), who created the most beautiful and accomplished of the old-fashioned gardens in Cornish, reportedly once threatened to train poison ivy over his porch to keep away visitors. What he did plant was much more alluring and, fortunately, was recorded in his gardening diaries, which date from May 19, 1893, when work started on his house, "Northcote." He began a flower garden in raised beds protected on the north and east by the white clapboarded house. Work was far enough along in October to allow him to establish grapevines against the south side of the house and to transplant a wild rose to a spot under his workshop window.

The next spring, Parrish planted an arborvitae hedge and enjoyed the hyacinths, crocuses, tulips,

Garden of Stephen Parrish, Cornish, New Hampshire. Photograph by Maxfield Parrish, c. 1900.
Dartmouth College Library, Hanover
Parrish's niece stands in the midst of his splendid garden overflowing with old-fashioned beauties in plank-bordered beds.
Clematis, Virginia creeper, and wild grapes cover the pergola.

and Madonna lilies put in the previous fall. He bought trees and shrubs in generous lots from nurseries in Boston and elsewhere and recorded setting out fifty Madame Plantier roses in a shrubbery to the south of the garden and a hemlock hedge to the west in 1895. He filled the flower beds with old-fashioned perennials, biennials, and self-sown annuals: peonies, iris, yellow lilies, hollyhocks, phlox, marigolds, pinks, sweet Williams, Oriental poppies, sweet peas, larkspur, campanulas, columbines, stokesias, asters, cornflowers, stock, Shirley poppies, English violets, and helianthuses. Box was set out in tubs. Vines and rambler roses draped other outbuildings. Native trees and shrubs were constantly being transplanted from the nearby woods.

As Parrish gained experience, his plantings spread outward and became more adventuresome and assured. The heart of the garden remained the exuberant cottage-style beds enclosed by the house and a newly built greenhouse. By the time the first article on the garden appeared, in 1902, its plan was complete. The particularly American charm of Parrish's masterpiece was stressed by Her-

bert C. Wise, author of the article and editor of *House and Garden.* "Modest retirement is the note which pervades it. Simplicity and absence of pretence are everywhere apparent. . . . It is a place to walk in, to live in, and be happy in, unconventional in its planting, easy in its growth and free from foreign objects which any native house gardener of these last hundred years would have scorned."[14]

For journalist Hazel W. Henderson, who visited "Northcote" the next year, it was the garden's informal exuberance that was most appealing. "One rambles through groves of head high larkspur, amid box bordered paths, and through labyrinthine tangles of hollyhocks, zinnias, and every known sort of old-fashioned flowering plant." Frances Duncan, writing about Cornish gardens, including that of Parrish, three years later saw a fresh and encouraging trend. "These Cornish gardens are small indeed compared with the great estates; yet a miniature may be as admirable a work of art . . . and in their sincerity, their rare-found harmony, and proportion, these gardens, unpretentious as they are, are yet blessedly indicative of a very hopeful development in American gardening."[15]

Maria Oakey Dewing. THE GARDEN IN MAY. 1895. Oil on canvas, 23 ⅜ x 32 ½ in. National Museum of American Art,
Smithsonian Institution, Washington, D.C.
In the Dewings's old-fashioned garden in Cornish, New Hampshire, old shrub roses were underplanted with dianthus in a box-bordered bed.
Maria Dewing's paintings provide a loving gardener's-eye view of her flowers where their sensual delights can best be appreciated.

Opposite: Maria Oakey Dewing. BED OF POPPIES. 1909. Oil on canvas, 25 x 30 in. Addison Gallery of American Art,
Phillips Academy, Andover, Massachusetts
This bed of Shirley poppies was in the Dewings's second garden begun after their move to Green Hills, New Hampshire, in 1903.
The close viewpoint here allows an intimate experience of flower texture, shape, and color, the bed seeming to stretch far
beyond the canvas edge and the viewer's sight.

Childe Hassam. IN THE GARDEN. 1892. Oil on canvas, 22 1/8 x 18 1/8 in. National Museum of American Art, Smithsonian Institution, Washington, D.C.
This painting of Celia Thaxter in the midst of her garden was used as the frontispiece to her An Island Garden *(1894).*

Two American Cottage Gardens

It is only a tiny garden,
Where the commonest flowers blow,
Where tangled vines are straying,
And shrubs all wayward grow.
No trim or stately hedges
Border our garden path,
No rare and lovely blossoms
With strange, new names it hath . . .

They are the flower-friends loyal,
Returning year by year,
Never from summer sowing
Comes bloom that's quite so dear.

Olive E. Dana, "Our Garden"

CELIA THAXTER'S COTTAGE GARDEN The old-fashioned cottage garden was typified in the 1890s in the garden of poet Celia Laighton Thaxter (1835–1894) on Appledore in the Isles of Shoals, off the coast of Maine. Thaxter's garden, enshrined in scores of paintings and watercolors by American Impressionist Childe Hassam, embodied the color, texture, and historical resonance that made the old-fashioned garden so appealing. Appledore House, a hotel on the island run by Thaxter's family, had attracted the educated and cultivated vacationer from New England and farther afield since mid-century. In the 1880s and early 1890s, Celia Thaxter held an informal salon in the parlor of her cottage that was a nexus for the cultural leaders of the day.

At the age of sixteen, Celia Laighton had married Levi Thaxter, a Harvard graduate, who had

Childe Hassam. A ROOM OF FLOWERS. 1894. Oil on canvas, 34 x 34 in. Private collection
In Thaxter's parlor, the paintings that lined the walls shared attention with the beautifully
orchestrated floral arrangements that covered the tabletops.

J. Appleton Brown. POPPIES IN A GARDEN. Before 1891. Oil on canvas, 21¾ x 18 in.
Isabella Stewart Gardner Museum, Boston
Beginning in the late 1870s, Brown often painted Thaxter's garden.

Celia Thaxter in her garden. Photograph, c. 1892
*Thaxter's dress was as distinctive as her garden; both had
an old-fashioned air.*

been briefly her father's partner and her own tutor. The Thaxters' first son was born in a cottage on Appledore. After a boating accident, Levi Thaxter refused to live on the island, and the Thaxters settled near Boston, where two more sons were born. Levi Thaxter, who was never gainfully employed, occupied his time in the cultivation of friendships with Boston painters and writers, and in the study of Robert Browning's work. Celia Thaxter's days were spent in endless housework, even after her published poems began to bring in much-needed income. In 1862 she wrote James Fields, editor of the *Atlantic Monthly,* who had requested prose sketches, "Here are some verses which have been evolved among the pots and kettles . . . verses can grow when prose can't." She added poignantly, "The rhymes in my head are all that keep me alive, I do believe."[1]

Thaxter was not able to write about her beloved island until she returned for an extended period in the late 1860s. Her sketches and stories, published as *Among the Isles of Shoals* (1873), did much to increase the popularity of the island as an exclusive vacation spot. As one visitor enthusiastically reported in 1874, "The Boston ton and upper crust are here—real gentle folk—courteous, affable, simple and natural in mien and manner. . . . The coarse and rough, the pushing and pretentious, are not here."[2]

J. Appleton Brown. OLD FASHIONED GARDEN. Before 1889. Pastel on paper, 21⅞ x 17¹⁵⁄₁₆ in.
Bowdoin College Museum of Art, New Brunswick, Maine
Brown spent many summers on Appledore, although this garden with its colonial archway
was perhaps in Newburyport, Massachusetts.

Childe Hassam. THE GARDEN IN ITS GLORY. 1892. Watercolor, 19 13/16 x 13 7/8 in. National
Museum of American Art, Smithsonian Institution, Washington, D.C. Gift of John Gellatly
*Celia Thaxter and her grandson stand in the entrance to her garden on Appledore Island. The trellis is
covered in climbing nasturtiums and morning glories and flanked by beds of Shirley poppies.*

Opposite: Childe Hassam. CELIA THAXTER'S GARDEN, APPLEDORE, ISLES OF SHOALS.
1890–93. Oil on canvas, 13 x 19 7/16 in. The Warner Collection of Gulf States
Paper Corporation, Tuscaloosa, Alabama
The steps leading from the piazza are shown here bowered in hop vines and flanked by hollyhocks.

During a winter spent in Boston in 1877, Thaxter had begun to study painting with J. Appleton Brown (1844–1902), a frequent guest on Appledore, along with fellow Impressionists Ross Turner and Childe Hassam. She continued to study informally with all three artists during summers on Appledore, where she began to garden seriously. At the same time, Thaxter launched a second career as a china decorator. Both china and the cultivated flowers from her garden found a ready market with visitors. A friend later recalled that "the garden was started entirely for pleasure, but in after years it became quite a source of revenue."[3]

Thaxter's cottage and garden on Appledore became the focus of her life and work. Her parlor (immortalized in Hassam's masterpiece *A Room of Flowers,* 1894), together with its encircling porch, or piazza, was extended in 1887 to accommodate her increasingly popular morning gatherings. Though modestly furnished, the room exemplified the Aesthetic interior and was Thaxter's own handiwork, from upholstery and drapery to flowers. All agreed, however, it was the flowers that gave the room its special distinction.

Thaxter's dress was equally distinctive recalling eighteenth-century fashions. Thaxter's garden, arranged in the dooryard of her cottage in plank-bordered beds enclosed with a board fence, looked back to colonial prototypes as well. Designed for use as much as for ornament, it was described by one visitor as "unlike any other garden, although more beautiful than conventional gardens I have seen lately; for it was planted all helter-skelter, just bursts of color here and there, and what color!"[4] The abundance and informality of Thaxter's garden, where "flowers grew luxuriantly at their own sweet wills, or at the will of the planter, never troubling their heads about agreeing with their neighbors," shocked textile designer Candace Wheeler, who could not understand how "a woman with so exquisite a sense of combination and gradation in the arrangement of flowers, should have so little thought of color effect in her garden." These were the very color effects, however, that charmed Hassam and inspired some of his loveliest watercolors, several used as illustrations in Thaxter's *An Island Garden* (1894). The formally orchestrated "long cords of color" in her parlor flower arrangements, so admired by Wheeler, gave way in her garden to a no less carefully thought out, if informal and painterly, organization.[5]

Thaxter's *An Island Garden,* a poetic evocation of one season among her flowers, was meant to instruct as well as to inspire. At the suggestion of Sarah Orne Jewett, Thaxter had included a planting plan of the limited fifteen-by-fifty-foot space. She explained rather apologetically, "I have not room to experiment with rock works and ribbon borders and the like, nor should I do so if I had all the room in the world. For mine is just a little old-fashioned garden."[6]

An ardent naturalist, Thaxter gave individual attention to each plant and in her book mentioned growing many more flowers than were included on her plan. Thaxter's secret was reliance on vertical space, on covering every inch of ground, trellis, and fence in successive plantings for continuous bloom. The long porch overlooking the garden, as well as the fence that enclosed the garden, was draped with vines—honeysuckle, wisteria, nasturtiums, sweet peas, wild cucumber, clematis, passionflowers, hops, and Dutchman's-pipe. The arch leading from the porch was embowered with the Tropaeolum cultivar 'Lucifer', *Cobaea scandens,* and Mexican morning glories and flanked with two beds of Shirley poppies. In most beds pansies, verbenas, Drummond phlox, and other low, spreading flowers were planted among the taller perennials for bloom when the earlier flowers had finished. Late bloomers like asters were placed in the corners of annual beds to take over in their turn. Thaxter's generous plantings overflowed the garden and tumbled down the bank toward the sea, where artemisias and California poppies bloomed.

Thaxter's marvelous garden grew not only from the rocky, treeless soil of Appledore Island, but from the New England cultural matrix that valued such distinctively American locales and celebrated them in verse, prose, and paintings. As were earlier dooryard gardens, hers was an intimate extension of the house, designed to be enjoyed from the piazza that formed one of the garden's boundaries. Its raised, plank-edged beds were both a reference to earlier usage and a practical solution to erosion in sandy soil. Thaxter's *An Island Garden,* painterly in its descriptive power, is a moving testament not just to the seductive beauty of such an old-fashioned American garden, but to the spiritual grace to be derived from its creation and nurture.

 WOMEN IN THE DECORATIVE ARTS MOVEMENT Ella Rodman Church, who wrote on both gardens and interior decoration, in *Money-Making for Ladies* (1882) recommended the two occupations practiced by Thaxter, china painting and gardening. For women in rural or suburban areas, Church felt the sale of garden flowers and vegetables offered the best opportunity both to earn money and maintain a middle-class semblance of leisure. "Many a careworn woman, struggling with her housework, and finding it next to impossible to make both ends meet, has only to look into her garden-patch . . . which might easily be made to culminate in an able-bodied Brigit in the kitchen, a half-grown boy at work outside, and the lady herself engaged in the lighter occupation of sorting fruit and vegetables, or tying up plants." Church considered china painting, however, to be "the most popular and profitable of art industries for ladies." Unfortunately, most women did not have Thaxter's advantage of a captive clientele for the sale of such wares. For these, Church pointed out the advantages of the New York Society of

Decorative Art, where "a number of ladies gifted with artistic taste find a most satisfactory depot for their productions."[7]

The New York Society of Decorative Art owed its existence to Candace Thurber Wheeler (1827–1923), the visitor who had disparaged Thaxter's garden while marveling at her flower arrangements. At the Philadelphia Centennial Exposition in 1876, Wheeler had been deeply impressed by the display of the Royal School of Art Needlework, recently founded in London. The skillful and artistic embroidery that filled the booth hung with panels designed by Walter Crane and William Morris suggested to Wheeler a solution to the difficulties of well-bred women who needed to become self-supporting yet wanted to avoid the stigma of working for a salary. In 1877, Wheeler, with several other well-connected New Yorkers, began the Society of Decorative Art as a center for the sale of embroidery, decorated china, and the like. A school of needlework was begun, at first using English instructors and designs. Wheeler, however, soon enlisted the aid of American artists to create original motifs that "appealed to our sense of beauty, both in spirit and subject, that were thoroughly American."[8]

Wheeler was not herself an amateur. Although she had been, as she confessed in her autobiography, "absorbed in family life, and country life, and social life" after her marriage, she had moved in artistic as well as social circles. She enjoyed friendships with many of the Hudson River School painters as well as with up-and-coming artists such as William Merritt Chase and she had studied painting for a year in Germany. With the society successfully launched, in 1879 Wheeler was able to accept Louis Comfort Tiffany's offer of a partnership, together with artists Lockwood de Forest and Samuel Colman, in a new firm specializing in interior decoration to be called Associated Artists. Here Wheeler endeavored to create an American style in the textiles she designed, believing that "Art applied to manufacture should have its root in its own country."[9]

After several years, Wheeler separated from Tiffany and took the textile department to different premises, retaining the Associated Artists' name and employing almost exclusively female designers and needleworkers. Rosina Emmet and Wheeler's daughter Dora, both students of Chase, worked for the firm, developing wallpaper and fabric designs based on American motifs for manufacture by American firms. Several of their designs for the "needle-woven" tapestries invented by Wheeler had subjects taken from American literature. Embroidery motifs were likewise drawn from native flora. Even some of the dyes—indigo, madder, butternut yellow, and walnut brown—were ones in use in colonial times. The firm was tremendously influential. At the height of its renown in 1893, Wheeler was put in charge of both the decoration and the display of decorative arts at the Women's Building at the World's Columbian Exposition in Chicago.

James Carroll Beckwith. ONTEORA LANDSCAPE. 1903. Oil on board, 14⅝ x 10⅜ in. Private collection

CANDACE WHEELER'S GARDEN OF OLD-FASHIONED FLOWERS AND NATIVE PLANTS Ten years earlier, when the Wheelers had bought land for a country house in the wilds of the Catskills, Wheeler was thrilled to discover hanging in the home of the original settler of the farm evidence of early American culture, "one of the needlework pictures which the daughters of prominent Colonial families educated in the famous Moravian school at Bethlehem [Pennsylvania] were taught to embroider." The site commanded a sweeping view of the Hudson Valley and the distant Berkshires and proved so appealing that the Wheelers and their friends bought more land and formed the cooperative Onteora Club.[10]

Wheeler wrote about the garden she made surrounding her cottage "Penny Royal" at Onteora in *Content in a Garden* (1901), illustrated with flower drawings by her daughter Dora Wheeler Keith. Wheeler's half-acre garden, bounded by a rough stone wall, was filled with native American plants and proven old-fashioned flowers. She had no time for demanding annuals, declaring, "It is out of my policy to plant seeds, unless they speedily make roots and take care of themselves." She likewise had no patience with modern blooms bred for exaggerated size, considering it "a wicked thing to tempt a flower into unnatural vagaries."[11]

Many of her flowers carried associations. Her lemon lilies came from an old Hudson River manor house, the iris from a friend in Cambridge, Massachusetts, her marigolds from an English garden, and her fragrant double-flowered violets from William Cullen Bryant's Long Island home. Some plants were volunteers, others were deliberately transplanted from the wild. Scores of the rare lavender-pink fringed orchis as well as the common bloodroot found a place in her garden as did sheets of stars-of-Bethlehem. Monardas were mixed with wild scarlet lobelias because "the difference in the shade of the blossoms gives the effect which painters call vibration, relieving and intensifying each other in color."[12]

Three principles governed the layout of Wheeler's garden: use quantities of flowers of the same kind for breadth of effect, plant intensively in the same spot for continuous bloom, and arrange blooms for gradation of color. Believing that "thousands of flowers of one variety . . . make an impression upon the eye and the imagination which is impossible to mixed masses," after carefully considering what would be blooming at the same time, and where, Wheeler planted in abundance. For Wheeler, as for Thaxter, intensive interplanting demanded an intimate knowledge of the cultural requirements of the plants. As she wrote, "I have set myself to learn which of the selected darlings of my garden love each other well enough to live together in the same few feet of earth, so that every inch of ground may blossom in a continuous wave of beauty." Those recalcitrant few, like nasturtiums, unwilling to live on congenial terms with other flowers, were condemned to single beds.[13]

Wheeler sought to suggest the lavishness of nature's plantings on a small scale through color modulations. She recognized that "many of those gorgeous effects are produced not by space, but by a gradual leading up to masses of color. One never finds a clearly cut outline, a sharp departure from one tint to another, in a wild garden." Gradual intensification of color produced by numbers of tints was her solution, "to plant out comparatively small spaces so that one tint may lie softly against another, each one leading up to and melting into deeper and more solid and compact blossom."[14]

Wheeler's description of color modulations recalls those of Gertrude Jekyll: "Red will melt into orange, and orange into yellow, and yellow into paler tints, until you reach white without anything like a shock of contrast; and in like manner blue can be trailed into the pink-lavender . . . and then into cold pink, and deeper again into crimson, or it may flow out in paler tints until it also reaches that absence of color which we call white." It was, however, to Celia Thaxter's arrangement of flowers in her parlor on Appledore Island, which she had seen just as she was beginning her Onteora garden, that Wheeler attributed the idea. "It was in this room, and enjoying its color as I have enjoyed few things in life . . . that I began to think of making a summer dream of it in my garden."[15]

Wheeler had been gardening for nearly fifty years when she wrote *Content in a Garden,* not just at Onteora, but at her home "Nestledown" on Long Island and at a recently purchased cottage in Georgia. Her garden at Onteora had not only native flowers but American roots, its arrangement and planting shaped by her knowledge of American painting and early embroidery, her love for the native flora of the Catskill region, and her familiarity with the original visions of American garden artists such as Celia Thaxter.

Charles Courtney Curran. THE LANTERNS. 1913. Oil on canvas, 30¼ x 30¼ in. Private collection
Japanese lanterns, so ubiquitous at this time, illuminate Curran's garden at Cragsmoor for an evening party.

The Arts and Crafts Movement and the American Cottage Garden

Far through years of wreck and riot

There's a garden sown with quiet,

Scented still with love that grew there with the blossoms long ago;

And the lake-winds whisper after,

Like a ghost of old-time laughter

In the half-choked alleys where the hollyhocks grow.

Still they watch for her untended,

Pinks and daisies, roses splendid;

Still the true, deep-hearted pansies turn their faces to the sky.

But the poppies grow unheeding

In the plots of love-lies-bleeding,

And the crushed hearts slumber as the years go by.

Frank Lillie Pollock, "The Garden"

WORKING WOMEN Candace Wheeler's New York Society of Decorative Art was one of the earliest manifestations of the Arts and Crafts Movement in the United States and was directly inspired by the Centennial Exposition, where the crafts ideals of John Ruskin and William Morris could be seen embodied in the art products of England and other countries. The New York Society of Decorative Art and similar societies that sprang up in other cities were desperately needed. As a later beneficiary pointed out, "The panic of 1873 literally turned out of doors thousands of women from homes grown luxurious in the exceptional prosperity that followed the war. The Centennial Exposition opportunely succeeded this crisis . . . what was then called 'decorative art' fur-

"Rookwood," home of Maria Longworth, seen from the garden. Photograph, c. 1890. Cincinnati Historical Society
Maria Longworth Nichols named her influential pottery "Rookwood" after her family home in Cincinnati. The old-fashioned garden had a pronounced Italian accent.

nished a polite way in which legions of women first conceived it possible to earn a living."[1] By 1890, the idea of a lady earning her own salary was no longer outrageous. Books on appropriate work for ladies and on successful women in various fields began to be published. Sarah K. Bolton's *Successful Women* (1888) included among the expected writers and educators Candace Wheeler and the proprietor of a nursery and greenhouse. The career woman appeared in popular fiction in the guise of the New Woman.

By the 1890s, the shift from an agricultural to a manufacturing economy, from dependence on local production to nationwide distribution of goods, from small-scale factories to huge industries meant that most workers, male or female, were no longer free agents but salaried employees at the mercy of impersonal and arbitrary economic forces. Many thoughtful members of the burgeoning middle class, increasingly alienated from this urbanized and industrialized America, saw in the ideals of the Arts and Crafts Movement an alternative to consumer culture, where rampant greed and commercialism seemed to have vanquished traditional values.

In England, the movement's theorists viewed the Middle Ages with nostalgia, while American participants looked back toward colonial times, when labor had been meaningful and satisfying and the home the moral center of family life. The movement became identified with nationalism and the quest for an American style and looked toward vernacular forms, folk traditions, and native crafts, particularly those of earlier times, for inspiration. Many of the craftsmen and craftswomen who began to produce pottery, needlework, furniture, textiles, metalwork, and baskets and to print fine books congregated in congenial communities across the country, a few of them established and maintained by more affluent supporters. Here they attempted to live the simple life, combining creative labor with artistic houses and old-fashioned gardens.

Benn Pitman and family in his wild flower garden. Photograph, c. 1890. Cincinnati Historical Society
Pitman's crafts classes at the School of Design were largely responsible for beginning the women's decorative arts movement in Cincinnati.

One of the first crafts to attract national attention was art pottery, with many of the craftswomen who decorated it having begun as amateur china painters. Cincinnati, Ohio, became a center for art pottery partly due to the efforts of an Englishman, Benn Pitman (1822–1910), who had settled there before the Civil War to popularize his shorthand method. Pitman turned to the decorative arts in the 1870s and began industrial-design classes at the Cincinnati School of Design. He organized the exhibition of Cincinnati crafts at the Women's Pavilion of the Centennial Exposition in Philadelphia, which included china decorated by his students Mary Louise McLaughlin and Maria Longworth Nichols. Considered the founder of the Cincinnati decorative-arts movement, Pitman was noted for his wild-flower garden as well as for his teaching.[2]

Maria Longworth Nichols (1849–1932), a Cincinnati native, was the daughter of Joseph Longworth, a noted patron of the arts, and grandaughter of Nicholas Longworth, who had institut-

Opposite: Charles Courtney Curran. A Corner of Grandmother's Garden. Oil on canvas, 30 x 20 in. Location unknown
This grandmother's garden includes pinks, bellflowers, phlox, foxgloves, and a girl whose tunic echoes the shape of the foxglove blossoms.

Elizabeth Robineau in the garden of "Four Winds." Photograph, 1916. Everson Museum of Art, Syracuse, New York
Adelaide Alsop Robineau's expansive, old-fashioned garden in Syracuse occupied the area between her house and pottery studio. Elizabeth was one of her three children.

ed grape culture in the West. After her marriage, she and her husband were instrumental in establishing in 1873 the annual music festival in Cincinnati. That same year, Nichols joined Benn Pitman's class in wood carving and his china-painting class in 1874. She visited the Centennial Exposition, where she was so impressed by the Japanese ceramics that she determined to start her own pottery. With her father's financial backing she began a concern named "Rookwood" after her family's estate, in 1880.

At first Rookwood Pottery was an amateur operation where independent studio work by members of the Cincinnati Pottery Club could be fired, but by 1890 it had become fully professional and a great commercial success. China painter Susan Frackelton in a 1906 article enthused that "the fundamental idea of Rookwood was to promote the national growth of an Art Pottery out of local

Frances Coates Jones.
A MIDSUMMER GARDEN.
c. 1907. Oil on canvas, 36¼ x
30 in. Private collection
This early white garden is one of a series of views, painted in different months, of the garden belonging to Jones's sister in Delaware.

Opposite: Frances Coates Jones.
AT THE GARDEN GATE. c. 1910.
Oil on canvas, 31 x 21 in. Private
collection
The combination of a pretty young woman wearing an old-fashioned dress in grandmother's garden proved irresistible to many painters.

conditions, both material and artistic . . . native clay, native decorative subjects and native artists."[3] Ironically, a pottery founded to encourage independent ceramic artists resulted in turning many women china painters into salaried employees of Rookwood.

More typical of independent potteries was the studio Adelaide Alsop Robineau (1865–1929) established beside her home, "Four Winds," in Syracuse, New York. In 1899, Robineau and her husband had bought the magazine *China Decorator,* and changed its name to *Keramic Studio.* Robineau's transformation from a china painter to a working potter, throwing her own wares and experimenting with clay bodies, including porcelain, paralleled the change of the magazine from one for amateurs to one exerting an important influence on the art-pottery movement.

Robineau had to care for three children and many domestic responsibilities; the physical integration of her work with her home life made both possible. She was always acutely aware of the "domestic problem," writing in 1912 when her youngest was seven, "It is because of the children and the home, that we cannot and will not give up, that the woman can never hope to become as great

in any line as man. Art is a jealous mistress and allows no consideration to interfere with her suprema-cy."[4] Nonetheless, Robineau managed to find time to tend an extensive and splendid old-fashioned garden filled with roses, which occupied the area between house and studio.

GRANDMOTHER'S GARDEN IN ARTS AND CRAFTS COMMUNITIES

In 1908, Robineau became the editor of a new mag-azine, *Palette and Bench*, that combined lessons in the fine arts with crafts instruction. Articles on painting and drawing were furnished by artists Charles Courtney Curran (1861–1942) and his wife, Grace Wickham, who later took over as editor. Curran's article, "The Outdoor Painting of Flowers," appeared in the June 1909 issue. The paintings used to illustrate the article, all of old-fashioned gardens and their flowers, included Willard Metcalf's *Purple, White and Gold* (1903), Robert Vonnoh's *The Edge of the Garden* (c. 1905), Frances Coates Jones's *August* and *September* (c. 1907), and Curran's *Among the Hollyhocks* (1904).

Vonnoh's unlocated painting of iris, daisies, roses, and other unidentifiable blossoms in great masses was described as "a luxurious riot of nature's strongest pigments—purples, blues, violets vie with vermillion, crimson, golden yellow and many shades of pearly white." Jones's two depictions of a garden in successive months employed a softer palette, with "beautiful silhouettes of white and delicate pink blooms against quiet grey green masses of foliage."[5] What seems to be the same garden can be seen in a midsummer version, possibly *July* in the series, of single-flowered white hollyhocks, pink and white gladioli, and phlox in informal beds separated by a grass path.

Curran's *Among the Hollyhocks* juxtaposed a young girl and old-fashioned flowers, as did his *A Corner of Grandmother's Garden* (1916). Curran made a speciality of such subjects and in his "A Class in Oil Painting" in the December 1908 *Palette and Bench* he described his intentions for a similar paint-ing. "The girl was meant to be as much as possible a flower herself, in the style of her dress, in the lighting of her face and neck, the way the figure loses herself among the flowers."[6]

Curran had painted young women in gardens even before having a garden himself. After the Currans became summer residents of Cragsmoor, New York, in the 1890s, such paintings came to dominate his work. His garden there of wild flowers, azaleas, and old-fashioned favorites served as the setting for many figure studies of his family and neighbors. *The Lanterns* (1913) documents the Currans' frequent use of the garden for parties. The inhabitants of Cragsmoor, one might judge from articles in the monthly *Cragsmoor Journal*, tried to outdo each other in their inventive entertainments as well as in their gardens.

Another specialist in paintings of women in gardens, Helen Turner (1858–1958), arrived in

"Wildweed" with Adah and J. Francis Murphy on the steps.
Smithsonian Institution, Archives of American Art, Washington,
D.C. Emerson Crosby Kelly research materials relating to J. Francis
Murphy
*The Murphys's cottage in Arkville, New York, was surrounded by an
exuberantly wild garden with natives like goldenrod and Joe-Pye weed
mixed with sunflowers and hollyhocks.*

Louise Huntington Collins in the garden at "Wildweed."
Photograph by Adah Murphy, c. 1890. Archives of American Art,
Smithsonian Institution, Washington, D.C. Emerson Crosby Kelly
research materials relating to J. Francis Murphy
*Adah Murphy posed friends in the garden and used the photographs for paintings
with titles such as* Among the Poppies.

1906. Infected by the Cragsmoor enthusiasm, Turner became a passionate gardener. Her garden climbed in three rock-bordered terraces beyond the porch of the cottage she built in 1910. She filled these beds with great masses of peonies, delphiniums, phlox, and foxgloves, which together formed a brilliant blur in the background of many of her paintings done on the porch. As did others in Cragsmoor, Turner domesticated native plants such as jack-in-the-pulpits, trilliums, and ferns, but had a special fondness for the hollyhocks that lined the south wall of her cottage and the old roses flanking the path to the front door.[7]

Girls in old-fashioned gardens were also the speciality of pastelist Adah Smith Murphy (1860–1949), wife of Tonalist painter J. Francis Murphy. As did the Currans, the Murphys summered in a congenial community of artists and craftsmen in Arkville, New York, where they had been introduced by fellow painter Alexander Wyant. In 1884, they built "Wildweed," a rustic cottage noteworthy for its shingle-style construction in native stone and timber and for its lack of a kitchen. The Murphys took their meals in a nearby hotel until they expanded the cottage and added a kitchen in 1899.

Adah Murphy was an amateur photographer who used her prints of models posed amidst her flowers as the basis for paintings of the 1890s with titles such as *Among the Poppies, Looking at Daisies, Old House and Hollyhocks,* or *Old Fashioned Flowers.* Both Murphys were keen gardeners, planting and tending their very informal garden, which included many transplants from the wild as well as the old standbys, annual and perennial. A description of the garden in 1908 gives something of its flavor. "They call it 'Wildweed' and because it is left so wild, and the weeds and the old-fashioned flowers grow in such reckless abandon . . . it is so charming. Wild vines clamber over its many piazzas, hollyhocks nod familiarly in at the kitchen door, and goldenrod hobnobs cosily with patches of scarlet poppies next [to] the front steps."[8]

The informal way of life and rustic architecture of many newly formed Arts and Crafts colonies seemed to encourage equally relaxed cottage gardens. Rose Valley was begun in 1901 as a cooperative community by architect William L. Price and a group of Quaker investors who bought a former textile mill near Philadelphia, converted it into workshops, and built a community center, guesthouse, and cottages. Among the crafts established there were a pottery, a furniture shop, and the Rose Valley print shop, which published the official journal of the association, *The Artsman: The Art That Is Life* (1903–7). Despite its auspicious beginning, by 1910 Rose Valley had become little more than a suburban commuters' enclave.

An equally ambitious settlement, Byrdcliffe Colony, was begun in 1902 near Woodstock, New York, by Ralph Radcliffe Whitehead (1854–1929), a wealthy Englishman who had studied with Ruskin at Oxford. That the colony was run as benevolent despotism rather than as a cooperative was seen as an advantage by one visitor: "Whitehead is the absolute monarch, and no one is tolerated who is not sympathetic to his rule. . . . Would not Onteora jump with joy were it subject to a Ralph Whitehead?" Whitehead had first attempted to found such a colony in Italy, where he met the well-connected Philadelphian Jane Byrd McCall, who became his second wife. McCall had studied painting in France and briefly in England with Ruskin himself. By the time she met Whitehead, she had embraced Arts and Crafts simplicity, exclaiming, "How little one needs—actually needs—in this life. . . . Here one change of raiment is enough . . . to be simple, to be at work is happiness."[9]

The Whiteheads swore allegiance to an Arts and Crafts life together in Italy before they were able to marry legally in 1892. Returning to America, they built a grand classical villa in Santa Barbara, California, where the gardens were planted with hollyhocks, lilies, roses, sunflowers, and iris. Their much simpler, vine-covered "White Pines" at Byrdcliffe was built in the same self-consciously rustic style as the artisan's bungalows, but on a vast scale.

Helen Turner. MORNING. 1919. Oil on canvas, 34½ x 44½ in. Zigler Museum, Jennings, Louisiana
Turner's old-fashioned garden at Cragsmoor was designed to be viewed from the porch of her cottage.

At Byrdcliffe, Whitehead attempted to foster distinctively American crafts. Graphic designers Zulma Steele and Edna Walker, hired by Whitehead to decorate the Byrdcliffe furniture with motifs taken from local flora, developed the Byrdcliffe fleur-de-lis trademark from drawings of lilies and iris in the Whitehead garden. Noted landscape painter Birge Harrison, who came as painting instructor during the summer of 1904, hoped that such efforts would produce "an art whose symbols will be the American flora and fauna as seen and felt through the American temperament."[10]

Byrdcliffe was never a commercial success, but Roycroft was. This colony at East Aurora, New York, had been established seven years earlier by Elbert G. Hubbard (1856–1915), a retired soap manufacturer who had visited William Morris in 1892 and determined to set up an American equivalent of Kelmscott Press. Hubbard began by publishing in late 1895 a periodical, *The Philistine*, full of ideas lifted from Ruskin and Morris. It became immensely popular, achieving a circulation of nearly

100,000. Other publications of Roycroft Press were equally in demand and admirers flocked to East Aurora, where Hubbard built an inn to accommodate them. His furniture industry, begun to supply the inn, expanded after 1900 to a business employing more than four hundred workers and depending in large part on mail-order sales.

Hubbard's charismatic personality and the success of his enterprises drew many artists and craftsmen to East Aurora. Among them was Minneapolis landscape painter Alexis Jean Fournier (1865–1948), who had been involved with the Minneapolis Craftshouse in the 1890s and came to Roycroft in 1903 to furnish mural paintings for the Roycroft Inn.

GUSTAV STICKLEY AND CRAFTSMAN GARDENS

The most far-reaching in its influence of all these Arts and Crafts enterprises was that begun by Gustav Stickley (1858–1942) in Syracuse, New York. Here in 1899 Stickley began to manufacture simply constructed furniture influenced by Morris designs he had seen on a trip to England; two years later he began the *Craftsman* magazine to spread his ideas and promote the products of his Craftsman Workshops. In addition to printing articles of general interest to both makers and purchasers of handcrafted products, in 1903 the magazine began to carry plans for Craftsman houses. A writer on "Suburban Homes" envisioned such a house as "a small building which shall be suited to our climate, our economics, our habits of life; which shall be distinctly American . . . consist of American materials treated in full American manner."[11]

Craftsman houses were meant to be simple, functional homes whose beauty was intrinsic to their structure, with the California bungalow frequently cited as a model. For Stickley, writing in the *Craftsman,* such homes and the opportunities they offered for rewarding labor both indoors and out were agents for moral good.

> In home life, in contact with nature and in constructive work rather than in the mere acquisition of fortune, lie happiness and beauty. . . . We American people are just beginning to emerge from a condition of unrest necessitated by immigration, migration, settling of new lands, developing of industries, sudden acquiring of wealth, and other forces due to the rapid growth of a large country, and I believe this is the time we should try to establish in our American life an ideal of home. It is the real family life that gives birth to the patriot's love of country. It is the real home that brings forth true citizens.[12]

Several articles in the magazine described in a general way gardens appropriate for Crafts-

Gustav Stickley's garden at Craftsman Farms, Parsippany, New Jersey. Photograph, c. 1914
In 1908 Stickley began work on what he hoped would be a cooperative community farm and crafts school in New Jersey. The intended clubhouse became his home and the garden combined vegetables with flowers as recommended in his Craftsman *magazine.*

man homes; all agreed that the garden should fit the house and the family's way of life. Landscape designer Arthur A. Shurtleff praised English cottagers' gardens, where flowers and neatly clipped hedges mingled with vegetables. An article called "Landscape Gardening" advised against the natural style of lawn and groups of trees for small properties because there was not enough available space to be effective. A writer on "Converting Backyards into Gardens" recommended for such a limited space an old-fashioned garden with brick paths and borders of box or privet. Illustrations showed such gardens, with plank- or box-bordered beds enclosed in picket fences.[13]

Only one article was addressed specifically to "Craftsman Gardens for Craftsman Homes," with plans and views given for four gardens for four different houses on small lots. The reader was cautioned to guard against discordant colors among the flowers and the house, while the arrangement of the flowers was to be informal and unpretentious. The vegetable garden was made an integral part of the designs; in two of the plans it occupied part of the front yard. This was in keeping with the belief that a "properly kept vegetable garden is in its way as beautiful as a flower garden, and by treating it decoratively and letting it have here and there a few clumps of flowers, it can be made a very charming spot indeed."[14]

Like colonial gardens, a Craftsman garden would combine the useful with the ornamental. A pergola, the modern equivalent of the colonial arbor, was viewed as a desirable component of the garden. As well as providing a sheltered living space, the pergola served another function, as pointed out in an article on "Pergolas: The Most Picturesque and Practical Feature of Modern Out-Door Life": "The orderly patches of vegetables . . . are no longer relegated to distant or hidden lots. They add a phase of beauty to their task of usefulness, are close comrades with flowers, united to them by the arches of the pergola."[15]

The old proven flowers were recommended for planting, both for their practicality and their links with the past. As one writer declared, "I shall plant the old-fashioned perennials because I am foolishly attached to the things of my fathers." Informality was preferred, with one Craftsman garden praised for its "maze of flowers . . . a haphazard arrangement that makes you doubt the superior law of discipline and order." All of the articles stressed the particularly American qualities of gardens appropriate for a Craftsman home and many urged the use of native plants. An article, "The Growing Individuality of the American Garden," illustrated with a photograph of an old-fashioned garden, pointed out that "America is wonderfully rich in the variety of its flowers, shrubs and trees. . . . We have no need to alter or import, if we desire beauty we have but to develop existing qualities."[16]

A beguiling first-person narrative of such a garden, "The Garden of the Many Little Paths," appeared in the March 1910 issue of *Craftsman,* and was written by the author of *The Garden in the Wilderness* (1903). This anonymous writer, identified as "a Hermit" on the book's title page, was Hanna Rion (Mrs. H. R. Ver Beck, 1875–1924), who wrote under her own name a manual for beginners, *Let's Make a Flower Garden* (1912). After college in Columbia, South Carolina, Rion, daughter of Mary C. Rion, the author of *Ladies' Southern Florist* (1860), came north to study art.

Rion's own two-and-a-half-acre garden was in the Catskills. Here with the forest as a background, great clumps of pines and cedars separated garden areas linked by narrow paths. Rion took particular pride in one very large, irregular bed planted with masses of goldenrod, wild purple asters, feverfew, black-eyed Susans, and ferns—with a border of hepaticas. A more conventional rose garden was underplanted first with annual phlox and California poppies and then with dianthuses, which did not need replacing each year. There was a moon garden of pale flowers designed for night viewing and fragrance with four-o'clocks, nicotiana, delphiniums, and moonflowers, and a border along the central walk with hollyhocks, perennial poppies, and Shasta daisies. Another garden area centered on a sundial surrounded with hyacinths, nasturtiums, phlox, and sweet peas.

Alexis Jean Fournier. HOLLYHOCKS IN THE GARDEN, THE BUNGLE HOUSE. After 1903. Oil on canvas, 26 1/8 x 40 1/8 in. Private collection
Assembled from a chicken coop and a blacksmith's shop, Fournier's picturesque "Bungle House" in East Aurora, New York,
had an apple tree growing through the roof and an old-fashioned garden in front.

Rion boasted of 150 Dorothy Perkins roses grown from cuttings but admitted having only one crimson rambler, exclaiming, "It is the most diseased, mildewed, bug-infested, shabby, common rose in the world!" Elsewhere were hundreds of lilies and iris, thousands of tulips and other bulbs, and self-sown sunflowers that appeared among the cornflowers, candytuft, coreopsis, and Shirley poppies sown each year. There was even a steep bank deliberately planted with dandelions.[17]

Rion's garden grew haphazardly, and as she admitted in her book, none of the flower beds would have pleased a landscape designer. Rather, she sought inspiration in old American gardening books (such as the one written by her mother), gardening magazines, and nursery catalogues. She probably had in mind, as well, her family garden in the South, with its "straggling, aged box borders . . . beautiful old traceries of paths—the curves of symmetrical beds."[18]

The Garden in the Wilderness had both precursors and followers. Almon Dexter (in real life, F. S. Dickson) described the making of a Craftsman house and garden on a remote Maine island in *And the Wilderness Blossomed* (1901). Among the six books he considered indispensable for a gardener's library, only one was English: William Robinson's *The English Flower Garden,* just beginning to be widely known. The others were Gray's *Botany,* Liberty Hyde Bailey's *Cyclopedia of American Horticulture,* Dana's *How to Know the Wild Flowers,* Charles Dudley Warner's *My Summer in the Garden,* and Celia Thaxter's *An Island Garden.*

Mrs. Theodore Thomas (1852–1929), wife of the noted conductor, wrote of their Bethlehem, New Hampshire, summer retreat in *Our Mountain Garden* (1904). In the Thomas garden, hardy perennials and wild flowers, many taken from the woods and meadows, were made at home in long borders above and below a rough stone retaining wall and in beds around the rustic cottage. Even though Thomas stated that "my garden is not in the least like any other of which I have read, for it is strictly a 'home-made' affair, and I write about it to show what one can do without a hot-bed, hose, greenhouse, or gardener, on a wild, rock-strewn mountain side, untamed by the hand of man," such a garden had been written about since the 1870s. As was often the case after 1900, these American predecessors went unacknowledged and perhaps unknown. Thomas felt that "nature and Robinson alone will furnish all the instruction any one can ask for." She attributed her use of American native "weeds" to Robinson, "the very wisest of the Wise Ones," who "recommended them so respectfully by their botanical names, and pointed out how effective they could be in the right surroundings."[19]

The author of what might be considered a manual for the American cottage garden, *Hardy Plants for Cottage Gardens* (1910), appeared first in the pages of the *Craftsman* as a champion of cottage industry. Helen R. Albee (b. 1864), who had settled in the small New Hampshire village of Pequaket on her marriage in the 1890s, established there in 1897 a cooperative hooked-rug industry among local women that received favorable notice in the magazine in 1902. In March of that year she wrote an article, "The Modern Craftsman: The Question of His Livelihood," arguing in favor of the use of machines in craft work. By this date her Abnakee Rug Industry had been in production for five years and she could boast of "my success in changing the supposedly worthless hooked rug into an artistic product."[20]

Albee's gardening book recorded her own apprenticeship under the tutelage of her husband, a New Hampshire native. Her garden seemed to follow the New England injunction, "Make over, make do, or do without," and with gratifying results, proving to her satisfaction "that where necessity is used as a guide, a certain kind of beauty inevitably follows." Her terraced garden was created out of a rock and rubbish heap, with the rocks reused to form raised beds threaded through with paths.

Albee became a serious plantswoman, the flexible, informal nature of her garden allowing

Helen Albee's garden. Photograph by Helen Albee in *Hardy Plants for Cottage Gardens* (1910) *Albee's free-form, old fashioned garden was in Bethlehem, New Hampshire.*

her to expand it at will to accommodate new passions, often old perennials and annuals. Her practice was to distribute color throughout the beds rather than restrict one color to one location. In an appendix to her garden book, she provided an annotated list of shrubs and flowers organized by color and time of bloom so that readers might make arrangements according to their own taste. Her model was the "conservative" gardener, "who preserves a remnant of her grandmother's garden. . . . who has retained for us the old-fashioned favorites, the almost forgotten things with aromatic odors."[21]

As was the case with so many women, Albee found her garden a source of spiritual growth as well as aesthetic enjoyment. In 1911, she wrote, "This bit of land less than seventy-five by a hundred and fifty feet, was to reorganize much of my thought; it was to be my confidante, my instructor, and my pulpit. Here I was to learn order . . . and foresight that would outrun the seasons; to develop a spirit of self-sacrifice . . . to perceive the inviolable workings of law and justice; to play a minor Providence in a miniature world, where neglect or ignorance paid swift and sure penalty."[22]

In an even more personal book, *A Kingdom of Two: A True Romance of Country Life* (1913), she embraced the Craftsman ideal of home life, which she considered to be "the aim and occupation of the whole feminine world." She held up the modest lily of the field as an example: "Being a conservative in social habits, she does not attend mass meetings . . . nor organize societies for equal suffrage in the garden, well knowing some plants are not qualified to associate with roses and lilies." For Albee, the old-fashioned flowers were "the perennial fruits of woman's love of beauty and home, fragile but imperishable monuments of human tenderness," and garden-making a way of affirming enduring values.[23]

Philip Leslie Hale. THE RED BARN. c. 1890s. Oil on canvas, 20 x 30 in. Private collection
Hale conducted a summer painting class at Matunuck, Rhode Island, where he advised his students to bring plenty of chrome yellow.
He himself delighted in painting strong color contrasts like that of goldenrod against a red barn.

Cottage Gardens for Laborers and Suburbanites

I want the old-time garden,
The dear sweet-scented flowers,
With yellow bees a-buzzin'
Through all the peaceful hours.

Low pinks and bouncin'-betties,
An' marigolds in rows,
Wee, snowy, sweet alyssum,
An' dainty button rose.

White phlox like girls in weddin' clothes,
Red poppies swayin' light,
And perky, gay snap-dragons
In velvet coats bedight.

Alice E. Ives,
"The Old-Fashioned Garden"

THE OLD-FASHIONED GARDEN AND THE AMERICANIZATION OF IMMIGRANTS Between 1870 and 1900, more than eleven million immigrants arrived in the United States, most of them coming from eastern and southern Europe after 1890. During these same years there was unprecedented labor unrest—the railway strikes of 1877, the Haymarket Riot in Chicago in 1886, a steel-mill strike in Pittsburgh in 1892, and more railway strikes in 1894. An economic depression that began in the 1870s contin-

Prize-winning garden at Bagley,
H. C. Frick Coke Company.
Photograph, c. 1910
*Gardens usually occupied all the space
around the miner's cottage and often
mixed flowers with vegetables.*

Below: Prize-winning garden at
Hecla #1, H. C. Frick Coke
Company. Photograph, c. 1910
*Mining companies used gardening
contests as part of their drive to assimilate
immigrant workers to American ways.*

ued through the 1890s. Many great industrial fortunes were being made, but more than eight hundred banks failed in the four years following the 1893 crash. Hundreds of thousands of previously independent small businessmen, farmers, and professionals were forced under. The middle-class abandonment of the cities accelerated while the only industry that experienced uninterrupted growth was that of trolley-line construction linking cities to the new suburbs. Political and industrial corruption was rampant and seemed to go hand in hand with an ostentatious display of wealth, fueling the fire of class conflict.[1]

Many thoughtful members of the established middle class feared that social order, particularly in cities and towns, was on the verge of disintegration. The assimilation of so many immigrants not of Anglo-Saxon stock was seen as the central problem of the time. Much of the political and social reform begun in the 1890s centered on educating the largely Catholic and Jewish immigrants about American ideals of government, community, and home exemplified in the values of the founding fathers.

In company towns and mining settlements on the frontier, the problem of the Americanization of a heterogeneous mixture of immigrant workers became acute. The town of Pullman, Illinois, had been thoughtfully planned in 1880 for the manufacture of sleeping cars. Despite its amenities, it was typical of towns where one industry was both employer and landlord and was not exempt from labor unrest, becoming the scene of a violent strike in 1894.

In an attempt to defuse tension and assimilate workers from widely divergent cultures, many companies offered English classes and lessons in homemaking. As a 1914 "U.S. Steel Corporation Bureau of Safety, Sanitation and Welfare Bulletin" put it, the workers had "been accustomed to ways of living which we must try to change." Cottage gardening was widely seen as an important tool in assimilation. In addition, company managers believed that the encouragement of gardening as well as the provision of a comfortable home would keep the men usefully occupied after working hours. As the U.S. Steel Bureau of Safety saw it, "The beauty of the gardens and lawns exerts a refining influence on the family. . . . In the making of a garden the members of the family are brought out into the open air and sunshine. This is especially beneficial to those who work in mines and mills. . . . The man who has learned to take pride in his garden hurries home from his work spending little time loitering and none in the saloon."[2]

In isolated mining villages far from other settlements, the need for gardens was pressing, not just for their recreational value and refining influence, but to provide food. Remote mines on the frontier ran farming operations, provided space for large vegetable gardens beside each miner's house, and often ran horticultural contests with cash awards.

Prizes could be substantial in these garden contests held in the early 1900s. The H. C. Frick Company in Pennsylvania offered gold pieces in the amounts of twenty, ten, and five dollars for first, second, and third prizes, respectively. A directive of October 6, 1910, to all superintendents of Frick plants ordered: "Commence, at once, and make a special effort to have every yard converted into a garden or flower patch next year. If necessary, plough up the ground and haul manure and give any necessary assistance and instructions." Nearly one-third of the United States coal companies had begun garden contests by World War I, with the companies providing plants and fences and awarding cash, certificates of merit, and gardening manuals.[3]

GEORGE WASHINGTON CABLE'S GARDENING CONTEST Others besides factory owners sponsored cottage-garden contests in an effort to Americanize foreign-born workers. In the factory town of Northampton, Massachusetts, best-selling author George Washington Cable (1844–1925) saw "irreligion, vulgarity and bad morals widening like a flood." Believing that preservation of the moral order depended on the family and the home, he began in 1887 the Home Culture Club for the encouragement of reading and discussion among factory workers, mechanics, and homemakers of the town.[4] Cable's insistence on the home as the basis for civic order paralleled that of Arts and Crafts reformers like Gustav Stickley. According to such thinking, women were still to be confined to the domestic sphere while men were encouraged to take on an executive role in the ordering of both home and garden.

Cable had grown up in the Garden District of New Orleans, the setting for several of his popular novels of antebellum Louisiana. Although a supporter of secession, and a Confederate veteran, he became a vocal advocate of civil rights for the newly emancipated slaves. At the time of his greatest acclaim as an author and lecturer, he was forced to move north with his family because of virulent opposition in the South to his stand.

A riveting public speaker, Cable attracted the devotion of a young art student, Adelene Moffat, who moved to Northampton, became his personal secretary, and in 1889 was made the first salaried director of the Home Culture Club. The club became the focus of Cable's reforming zeal and rapidly expanded into public rooms where classes in English, American history, and other subjects were conducted by Smith College students. Housed in a colonial-style building, described in 1904 as "glistening white and shedding light on a region rather dark," the club provided its foreign-born members surroundings of "cultured taste" as well as instruction.[5]

Cable paid a visit to Andrew Carnegie in Scotland in 1898, seeking funding for the club and returned inspired with the idea of a flower-garden competition, with Carnegie to underwrite the cash prizes. From the beginning, the contest was designed to encourage real cottage gardening—professional gardeners or those who hired any help at all were excluded. According to the rules printed in 1899, special merits were considered to be "economy of money outlay; abundance of flowers; artistic taste in the laying out of the garden; artistic harmonies and contrasts of color; condition of the lawn."[6]

The sort of garden that Cable envisioned as an American one, revealed in his book *The Amateur Garden* (1914), was predictably the old-fashioned garden of perennials and flowering shrubs, many of them natives, arranged in informal masses within a fence, since "the poor man—the poor woman—needs the protection of a fence to a degree which the well-to-do know nothing of." The home itself was to be the focus: "The garden as it approaches the house, should accept more and more discipline—domestication—social refinement." Cable disliked small-scale bedding-out schemes, which he identified with foreign gardens. "In such gardening there is a constraint, a lack of natural freedom, a distance from nature and a certain contented subserviency, which makes it wholly unfit to express . . . the American home."[7]

Cable's own garden exemplified his ideas. His two boundaries with neighbors were defined with wire fences covered in vines. Wide borders were planted with shrubs and old-fashioned perennials. His back lawn merged into a carefully edited woodlot and his house was shaded by mature trees and cloaked in flowering shrubs. He saw his work in his garden as paralleling his work with the Home Culture Club: "Gardening is a benevolent, gracious *naturalization* [emphasis Cable's] of nature to citizenship under the home's domain, and an American garden should remain American whatever it borrows from Japan, England, Italy or Holland. . . . As a matter of fact, at least four-fifths of all the commonest and most beautiful things in our gardens are exotics, but they are naturalized citizens and have themselves long forgotten that they came from China, Scotland, Persia, or the islands of the seven seas."[8]

In the first year of the garden competition, sixty gardens were entered; fifteen years later, more than a quarter of the households in Northampton had joined in. As early as 1905, Cable could write exuberantly to his sister, "I never expected to have a whole town for my garden but that's how 'tis." This was an exaggeration, but Cable's gardening ideas held sway over as many as one-fourth of Northampton's gardens before 1915. Some of the immigrant gardens of "cerulean sewer pipes crested with scarlet geranium . . . purple paint kegs of petunias . . . crimson wash-kettles of verbenas" that he cast into oblivion seem as appealing today as his insensitive patriarchal stance does not.[9]

One of the prize-winning gardens, kept by Mrs. Bardwell and Mrs. Flower, exemplified for Cable what an American cottage garden should be. As he described it, "The flowers rise in dense abundance, related to one another in clever taste and with a happy care for a procession of bloom uninterrupted throughout the season." As well as flowers, "in charming privacy, masked by hollyhocks, dahlias and other tall-maidenly things, lie beds of strawberries and lettuce and all the prim ranks and orders of the kitchen garden."[10]

Cable, however, intended the cash prizes to encourage the male head of the household to garden. He proclaimed, "We want to dispel the notion that flower gardening is only women's work and child's play." To this end, in 1906, professional horticulturist H. D. Hemenway was brought in. Cable's insistence that "administrative work must be done by one secretary who must be a man" led to Hemenway's appointment as director of the Home Culture Club and the unfortunate forced resignation of Adelene Moffat, who nearly singlehandedly had overseen the development of the club into an important social service agency and the garden contest into an event of national interest.[11]

GRANDMOTHER'S GARDEN IN THE SUBURBS By the turn of the century, cottage gardening was seen as therapeutic not just for workers but for middle-class dwellers in the new suburbs, where people of widely divergent backgrounds were thrown together. In 1909, the magazine *American Homes and Gardens* announced a gardening contest directly inspired by that in Northampton. The editor was impressed by the "cottage gardens so tastefully laid out and so admirably kept" that illustrated what could be done on a small plot. The contest was instituted "to encourage the suburban house owner to embellish what little land he owns by the judicious planting of flowers."[12]

Nearly all the prizewinners modeled their gardens, published in successive issues in 1910, on the old-fashioned one with masses of hardy perennials and shrubs often arranged in rectangular beds bisected by grass or gravel paths and enclosed by vine-covered fences or hedges. A garden in Troy, New York, was divided into large beds backing on a fence and planted with rudbeckias, hollyhocks, larkspur, foxgloves, phlox, sweet Williams, primroses, tiger lilies, and dahlias. Another in Lexington, Massachusetts, had many rectangular beds with a grape arbor in the old style.

The garden of the fourth-prize winner, Mrs. Anna H. Condict of Essex Falls, New Jersey, was closest to the old-fashioned plan of enclosed flower beds intersected by grass paths with an arbor screening the kitchen garden. In Mrs. Condict's case, the creation of the garden was literally therapeutic. Having been advised to lead an outdoor life because of ill health, she exclaimed, "I have in this my fourth summer not only improved my health, but I have also a fine kitchen garden and a formal garden of which I am quite proud. Flowers are everywhere of fifty different kinds." She attributed her success to *A Woman's Hardy Garden* (1903) by Helena Rutherfurd Ely (1858–1920). Empowered by reading that "the best success in flower culture was obtained by people in middle life," she

Bordered path looking south, "Meadowburn Farm." Photograph, c. 1900. Collection B. Danforth Ely
This path lined with lindens and the hardy perennials recommended in A Woman's Hardy Garden *(1903)*
led from the pool garden near the house to a rustic arbor and seat.

The pool garden with lilies, "Meadowburn Farm." Photograph, c. 1900. Collection B. Danforth Ely
Helena Rutherfurd Ely's garden at "Meadowburn Farm" in Sussex County, New Jersey,
had several garden rooms connected by bordered paths.

Elizabeth Lowell. Judge A. Aiken's Garden, Greenfield, Massachusetts. c. 1900. Watercolor on paper,
18 x 14 in. Collection Mr. and Mrs. G. Ernest Dale, Jr.
*This old-fashioned garden was made by Judge Aiken and his wife after their marriage in 1895 and is a
splendid example of many such gardens made in New England in the 1890s.*

was filled with enthusiasm and determined "to strive for masses of color and succession of bloom. Not one plant of a kind, but a hundred of each, all of my own raising."[13]

Ely's book did not assume the existence of either a gardener or a greenhouse, but was intended, as she wrote her editor, "to help people . . . who do most of the garden work themselves by telling concisely what to do and how to do it."[14] It was one of the clearest and most realistic of the manuals written after 1900 by educated and energetic women gardeners. Designed for the growing ranks of women like themselves who married and settled in droves in the new suburbs or took on the responsibility of a summer or weekend house, the manuals of these writers presumed a modicum of both leisure and money, if not gardening know-how, on the part of their audience.

These books were illustrated with photographs of the authors' own gardens, which were seldom so elaborate that at least some part of them could not be duplicated by the reader. Ely's description of one of her own gardens at "Meadowburn Farm" in Sussex County, New Jersey, with four beds centered on a sundial and backed by a pergola, served as a model for probably thousands of suburban gardens made on a smaller scale. One of these, "A Woman's Two-Year-Old Hardy Garden from Seed," was published in *American Homes and Gardens* (March 1911) and described as a "real old fashioned garden of perennial plants" arranged in four beds around a sundial with a pergola along two sides. All the expected flowers, some started from seed, others moved from an old garden, still others dug from the woods, furnished bloom from June to frost.[15]

Occasionally the author herself, dressed for work, appeared in photographs in these manuals. In *The Flower Garden* (1903), a book which unlike Ely's, did assume the presence of a gardener, author Ida Bennett made a point of participating in all the activities shown, wearing her recommended denim skirt, calico blouse, and apron. Ely advocated suede gloves and an old-fashioned sunbonnet. The cover of Edith Fullerton's *How to Make a Vegetable Garden* (1905) sported a photograph of a suitably attired woman guiding a tiller.

A knowledge of the latest gardening literature in England as well as in America was now expected of these authors and resulted in an increased concern with "continuous bloom" or "succession of bloom." Louise Shelton's 1915 handbook, for example, was titled *Continuous Bloom in America*. Nonetheless, the old-fashioned American garden with its informal, even haphazard planting and rectilinear bordered beds was praised by nearly all writers and preferred by many.

HELENA ELY'S GARDEN Ely in *A Woman's Hardy Garden* welcomed the growing popularity of old gardens and their flowers not only because of their association with America's past but also because she saw these gardens as classic and always in good taste. "The

"Bouncing Betts." Photograph by Mabel Osgood Wright, n.d.
Wright was an accomplished photographer who delighted in picturing the plants that had escaped from colonial gardens, such as the Saponaria officinalis *seen here.*

simple, formal gardens of a hundred years ago with box-edged paths, borders and regular box-edged beds, are always beautiful, never tiresome, and have the additional merit of being appropriate either to the fine country place or the simple cottage."[16]

Ely's own garden filled several acres beside her "stern and very simple" eighteenth-century house, "Meadowburn Farm." For such a house, only an old-fashioned garden would do, albeit a very grand one. A memoir written by her daughter relates that Ely's first gardening efforts after her marriage in 1880 had been geometric beds of annuals but that, "as she drove about the countryside, she noticed the old fashioned flowers in the dooryards of the farm houses. These charmed her beyond measure, and she longed for them on her own place. So she started her first long border. . . . and begged from her friends among the farmers' wives roots and divisions of their hardy flowers."[17]

In 1894, Ely went to Europe, where she was particularly moved by English gardens. She began to think of her garden in terms of a series of rooms connected by bordered paths and rose-

"Osborne House." Photograph by Mabel Osgood Wright, n.d.
Wright photographed many old houses in Fairfield, occasionally including a suitably costumed resident.

covered arches. At the turn of the century, her garden had three principal rooms: the formal garden with box-edged grass walks centered on a sundial; a rose garden with beds underplanted with pansies and surrounded with a barberry hedge; and a rustic summerhouse, covered in clematis and crimson rambler roses, enclosed by a perennial border backed with alternating pink and white altheas. Other rooms were added, including a pool garden filled with lilies. The lilies, which proved a disappointment, were later replaced by evergreens, as were many of the flower beds.

Although Ely's garden was maintained by a number of gardeners, in her book she stressed her own active planning and planting and envisioned simple arrangements for those with small grounds and no help. She suggested plants from the woods—Virginia creeper, rhododendron, ferns, columbines, cardinal flowers, and other wild flowers—and recommended a simple border lining a walk, with spring bulbs, peonies, lilies, and chrysanthemums. Ely's advice was practical and down-to-earth, and she readily admitted when her knowledge was scanty. She recommended only those plants she herself had grown and that had proved reliably hearty. She noted ruefully, "Well, they have climate in England, even if we have weather, and English gardens will always fill American gardeners with despair."[18]

Ely believed that "the garden of hardy perennials, annuals and bulbs will give us a continual sequence of flowers . . . from April to November." Her chapter devoted to perennials listed all the old favorites, including valerian, "seen now-a-days only in old-fashioned gardens." She was particularly fond of delphiniums and hollyhocks, asserting, "No one can have too many Hollyhocks." She noted happily, "Even as the mahogany of our grandfathers is now brought forth from garrets and unused rooms . . . so we are learning to take the old gardens for our models, and the old-fashioned flowers to fill our borders."[19]

Many of the women writers of gardening books were able to translate the knowledge derived from creating their own gardens into actual financial rewards and often a professional career. In Ely's case, the advance she received for her manuscript was, as she revealed to her editor at Macmillan and Company, the first money she had ever made. The book continued to earn money, remaining in print until 1930, and was reprinted in 1990. Ely wrote two other manuals, *Another Hardy Garden Book* (1905) and *The Practical Flower Garden* (1911). The last closed with a chapter on wild gardening inspired by the splendid woods garden in Greenwich, Connecticut, of a close friend, Benjamin F. Fairchild, whom she married two years after the death of her first husband in 1914.

MABEL OSGOOD WRIGHT AND THE ROMANCE OF THE OLD-FASHIONED GARDEN The value of Ely's first book was recognized by another popularizer of the old-fashioned garden, Mabel Osgood Wright (1859–1934), who had been asked by Macmillan and Company to critique the manuscript. While pointing out that there was no new material in the book, she continued: "The simplicity of the directions, their directness and the elimination of all but the most satisfactory plants and bulbs, will, I am sure, make the book valuable to the novice." Wright's caveat that "the author is affluent—those who use the book are not likely to be" prompted a heated rejoinder from Ely. "I should really be obliged if you could disabuse the reader's mind of her opinion that I am an 'affluent' person. The term so horribly savors of a calico gown and diamond ear rings!"[20]

Wright herself had enjoyed a privileged upbringing and by any standards was affluent. The daughter of the Reverend Samuel Osgood, she had lived during the winter in a New York brownstone and during the summer at the Osgoods' ten-acre country place, "Waldstein," in Fairfield, Con-

Philip Leslie Hale. THE CRIMSON RAMBLER. C. 1908. Oil on canvas, 25 1/4 x 30 3/16 in.
The Pennsylvania Academy of the Fine Arts, Philadelphia. Joseph E. Temple Fund
Hale's vigorous Impressionist brushstroke and brilliant palette enlivens this now common combination of a
lovely young woman and flowers seen in strong sunlight.

Garden at "Waldstein," Fairfield, Connecticut. Photograph by Mabel Osgood Wright, n.d.
Wright included this photograph of a grape arbor and perennial beds, with fraxinella in the foreground in The Garden, You and I *(1906).*

necticut. After her father's death and her marriage to an antiquarian bookseller from England, she and her husband moved into "Waldstein," where she became a commuter's wife.

Unlike Ely, soon after her marriage Wright began to forge a career as a nature writer of newspaper pieces, which were collected in *The Friendship of Nature* in 1894. Her absorbing passion, besides gardening, became wild-bird protection, and her second book was the highly regarded manual *Birdcraft* (1895). She was one of the founders of the Connecticut Audubon Society, which had grown from the Fairfield chapter of the Daughters of the American Revolution (which Wright had helped found in 1894). She served as the society's president for twenty-five years and edited the Audubon section of the magazine *Bird Lore*.

Despite the success of *Birdcraft* and several children's books on nature subjects, Wright wrote to her editor at Macmillan and Company in 1899, "I have several ideas, new unless Neltje has thought of them."[21] Neltje was Mrs. Frank Doubleday, wife of the publisher, who had to her credit several lavishly illustrated books on birds written under the pseudonym Neltje Blanchan and at the time was working on *Nature's Garden* (1900), a large-format wild-flower manual with color photographs.

Blanchan's cultural gentility exceeded even Wright's and found expression in *The American Flower Garden* (1909) where, together with gardens of great estates, she illustrated examples of the old-fashioned garden. She confessed, "However great may be one's intellectual enjoyment of a fault-less piece of formal garden composition, one is compelled to really love far better the little cottage garden where roses tangle over the doorway, hollyhocks peep in the lattice, tawny orange lilies that have escaped through the white picket fence brighten the roadside, clematis festoons fleecy clouds of bloom over the unpruned bushes along a lichen-covered wall where chipmunks play hide and seek, and tall, unkempt lilacs send their fragrance through the kitchen door."[22]

Wright's ideas were for a different sort of garden book than Blanchan's. Captivated, as so many were, by *Elizabeth and Her German Garden* (1898) and its first-person narrative, Wright determined to produce a similar garden "romance" combining story line with instruction. Her first effort in this genre was *Flowers and Ferns in Their Haunts* (1901), an engaging if episodic chronicle of the wild-flower explorations of the narrator and her companion, "Flower-Hat" (no endangered bird feathers there!), under the tutelage of an old Yankee farmer. The book was illustrated with Wright's own photographs as well as those of professional garden photographer J. Horace McFarland.

Her second effort, *The Garden of a Commuter's Wife* (1901), a semiautobiographical account of life in a suburb written under the pseudonym "Barbara," was a resounding success. She continued the formula in two sequels, *The People of the Whirlpool* (1903) and *The Garden, You and I* (1906), using letters and diary entries as well as a first-person narrative. Wright envisioned the books as "social comedy" as well as manuals of garden instruction. Through her alter ego, Barbara, she examined both the social turmoil occasioned by the influx of suburban commuters and new money into the rural community of Fairfield and the changing position of women within the new social order.

Earlier in the century, family background rather than wealth had determined social position, but by the 1880s, as Wright wrote in her autobiography, "the frank and cordial understanding that had existed between congenial groups of widely different financial standing was being upset. A new and quite un-American way of making money on the one hand and being received socially on the other, developed." Those from old families like Wright's, who felt displaced both by the nouveaux riches who lived on a grand scale and by other suburbanites on a financial par with the old families but with no background, sought concrete signs of affiliation with those in a similar situation. As Wright put it, "the first general groping about for origins began, both in life and furnishings. Roots, feelers, anchorage in the new soil became desirable—the deeper the better."[23]

An interest in grandmother's garden as well as her house and furniture was one obvious manifestation. Thus the pseudonymous Barbara's garden, inherited from her mother, was "of that respectable no-period style of the [eighteen] forties. . . . a style best summed up in the words Early American." A "purely American" garden, it boasted "no single plants but great masses and jungles of

Philip Leslie Hale. WISTERIA. C. 1915. Oil on canvas, 30 x 25 in. Private collection
In 1912 the Hales bought a 1727 farmhouse in Dedham called "Sandy Down" where Lilian Westcott Hale
made a suitably old-fashioned garden, which was the setting for many of her husband's paintings.

Ross Turner. SALEM GARDEN. c. 1887. Watercolor on paper, 9³⁄₄ x 11¹⁄₂ in. Collection of Kathryn and Jeffrey Brown
Turner was an avid gardener, but in his paintings it was the patterns created by the flower colors that interested him.

flowers without bare ground showing anywhere."[24] Barbara's garden, quite obviously Wright's own, included broad beds filled with hardy perennials and shrubs lining the walk from house to stable, a formal flower garden forty feet square centered on a sundial, and a wild garden in the adjoining woods. Photographs by Wright of her own garden as well as of other old-fashioned gardens such as that at "Van Cortlandt Manor" illustrated all three books.

The circumstances of Barbara's life, while also paralleling Wright's, differed in significant details. Herself childless, Wright felt obliged to make Barbara the mother of twin sons. Wright enjoyed a dual career as nature activist and popular author, but Barbara was content to stay within the protecting walls of her home and garden ministering to the needs of her male family—father, husband, and sons. Barbara viewed gardening not only as a socially appropriate activity for a woman, but more importantly, a moral one. "Gardening is the truly religious life, for it implies a continual preparation for the future, a treading in the straight and narrow path that painful experience alone can mark, an absorption beyond compare, and the continual exercise of hope and love, but above all, of entire childlike faith."[25]

 **PAINTERS' SUBURBAN GARDENS** Fairfield was only one among many ancient villages in New England rapidly becoming bedroom communities as improved transportation made commuting to cities from a distance quite simple. Salem, near Boston, had long been noted for its ancient gardens, lovingly maintained, as well as for more recent ones in the old style. That of Susan Osgood on Essex Street, for example, exhibited the plank-bordered beds, vine-covered archway, and picket fence that were markers of grandmother's garden. Ross Turner, who specialized in painting such gardens, found his Salem house and cottage garden a convenient commute from his Boston studios.

Turner's friend Dwight Blaney, who also lived in Salem, eventually owned an early house in Weston, Massachusetts, and a town house on Beacon Hill in Boston as well as a farmhouse on Ironbound Island, Maine, where he had an informal garden, as noted earlier. The residences were required to house his formidable collection of colonial furniture and decorative arts, all of it made possible by his marriage to an heiress in 1893. Blaney was an original member of the Walpole Society, a rarefied club of antique collectors founded in 1910. He was also a craftsman in wood and an ardent fisherman as well as gardener.[26] His garden and that of his friend Ross Turner, seen in their own paintings and those of fellow Impressionist John Leslie Breck, were lush and highly colored tapestries of old favorites.

Dedham, Massachusetts, was chosen by painters Philip Leslie Hale (1865–1931) and Lilian

Susan Osgood's garden, Salem, Massachusetts. Photograph, c. 1910
The plank edgings of the beds, picket fence, and arbored gate could be found in both old and old-fashioned gardens in Salem.

Westcott Hale (1880–1963) for residence after the birth of their daughter in 1909. Lilian Hale's studio was in the house, but Philip commuted each day to Boston. His daughter later wrote, "The only thing that kept my father home from his Boston studio in the daytime was to be at work on a painting of the white hollyhocks in our garden, or of a model in a veiled hat standing beside his favorite white standard rose tree." As a student Philip Hale had spent several summers in Giverny. Back home, he often summered in Matunuck, Rhode Island, where his aunt, painter Susan Hale, had a noted garden.

Lilian Hale seems to have been as gifted a gardener as she was a painter, and like her work, her gardens were steeped in the American past. Her studies of antiques-filled interiors painted in a fine-grained academic style represented, as did her garden, a refuge from the industrial present and a link with an aestheticized New England past. Her daughter wrote of her that "the standard for her gardening afternoons was the same as for her painting mornings—quite simply perfection . . . with wide beds of Rosa Mundae . . . delphinium and irises in the borders . . . climbing yellow rose beside the front steps."[27]

Adrien Persac. SHADOWS-ON-THE-TECHE, NEW IBERIA, LOUISIANA. 1861. Watercolor on paper, 22 x 16⅝ in.
Shadows-on-the-Teche, a museum property of the National Trust for Historic Preservation
The kitchen garden across the main street from this house in New Iberia included flowers among the vegetables.

GRANDMOTHER'S GARDEN IN THE MIDDLE ATLANTIC AND SOUTH

The larkspur lifts on high its azure spires,

And up the arbour's lattices are rolled

The quaint nasturtium's many-coloured fires;

The tall carnation's breast of faded gold

Is striped with many a faintly-flushing streak,

Pale as the tender tints that blush upon a baby's cheek.

The old sweet-rocket sheds its fine perfumes;

With golden stars the coreopsis flames;

And here are scores of sweet old-fashioned blooms,

Dear for the very fragrance of their names,

Poppies and gillyflowers and four-o'clocks,

Cowslips and candytuft and heliotrope and hollyhocks.

John Russel Hayes, "The Old-Fashioned Garden"

INSTRUCTIONS FOR PLANTING THE OLD-FASHIONED GARDEN   After 1900, amateur gardeners across the country who wanted to create an old-fashioned American cottage garden were offered advice in many publications. They could read about a romanticized cottage garden, "The Garden of Forgotten Flowers," in *Good Housekeeping* (April 1907); actual old-fashioned gardens, such as one in New Jersey featured in *American Homes and Gardens* (November 1906) and another in Pennsylvania in *Indoors and Out* (March 1907); or remembered ones, such as "My Grandmother's Garden and Orchard Ancestral," described in *Atlantic Monthly* (June 1909). They were offered advice by Frances Duncan, garden editor of *Ladies' Home Journal,* on "How to Make an Old-Fashioned Garden" (April 1909).

Country Life in America ran a two-part article, "Old-Fashioned Gardens" and "Old-Fashioned Flowers," in March 1907. The first was illustrated with photographs of two gardens whose plans dated to colonial times and the second offered an annotated list of plants, prepared by horticulturist Wilhelm Miller, whose use predated 1776. The kitchen garden was not neglected: the following year a list of "Herbs and Vegetables for Old-Fashioned Gardens" was published (April 1908).

It remained for landscape architect Grace Tabor to attempt a scholarly treatment of the subject in *Old Fashioned Gardening: A History and Reconstruction* (1913), tracing the English, Dutch, and Spanish roots of American gardens and appending a list of "old-time flowers." For Tabor, the characteristics of an old-fashioned garden were simplicity, convenience, and a certain formality and symmetry. She included a plan of a flower garden "in the old style," with geometric beds bordered in box planted with appropriate flowers. Such plans appeared in many publications of the time—not just gardening ones—for example, in Charles Edward Hooper's *Reclaiming the Old House* (1913), which offered diagrams of both restored early gardens and more recent reproductions.

In her earlier *The Landscape Gardening Book* (1911), Tabor had pleaded, "Let us have, here in America, American gardens—not imitation Italian, or English or Dutch gardens, or any other sort." For Tabor, as for so many other writers, old-fashioned gardens with their regular layout, generous planting, and intimate relation to the house were a welcome relief from pretentious shams. Tabor viewed such houses and gardens as a standard Americans ought to hold to: "The simple old white houses of New England are classics quite as truly as any Grecian temple—and in the midst of their prim, old, box-bordered little gardens, they present far saner and safer models for us generally."[1]

OLD-FASHIONED GARDENS IN MARYLAND AND PENNSYLVANIA

Gardeners in the Middle Atlantic states and the South, of course, did not need to look to New England for examples—they had their own old gardens, and not just those of country estates and great plantations. Many more modest gardens on small town lots or in more rural villages had been lovingly maintained by the same families over several generations. The renown of these gardens may have been only local but they served as models for their immediate neighborhood and kept alive a taste for the old perennials and flowering shrubs. It was to these gardens that many novice gardeners turned.

In the 1890s, writer Helen Ashe Hays began a garden in Maryland within an old encircling wall. For guidance in planting she relied on neighboring gardens and also on Bernard McMahon's *The American Gardener's Calendar* (1806), which she stumbled on just as she began. She wrote in her account of its making, *A Little Maryland Garden* (1909), "I had never heard of William Robinson. . . .

It was then instinct that led me to keep my flowers back in borders rather than cut up the lawn in circles and ovals. And it was necessity that guided me in the choice of hardy plants to fill the borders."[2] As she became more experienced, she was able to plan bloom from March to November, relying heavily on American natives as well as on old favorites.

In Pennsylvania, as in New England, many painters sought out villages with historic associations. The art colony in New Hope was begun when Edward Redfield bought an old farmhouse there. Thomas Anshutz (1851–1912) and Hugh Henry Breckenridge (1870–1937), teachers at the Pennsylvania Academy of the Fine Arts in Philadelphia, gave summer classes in Fort Washington, near Valley Forge, beginning in 1902. Here Anshutz had a studio, according to a visitor a few years later, in the midst of an "old-fashioned flower growing garden, which antedates Revolutionary days." Breckenridge named his home "Phloxdale" and surrounded it with an informal cottage garden filled with phlox and other hardy perennials, the subject of many of his paintings.[3]

A more modest garden in rural Pennsylvania, recalled by the gardener's granddaughter, filled the yard beside the house with the blossoms of spring bulbs, peonies, iris, phlox, sweet peas, and many self-sown annuals such as larkspur, poppies, and daisies. There were lilacs but also currants and gooseberries, usually confined to the kitchen garden. The porch was covered with crimson rambler and pink seven sisters roses, and other climbers, including an enormous purple clematis.[4]

At a time when a taste for privacy and enclosure was no longer seen as un-American, the old walled gardens of Germantown, Pennsylvania, had fresh appeal. Painters Elizabeth Shippen Green (1871–1954), Violet Oakley, and Jessie Willcox Smith shared a studio home there beginning in 1905. Many of Green's magazine and book illustrations used their old-fashioned garden as a background. These caught the fancy of noted gardener Anna Gilman Hill who, in her *Forty Years of Gardening* (1938), attributed the inspiration for her well-known "Grey Gardens" in Southampton, Long Island, begun in 1913, to seeing some of Green's illustrations. Just as the work of Kate Greenaway and other popular book illustrators in England reflected a taste for the old walled gardens of the seventeenth century espoused by Reginald Blomfield in *The Formal Garden in England* (1892), such American illustrations fueled the popularity of the old-fashioned garden.

POET ANNE SPENCER'S GARDEN IN VIRGINIA In small towns throughout the South, old family gardens continued to be maintained and imaginative new ones made in the old style. In Lynchburg, Virginia, in 1903, poet and civil-rights activist Anne Spencer (1882–1975), who became an important figure in the Harlem Renaissance of the 1920s, began a garden behind the house her husband, Edward, had built. The long, narrow space of the gar-

Hugh Henry Breckenridge.
WHITE PHLOX. 1906. Oil on
canvas, 26 x 39 in. Terra Museum
of American Art, Chicago. Daniel
J. Terra Collection
*"Phloxdale" was Breckenridge's name
for his house and garden in Fort
Washington, Pennsylvania.*

Opposite: Hugh Henry Breckenridge.
THE FLOWER GARDEN. c. 1910.
Oil on canvas, 25 x 30 in. Private
collection
*Breckenridge's garden had climbing roses
on a trellis fence as well as masses of
phlox which he often painted in vivid
Fauve style.*

den was enclosed with a wire fence ornamented with iron trim and covered in vines. Clipped privet bordered the path leading from the house through three areas defined by a latticed entrance, a grape arbor, and a wisteria-covered pergola. The path terminated in a fishpond circled with box and flanked by cedars.

This formal structure was filled to overflowing in cottage-garden style. Scores of old roses occupied a bed near the back door, while bulbs, perennials, and shrubs were planted in beds flanking the central path and in narrow borders running the length of the garden. Identifiable in photographs taken in the 1920s, used in the recent restoration of the garden, are poppies, peonies, iris, day lilies, hollyhocks, rose-of-Sharon, daisies, phlox, chrysanthemums, coralbells, and foxgloves. Spencer was keenly interested in the latest introductions as well as old favorites. Her roses included the 1902 American pillar rose, and she continued to add new varieties through the 1940s. A nursery catalogue from the 1930s, on which she had written a poem, was marked with flowering shrubs to add to the borders.

References to the garden and its flowers abound in Spencer's poetry. Most was written in the garden in a one-room cottage covered in trumpet vines built for her by her husband. Despite responsibilities of children and housekeeping, Spencer was able to work in both garden and garden room thanks to her sympathetic husband and a housekeeper. The garden was to be not only an inspiration and refuge for Spencer and her family, but a haven for visiting intellectuals such as W. E. B. Du Bois, who presented her with *Prince Ebo,* named for the African Ebo tribe, a cast-iron head that served as a fountain for the pond.[5]

Old gardens filled with a wealth of perennials and fragrant shrubs not reliably hardy farther north abounded in Virginia. The box-bordered beds of gardens like that at "Reveille" plantation near Richmond, a garden enclosed by flowering shrubs where intersecting paths centered on a sundial, came to typify the southern old-fashioned garden. Such gardens were revered in the South even more than in New England as they provided a palpable link with the halcyon time "before the war" and seemed to suggest a leisured existence where social ties and family life could be cultivated.

Anne Spencer in her garden, Lynchburg, Virginia. Photograph, c. 1920. Collection Chauncey E. Spencer
Spencer's husband, Edward, made the arbors and purple martin houses that furnished the garden, as well as her one-room retreat, the "EdanKrall," in which she wrote her poetry.

SOUTH CAROLINA
GARDENS
OLD AND NEW

Planters in South Carolina like those in Virginia had enjoyed a semifeudal way of life before the devastation of the Civil War. Afterward in the garden, as elsewhere, any work had to be done by the owner or by undependable hired labor. Nonetheless many old gardens with their box-bordered beds did survive to serve as models for new ones, despite difficulties such as those so poignantly described by Elizabeth Pringle in her account of her struggles to maintain her own plantation in *A Woman Rice Planter* (1913).

In Columbia, South Carolina, Sarah Boylston (1871–1963), a transplanted northerner and newly married in 1909, inherited an early-nineteenth-century house with an extant garden on three levels. Boylston rejuvenated the plantings and acquired land to add a series of brick-walled garden "rooms." On the lowest level she created a garden of box-bordered paths intersecting at a fountain. She filled each quadrant, further divided into four, with bulbs, planted among the perennials native wild flowers and ferns, and added crape myrtles, camellias, and other flowering shrubs throughout the garden.[6]

Not far from Boylston's residence was the splendid walled "Hampton-Preston" garden which may have inspired her. Begun in 1818 and once the home of Governor Wade Hampton, it was noted for its evergreens. By Boylston's time it had become a romantic tangle where, as Helen Ashe Hays described it in *Country Life in America,* overgrown wisteria "unites the whole garden in its embrace, casting ropes and nets between the branches, leaping over the walls and twining to the tops of the tallest trees." Its geometric box-edged beds were still intact, however, and kept well-trimmed and filled with roses and old-fashioned perennials. Such gardens had for Hays, and undoubtedly Sarah Boylston, an ineffable charm. As Hays wrote, "Not at a glance does one discover the secrets of its numerous paths and winding ways; and a more than superficial acquaintance is needed to find out all its treasures of plant life."[7]

With the breakdown of the rice-based economy of coastal South Carolina after the Civil War, many plantation-bred ladies often found their flower and vegetable gardens a source of much-needed cash. Married and living in her own small house built partially with proceeds from her garden, Anne Porcher Gregorie of "Oakland" plantation wrapped thousands of flowers from her garden for sale in nearby Charleston each spring. In her diary for February 1914, Gregorie's daughter recorded, "Two afternoons this week I have given to helping Mother gather and bunch jonquils to be sold at the Ladies' Exchange. We picked 1811 stems."[8]

Alice Ravenel Huger Smith (1876–1958) was born in Charleston and lived all her life at 69 Church Street, an eighteenth-century house bought by her widowed grandmother as a family refuge after the war. She faced the necessity of contributing to the family income, and never married. Although Smith studied drawing at the Carolina Art Association and had the encouragement of Tonalist painter Birge Harrison, who wintered in Charleston for several years, she was mostly self-taught as a watercolorist.

The growing attraction of Charleston for tourists created a market for Smith's charming views of the low country and town. What Eliza Greatorex had done for old New York in the 1870s Smith determined to do for Charleston. She wrote a friend on April 6, 1915, "For some years I have been making drawings of old houses in Charleston and on the coast which are rapidly disappearing." With her father, an amateur historian, she collaborated on *Twenty Drawings of the Pringle House on King Street* (1914), now known as the "Miles Brewton House," followed by *The Dwelling Houses of Charleston* (1917), both with a preservation message. The second book proved influential far afield as well as in Charleston, where it gave a boost to the nascent historic preservation movement. Smith also painted the gardens at "Middleton Place" and other plantations, although in her watercolors, as in reality, field crops took precedence over flower gardens.[9]

Gardeners outside the South seemed especially charmed by South Carolina gardens, large or small. Hildegard Hawthorne in her nostalgic *The Lure of the Garden* (1911) included among "Our Grandmother's Gardens" the expected New England ones but also a South Carolina plantation and the walled gardens of Charleston. For Hawthorne and many others, Charleston gardens were worthy of imitation, "made to lend seclusion and quiet to the house, as well as loveliness, and to be lived in as part of the home." The garden illustrated showed the path that in most Charleston gardens led along the house from the street to the back garden, and was arched over with climbing roses, wisteria, or Carolina jessamine and flanked with flowering shrubs.[10]

Northerners in increasing numbers made towns like Charleston, Camden, and Aiken fash-

Opposite, above: "Reveille" plantation, Richmond, Virginia. n.d. Glass slide. Smithsonian Institution, Archives of American Gardens, Washington, D.C., Garden Club of America Collection
Many old southern gardens survived the Civil War to serve as models for those making an old-fashioned garden.

Opposite, below: Miles-Brewton house, Charleston, South Carolina. n.d. Glass slide. Smithsonian Institution, Archives of American Gardens, Washington, D.C., Garden Club of America Collection
Charleston artist Alice Ravenel Huger Smith documented this early house and garden in her book Twenty Drawings of the Pringle House on King Street *(1914).*

Right: "In a Charleston Garden." Illustration by Anna Whelan Betts
This romantic depiction of a walled Charleston garden appeared in Frances Duncan's article in Century Magazine *(March 1907).*

ionable wintering places. Following the lead of residents, new owners tended to eschew professionally made gardens for more informal and old-fashioned ones. The garden made by Celestin Eustis in Aiken in the 1870s, for example, which served as the model for many others, was enclosed by a picket fence and filled with fragrant shrubs and vines. The house itself was draped in Lady Banks' roses, a southern favorite.

PAINTER BLONDELLE MALONE'S GARDEN

One resident of Aiken, painter Blondelle Malone (1877–1951), had arrived in 1916 from no farther away than Columbia. Her garden occupied only the front yard of her cottage in Aiken, but her first garden, begun by her mother, had been that surrounding her parents' home in Columbia. Malone's father, the proprietor of a piano emporium and music store, could afford to pay for his daughter's

Malone garden, Columbia, South Carolina. Photograph, c. 1910
Painter Blondelle Malone, seen here with a suitor in the Malone family's lush, old-fashioned garden,
preferred the artist's life in France to her genteel and restricted life in Columbia.

Blondelle Malone's studio garden, Aiken, South Carolina. Photograph, c. 1916
After her mother's death, Malone moved to Aiken where she is seen here with another gentleman friend.

education at Converse College followed by two years of painting study in New York with John Twachtman and William Merritt Chase.

After a stay at home, where she painted her own and neighbors' gardens, Malone persuaded her father to finance a two-year stay in France. In 1904 in Giverny, where she spent several months, she met Monet. Inspired by his garden, Malone wrote to her mother requesting hollyhock seed, passionflower vines, and Japanese-lily bulbs from their garden to give to friends there. At last prevailed upon to come home, she wrote, "We must have the garden so people cannot see in when I return, for I expect to live in it and paint it when I return. If you can plant a high hedge all around it would suit me exactly."[11]

Back in Columbia in April 1908, she noted in her diary that her studio overlooked a Lady Banks' rose white with blossom and that she was painting the iris in the garden. Several days later she complained, "For the last two weeks I have been killing myself painting the wisteria in Miss Hughes' garden." Other subjects were the "Hampton-Preston House" garden and in Charleston, the "quaint and charming" gardens of the Colonial Dames headquarters and nearby "Magnolia Gardens."[12]

Malone's own garden became her refuge as well as the subject of many paintings. Malone had always felt trapped in Columbia, by the proprieties, by her father's lack of sympathy with her vocation (in which admittedly she had difficulty supporting herself), and by lack of kindred spirits such as she had found among English and French painters. Her move to Aiken followed her mother's death. The remainder of her life seems to have been spent in flight from Columbia and her father, with trips to Europe alternating with forays along the East Coast painting garden portraits.

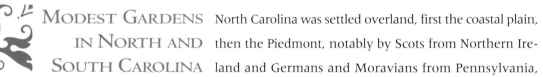 MODEST GARDENS IN NORTH AND SOUTH CAROLINA North Carolina was settled overland, first the coastal plain, then the Piedmont, notably by Scots from Northern Ireland and Germans and Moravians from Pennsylvania, who considered themselves farmers, not planters. The baronial character of both Virginia and South Carolina was absent in North Carolina, giving rise to its tongue-in-cheek description as a vale of humility between two mountains of conceit. Certainly there were grand plantations, but more typical were spacious houses built on lots of several acres in prosperous small towns not so different from those in New England.

As described in 1850 with its "two straight, broad shady streets crossing each other at right angles; other and narrower streets running parallel with these; a little church or two; a newspaper; an academy; two ancient, spacious taverns, more like hamlets than houses; a few prosperous-looking stores; a score of comfortable village houses," Salisbury in the Piedmont was typical of these

Paul Sawier. LIBERTY HALL GARDEN. Before 1915. Oil on canvas, 17½ x 11 in.
Collection Liberty Hall, Historic Site, Frankfort, Kentucky
Overgrown box was an appealingly picturesque feature of many old southern gardens.

towns. At the turn of the century, several notable old gardens survived there. The Murdock garden on Bank Street, begun by Mrs. William Murdock before the Civil War, was given even more box-bordered beds in the 1890s.

The Boyden garden on Fisher Street, begun in the early 1800s by Sarah Alexander Henderson, was continued by her daughter Jane Henderson Boyden. Occupying a city block of several acres, it included a vegetable plot, orchard, and pasture for livestock as well as an extensive box-bordered perennial garden, described in the *Carolina Watchman* as it was in 1868: "The beds and borders of this garden are all aglow with gold, and white and crimson beauties; and all through the Spring, and all through the summer, and autumn, the scene is only shifting. . . . There is one rose bush alone worth a long walk to see. . . . But we dare not attempt a description, much less to single out one thing as chiefly attractive. It must be taken as a whole; the giant old oaks which form the back ground, the creepers and thick shrubs, and then the easy, and apparently designless, mingling of fruits and flowers, vegetables and flowers, and flowers and herbs—all in their most natural places."[13]

In time, the garden was lovingly maintained by Mrs. Boyden's daughter-in-law May Shober Boyden. This Mrs. Boyden's daughter May, on her marriage in 1907, moved into a newly built Queen Anne–style house on the family block and made her own old-fashioned garden connected to her mother's domain by a box-bordered path. Both mother and daughter died in 1929. The gardens gradually disappeared, and both houses are now gone as well. In the memory of another May (the author), granddaughter and great-granddaughter of the gardeners, traces of their gardens linger, marked by overgrown box, indomitable old shrub roses, giant crape myrtles, rampant wisteria, a forest of fig bushes and an ailing orchard, persistent flowering shrubs, and an indestructible peony hedge.

Until well into the present century, the mountains in the western part of North Carolina were thinly settled and isolated from much of the state. Here, around cabins on small holdings, flower gardens were of necessity frugal but no less part of a long tradition. A visitor in the 1930s wrote, "In these modest gardens are many tender annuals of the North . . . whose remote ancestors may have travelled, long before the Revolution, in covered wagons over rough trails down from Western Pennsylvania and New York State."[14] Many children raised on these small farms headed east and south in the 1890s to the booming cotton-mill towns in both North and South Carolina.

As had happened in the North, some southern mill owners hit upon cottage gardening as a method of keeping their workers at home and happily occupied. In Greenville, South Carolina, Thomas Parker, president of the Monaghan Cotton Mills, and Ellison Smyth, president of the Pelzer Manufacturing Company, in the 1890s erected model villages with public gardens. Parker offered annual prizes for the most attractive gardens in the space allotted each worker's house, encouraging flower as well as vegetable gardens in cottage-garden style.[15]

GARDENS IN TENNESSEE, KENTUCKY, AND GEORGIA In Tennessee in the 1890s there were still a few old gardens begun years earlier when it was on the frontier. Most gardens featured box as did the one begun before the Civil War by the Rev. F. A. Thompson at his home near Spring Hill, still lovingly maintained by his great-granddaughter, who inherited it in the 1890s. The ninety-foot-square enclosed garden was bordered with spring bulbs and the box-bordered beds were planted with roses, irises, Scotch broom, lilies, chrysanthemums, spirea, snowball, crape myrtle, camellias, honeysuckle, jasmine, bridal wreath, dogwood, and flowering almond. The garden of President Andrew Jackson's home, "The Hermitage," near Nashville, combined both vegetables and flowers in square beds separated by gravel paths. A border including crape myrtle, lilacs, roses, peonies, and other shrubs lined the fence enclosing the garden. In 1889, the care of the garden, its brick-bordered flower beds still intact, was assumed by the Ladies Hermitage Association.[16]

A diary of the late 1820s described Kentucky log cabins covered with climbing roses and in the yard lilacs, altheas, cinnamon roses, and beds of spring bulbs. On a grander scale, the garden of "Liberty Hall," begun about 1800 in Frankfort, Kentucky, was being maintained in the 1890s by Mary Mason Scott, a vice-regent of the Mount Vernon Ladies' Association. A plan of the garden as it was then showed four large beds, one devoted to vegetables, surrounded by flower borders and backed with roses and a box hedge, with box bushes marking the inside corners.[17]

In Georgia, many antebellum gardens remained, among them in Savannah the walled garden of the Richardson house, where oval beds edged with dwarf box were planted with camellias, banana shrub, sweet olive, jasmine, roses, lilacs, spring bulbs, and perennials. At the Champion-McAlpine house garden, an arbor of yellow Banksia roses joined beds bordered with dwarf box. On "Veasy Plantation," a house built after the Civil War was given a front flower garden surrounded by a picket fence, the geometric beds edged with box, the corners marked with box trees.[18]

THE OLD-FASHIONED GARDEN IN THE DEEP SOUTH

Old-fashioned gardens were the rule at the turn of the century in much of the deep South. In the nearly subtropical climate, with its mild winters and a long growing season, gardens could not help being lush; constant vigilance and rigorous pruning was necessary just to keep them within reasonable bounds. Many of these gardens still exist in the memories of grandchildren, now grandparents themselves, and in precious family photographs.

A garden in Sion Hill, Mississippi, made by Leona Jones Aaron after her marriage in 1880, was, as her granddaughter recalled it, a lush and fragrant place. The dooryard garden was enclosed by a white picket fence smothered in sweet peas. Rectangular beds along the fence were filled with flowering shrubs and taller perennials like hollyhocks. Four box bushes clipped into neat circles formed accents in the fence border.[19]

At "The Cedars" in central Louisiana, still occupied by the same family since just after the Civil War, huge unpruned crape myrtles guarded the front gate. The front fence was lined with fragrant banana shrub, deutzia, and sweet olive. Flanking the central path an enormous Banksia rose grew up through the branches of a cedar, the ground beneath carpeted in the fall with red spider lilies. Under the cedar's twin across the path was a bed of red American amaryllis. The whole of the fenced inner yard was generously planted. Narcissus filled bordered beds before the porch, followed by drifts of amaryllis, phlox, cornflowers, gaillardias, coreopsis, and four-o'clocks. Winter jasmine clambered over the porch.[20]

Louisiana gardens, even after the Louisiana Purchase of 1803, owed much to the still per-

House and dooryard garden of
Leona Jones Aaron, Zion Hill,
Mississippi. Photograph, c. 1910.
Collection Viola G. Harrison
*In this garden begun in 1880, roses and
other fragrant flowers filled small beds
near the house with two Cape jasmine
flanking the front steps.*

vasive French culture. New Orleans garden owners before the Civil War were a cosmopolitan mixture of old Spanish and Creole families, free persons of color, and newcomers from other states as well as immigrants from Ireland and Gemany. Houses ranged from small Creole cottages in the Vieux Carré, which opened directly on the street with tiny back gardens, to grand three-story mansions on substantial lots in the Garden District flaunting elaborate flower beds arranged in fanciful geometric figures. As in the rest of the South, the enclosed gardens made at the turn of the century were strongly influenced by the old ones that remained.

Plantation gardens could be more expansive. The garden at "Rosedown," near St. Francisville, owed its plan and planting to Martha Turnbull (1810–1896), who recorded in her journals, beginning in 1836, nearly sixty years of work in her garden. She experimented with all sorts of plants, including the old-fashioned flowers popular in New England, and as late as the 1890s was ordering more roses to fill circular beds centered on a gazebo. The garden's central axis was flanked by discrete spaces, including that for roses, divided by hedges. Privet, Banksia or Cherokee rose, mock orange, holly, Cape jasmine, and cherry laurel were usual choices for hedges; Turnbull also used wild peach and myrtle.[21]

Throughout the South, true cottage gardens existed anywhere there was a yard big enough and a gardener with enough heart to cultivate flowers as a gesture of graciousness in an otherwise difficult life. Such gardens were usually made in the front yard close to the road to encourage visiting. These small gardens could not boast box borders or many shrubs but depended on perennials, wild flowers, and self-sown annuals, not massed for effect but individually cherished.[22]

A. F. Brader. PROPERTY OF ANDREW CRIM, OHIO. 1893. Watercolor on paper, 26 x 39 in.
Collection David A. Schorsch Company, New York

GRANDMOTHER'S GARDEN
ON THE FRONTIER

Grandmother's garden was edged with box,

And quaint were the flowers that grew;

Foxglove and fennel and ladylocks,

Marjoram, mint and rue;

Fragrant it was with mullen pink,

And lilies of white and gold;

Never was sweeter a spot I think,

Grandmother's garden of old. . . .

Rose Mill Powers, "Grandmother's Garden"

GARDENS IN THE MIDWEST In the border states and on the western frontier, the old-fashioned garden found in New England and the South appears. As settlers moved west, they brought with them ideas of what a garden should be, as well as plants and seeds; the first gardens made in new settlements were often more or less successful attempts to re-create what had been left behind, but the exacting climate, the often spectacular landscapes, and a native flora different from that of the East Coast had an effect on even the most determined gardener.

A writer in the *Atlantic Monthly* (March 1866) noted the cookie-cutter quality of Midwestern settlements, many of them built in weeks with prefabricated houses shipped from eastern factories. "Locomotives, like huge flat-irons, are smoothing customs, costumes, thoughts and feelings into the plain, homogeneous surface. . . . Coming from the West you are whirled through twelve hundred miles of towns, so alike in their outward features that they seem to have been started in New England nurseries and sent to be planted wherever they might be wanted." Mary Austin (1864–1934), a California writer whose childhood was spent in Carlinville, Illinois, in her autobiography described her house there as "clapboarded, white-painted with green blinds, its original Colonial lines corrupted

Garden walk of Miss Sherwin, Gates Mills, Ohio
This old-fashioned garden, complete with colonial arbor and picket fence, was the frontispiece to Harriet L. Keeler's book on hardy perennials and annuals, Our Garden Flowers *(1910).*

Opposite: Residence of A. H. McLain, Newton, Kansas.
Photograph by A. H. Foss
Foss was a traveling photographer who specialized in portraits of houses like this spanking new one bristling with lightning rods. Hopeful flower beds border the walk, where two of the owner's children show off their penny-farthing bicycle and tricycle.

by what in the course of the next decade or two broke out irruptively into what is now known as the 'bungalow' type." Many such homes as well as more modest ones had cottage gardens. Austin reported that even "log-cabin gardens were thick set with old-fashioned flowers, touch-me-nots, kiss-me-quicks, balsam apples, love-in-a-mist, and scarlet runners."

Such gestures toward New England homes and gardens were part of an affiliation with what was seen to be the best of American culture. Austin noted the pervasiveness of New England taste in the Midwest and recalled being brought up on the works of New England authors, particularly Henry Wadsworth Longfellow. As she put it, "you climb to Culture as the climax of a series of attitudes which Mr. Longfellow so satisfyingly fulfills that along in the seventies he became the true gesture of National Aspiration."[1]

In the small town of Wheaton in the northern part of Illinois, gardens were not very different from New England ones. Flowers were grown together with vegetables, often in raised beds bordered with a low-growing plant. Hollyhocks, other tall perennials, and shrubs grew along the fence that enclosed the garden while morning glory, matrimony vine, honeysuckle, and Virginia creeper ornamented the porch. There was no attempt at color harmonies but, according to recollections of a resident, just "a succession of flowers and plenty of them." This resident listed among the commonly planted flowers and shrubs in the 1880s portulaca, hollyhocks, morning glories, impatiens,

marigolds, buttercups, lychnis, grass pinks, clove pinks, sweet Williams, periwinkles, moneywort, Johnny-jump-ups, larkspur, ribbon grass, blue flag, live-forevers, southernwood, honeysuckle, flowering currant, flowering almond, syringa, lilac, snowball, peonies, and blush, yellow, and moss roses.

In 1882, Julia Duncan Kirby of Jacksonville, Illinois, created an old-fashioned garden on the site of a garden of the 1830s made by her grandfather, a former state governor. Here a grape arbor bordered the west side of the rectangular plot enclosed by a board fence and divided into four large beds. The central path running the length of the garden was bordered with irises, foxgloves, larkspur, and other old perennials; the crossing path was marked by four yuccas.[2]

After the turn of the century, Chicago-based painters like Louis Ritman (1889–1963), Lawton S. Parker (1868–1954), and Pauline Palmer could record gardens very much like New England ones. Palmer's own garden, seen from her studio window, had the requisite picket fence with hollyhocks, climbing vines on a trellis, a birdhouse, and lanterns. The splendid delphinium garden and colonial-style house painted by Parker could have been found anywhere from the Great Lakes to the Atlantic, while the lush cottage gardens Ritman painted would have been as much at home in France as in the Midwest.

The northeastern part of Ohio, once part of Connecticut's Western Reserve, was first occupied by New Englanders who came overland; the southern part was settled mainly from Pennsylva-

Otto Stark. SUZANNE IN THE GARDEN. 1904. Oil on canvas 35 x 16 in. Collection Bob and Ellie Haan

Opposite: Lawton S. Parker. WOMAN IN A GARDEN. Oil on canvas, 24 x 24 in. Private collection.
Although this splendid old-fashioned garden would have been equally at home in New England, it was probably painted near Chicago.

nia, Maryland, and the southern states. By the early nineteenth century, old-style southern flower gardens laid out in terraces or "falls" began to appear in southern Ohio as did New England cottage gardens in northern Ohio and in states farther west.

Hortense Share, who moved with her husband to a Minnesota farm in 1864, re-created there the garden she had known at home in the East. A plan published in the April 1874 *Ladies Floral Cabinet* showed a rectangular space divided into geometric beds filled with old-fashioned perennials—peonies, asters, pinks, salvias, and tiger lilies as well as reliable annuals and vines, including Drummond phlox, stock, balsam, morning glories, and daturas. By the 1870s, pioneer nurseries, such

William Forsyth painting
hollyhocks. Photograph, 1903.
Collection Eckert Fine Art,
Indianapolis
*Forsyth's painting was made into a
folding screen suitable for an Aesthetic
interior.*

as Anoka Nursery in Minnesota, were able to "furnish everything that is found to be hardy and reliable for our climate and soil."[3]

Gardens along the lake shores of Wisconsin, Michigan, and Minnesota had the advantage of a short but spectacular growing season aided by the moist atmosphere that mitigated the extreme heat and drought. After the turn of the century, newcomers there were still making old-fashioned gardens remembered from home. A visitor in 1908 to a garden in Minnetonka, Minnesota, where a Virginia native had established a summer home, was startled to find that "many wonderful things flourish here as valiantly as in the South." The garden was entered through an arch covered in honeysuckle, Carolina jessamine, moonflowers, and *Cobaea scandens,* while a crimson rambler sprawled over the fence. Among the shrubs were such southern favorites as calycanthus and rose-of-Sharon and among the flowers, nicotiana, yuccas, hollyhocks, sweet Williams, peonies, Canterbury-bells "all tangled in together" with foxgloves, poppies, Madonna lilies, and columbines. A herb garden included artemisia, rosemary, thyme, marjoram, lavender, rue, caraway, fennel, ambrosia, and okra, which the visitor, obviously not southern, thought a "distinctly new herb."[4]

In Nesho, Missouri, Ida Woodside Dougan, a divorced woman with three children, began a garden surrounding the house bought for her by her father, a judge in nearby Salem. Here on a restricted town lot she created a charming old-fashioned garden that was recorded in many photographs taken by herself and by her daughter Kathleen, who became a professional photographer. The garden was meant to be enjoyed from the vine-covered porch, and many photographs show friends gathered in its shelter. A wide gravel path led from the side of the porch across the lawn, through a grape arbor furnished with seats, and on to the barn. To the right, a vegetable garden was

Ida Woodside Dougan in her garden in Neosho, Missouri. Photograph by Kathleen Dougan, c. 1915. Collection Michael B. Dougan *Towering* Nicotiana sylvestris *and broad-leafed cannas bordered one path in the garden, while hydrangeas and other shrubs flanked a latticed porch covered in vines.*

hidden behind a lush growth of vines and a border of hardy flowers. Nicotiana was a particular favorite. Flowering shrubs, roses, viburnums, hydrangeas, hibiscus, and many plants surrounded the house and masked the property line.[5]

The perils of amateur photography were amusingly recorded by Alice French (1850 -1934), who, under the pseudonym of Octave Thanet, wrote *An Adventure in Photography* (1893). French was a writer, not a photographer, although her photographs were quite creditable if not up to Kathleen Dougan's standards. Born in Massachusetts, brought up in Iowa, and educated at Vassar College, she became known in the 1890s for her colorful stories of the Arkansas delta. Her life companion, Jane Allen Crawford, had inherited the plantation "Clover Bend," six miles from Minturn, Arkansas, where they spent their first winter in 1883. French used earnings from her best sellers to build a commodious frame mansion with a vine-covered porch called "Thanford," a name combining French's pen name with Crawford; the two friends returned there each year until 1909. At "Thanford" French (a formidable woman over six feet tall) could indulge her passions for photography, carpentry, cooking, and entertaining lavishly as well as gardening.

French's illustrated newsletter, the *Clover Bend Poke Root,* published sporadically from "Thanford" and sent to friends including Margaret Deland, Mary Wilkins, and Sarah Orne Jewett, gives a vivid picture of the garden. The issue of May 25, 1905, has an amusing account of the never-ending battle against weeds, specifically ragweed. "Bro Thanet has used salt, lye, hoes, spades, hands, and profanity with but slender results; the conqueror of the Poke Root, the narrow dock and the army worm declares himself at the end of his wits."[6] Intended for winter and spring months, the garden included a kitchen garden, a peony bed of more than two hundred plants, a formal garden

J. Otis Adams. THE COTTAGE GARDEN. 1899. Oil on canvas, 29 x 22 in. Collection Bob and Ellie Haan
A suitably costumed young woman sweeps a neat brick terrace leading to a bed of spring bulbs and a trellis for climbers.

Opposite: T. C. Steele. PEONY GARDEN. c. 1913. Oil on canvas, 30 x 40 in.
Collection Mr. and Mrs. Barton L. Kaufman
This peony garden was made by Steele's new wife, Selma, at the "House of the Singing Winds"
in Brown County where they moved after their marriage in 1907.

with petunias, verbenas, and geraniums among the bulbs, a crescent rose garden featuring multiflora, Dorothy Perkins, red ramblers, and other climbers over iron frames, and many flowering shrubs, all enclosed in a privet hedge.

Artists throughout the Midwest attempted to re-create the summer painting colonies and their gardens that they had enjoyed on the East Coast and in Europe. In 1899, Chicago artists, led by sculptor Lorado Taft (1860–1936), established "Eagle's Nest," a rustic camp near Oregon, Illinois. Here they surrounded stone and log bungalows with native plants and trained vines over porches and rustic pergolas.

HOOSIER PAINTINGS AND THE OLD-FASHIONED GARDEN

In Indiana, artists returning from study in Munich and Paris likewise sought rural locations for landscape painting. Theodore C. Steele (1847–1926), an early convert to Impressionism, settled in Indianapolis in 1885. Here he painted his vine-covered house and cottage garden filled with

Mrs. William Newton Byers with flowers from her garden. Photograph, c. 1910

roses, irises and tiger lilies when he was not able to get out into the open country.

In 1897, on a painting excursion with fellow landscapist J. Otis Adams (1851–1927) along the Whitewater River near Brookville, Steele discovered a derelict but grand old house surrounded by the woods and water he loved to paint. Steele and Adams bought the house together, Adams making it his full-time residence and Steele and his family occupying half during the summer. Steele's wife, Libbie, named the old house the "Hermitage" and began a garden by bringing old lilacs from the Indianapolis house.[7]

Steele, following his wife's death and his remarriage in 1907, left the "Hermitage" and began spending summers in a new studio home in rural Brown County, near Belmont, Indiana. At the hilltop "House of the Singing Winds," Selma Steele began a vegetable garden and flower beds along the walk leading from the house to several outbuildings. Since the site was on a slope with shallow soil, topsoil and leaf mulch from the surrounding forest had to be hauled in. Here she grew many of the

Dr. Howard Gates in his garden adjoining the original Van Briggle Pottery Company. Photograph, c. 1901.
Starsmore Center for Local History, Colorado Springs Pioneers Museum
Colorado Springs drew many tubercular patients, among them potter Artus Van Briggle, who set up a pottery there in 1901.

old favorites despite discouragement from the neighboring farmers, for whom, as she wrote, "it was an inexcusable waste of money and labor to grow flowers."

A novice gardener, she studied bulletins from the U.S. Department of Agriculture and planned carefully, but admitted that "even then my enthusiasm got the better of me in trying to force a growth of plants and shrubs unfitted to the local conditions. It happened because of certain early associations in flower gardening that made me believe no garden of mine, no matter where, could be satisfying without the plants I had learned to love so dearly. Experience was to teach me otherwise." Ultimately her garden design was suggested by the site and its background of forest, her intention being to "naturalize flowers over my own hillsides . . . along lines supplementary to the character of the natural setting."[8]

Virginia-born artist Will Vawter (b. 1871) came to Brown County a year after the Steeles, in 1908. Here in the hills overlooking Nashville, his noted old-fashioned flower garden served as a set-

ting for many paintings as well as a model for neighboring gardens. Other painters drawn to the new artist colony recorded the picturesque cabins and cottage gardens there, as did printmaker Gustave Bauman.

Otto Stark (1859–1926) moved to Indianapolis in 1893 as a widower with four children. His garden, though much simpler than that of the Steeles or Vawter, was the setting for many paintings of his family. William Forsyth (1854–1935) seldom dignified the subject of his paintings done at his home in Irvington with the name "garden," calling it instead "backyard" or "our yard." Nonetheless he was proud of his garden and of coaxing bloom from his flowers "from frost to frost." He encouraged native vines and shrubs as a background for his informally massed flowers.

These Hoosier gardens tended to be free-form and as open-ended as the landscape of which they were a part, including many native shrubs and wild flowers in informal associations. They were as much a deliberately American creation as the paintings of the Hoosier Group, an informal association of five of these artists whose aims, described by Forsyth on the occasion of their first exhibition together in 1894, were "to paint their pictures here at home, to express themselves each in his own way and yet hold closely to that local truth characteristic of our particular spot of earth and interpret it in all the varying moods that are its charm."[9]

![decorative初始字母] GARDENS ON THE WESTERN FRONTIER   The vast prairie covering much of the Midwest was still seen as a uniquely American garden by painters long after William Cullen Bryant had celebrated these "Gardens of the Desert . . . / For which the speech of England has no name" in his poem "The Prairies" (1832). Harvey T. Dunn, a South Dakota native who moved east at the turn of the century but returned home each summer, specialized in paintings of the prairie and its isolated settlements, where often the only flower gardens were, as Bryant put it, the "unshorn fields, boundless and beautiful." The landscape inevitably played a role not only in such natural Edens but in gardens planned by men and women. The latter were made by professionals, who developed the Prairie Style in landscape design, and by many amateurs as sensitive to site as landscape painters had to be.

Colorado, the gateway to the Rocky Mountains, reached by the transcontinental railway in 1869, offered myriad attractions to flower lovers as well as to such landscape painters as Albert

Bierstadt and Worthington Whittredge, both of whom came in the 1860s. Eliza Greatorex, quick to capitalize on a trend, visited Denver and Colorado Springs with her two daughters who specialized in flower paintings. Her own drawings of the landscape and picturesque settlements were published as *Summer Etchings in Colorado* (1873). The native wild flowers attracted many other painters and writers, including poet Helen Hunt Jackson, whose *Procession of Flowers in Colorado* (1885) was illustrated by Alice Stewart Hill, a resident of Colorado Springs. If the stunning natural scenery and native flora drew tourists, they were not necessarily appropriated by full-time residents. Even at the base of the spectacular rock formation the Garden of the Gods near the town, William Jackson Palmer, the founding father of Colorado Springs, wanted an East Coast garden with bordered flower beds, lawn, and rustic, vine-covered pergolas.

Palmer had envisioned Colorado Springs as a health resort for tubercular easterners. The building of a railroad link and the discovery of gold in 1893 made it something of a boom town as well. Art potter Artus Van Briggle, who had been chief designer at Rookwood in Cincinnati, came to Colorado Springs as a tubercular patient in 1899. Two years later, with the backing of Maria Longworth Nichols, he built a new pottery there, which was an immediate success; one of the resident doctors made an expansive cottage garden adjoining it. Both pottery making and gardening were viewed as particularly therapeutic for those with tuberculosis. In Van Briggle's case, neither was successful as he died within five years of establishing his pottery.[10]

Denver, a thriving town in 1860, had begun by the 1870s to sprout suburbs where substantial houses were often surrounded by old-fashioned gardens. The suburb of Rosedale, for example, was reputedly named for the abundance of yellow roses that covered the frame house of resident Amanda Field. Elizabeth Byers, wife of William Newton Byers, the publisher of the *Rocky Mountain News,* was justly proud of the masses of old-fashioned blossoms gathered from the garden of her new home built in the 1890s. Successful businessman Avery Gallup, noted for the collection of rare plants and trees surrounding his suburban estate, had first lived on the property with his wife, Charlotte, "in a rustic cottage covered with vines" while his house was being built in 1881. Charlotte Gallup subsequently ran a thriving nursery business from their greenhouses.[11]

THE SPANISH HERITAGE OF THE SOUTHWEST   In their search for a usable past, a trend that had accelerated by the turn of the century, gardeners in Florida, Texas, southern California, and parts of the Southwest no longer ignored their Spanish garden heritage. They studied the gardens of missions, ranches, and walled town houses both for their climate-sensitive plantings and their plans. Grace Tabor began her *Old-Fashioned Gardening* (1913) with a

Gustave Baumann. GRANDMA BATTIN'S COTTAGE. c. 1910. Color woodblock, 13 x 13 in. Eckert Fine Art, Indianapolis
Grandma's neat cottage in Brown County, Indiana, has a white picket fence covered with hollyhocks, morning glories, and other old favorites.

consideration of the historic gardens of St. Augustine, Florida, the site in 1565 of the first outpost of the Spanish Empire in North America. After 1865, there were still ancient walled gardens overlooked by the loggias of houses where figs, peaches, grapes, plums, and oranges as well as flowers flourished. Harriet Beecher Stowe, who visited then, wrote that St. Augustine resembled "some little, old, dead-and-alive Spanish town, with . . . the indolent, dreamy stillness that characterizes life in old Spain." [12]

Santa Fe, New Mexico, founded in 1609–10, did not become part of the United States until after the Mexican War of 1846–48. The railroad reached Santa Fe in 1880 over the route of the old Santa Fe Trail, and, soon after, many artists were drawn there both by the dramatic landscape and by interest in the distinctive cultures of the Zuni and Pueblo Indians. The horticultural heritage there was not easily assimilated. As Tabor had written about the gardens of St. Augustine, "It is the interest of the strange and foreign rather than of homely familiarity." [13]

In San Antonio, Texas, Adina de Zavala (1862–1955), a leader in the local efforts to preserve the Alamo mission and the Spanish Governor's Palace and the author of *The Alamo and Other Missions* (1917), sparked interest in old gardens and their flowers. She was frequently called on for recollections of her own grandmother's garden, noted for its collection of roses, in Galveston, Texas. Lorenzo de Zavala, her grandfather, had been Mexico's ambassador to France. When he returned to Texas, then a province of Mexico, in 1838, he brought with him a number of fine French roses.

The first de Zavala house, near Lynchburg, Texas, the destination of these roses, burned. Their

Will Vawter. OUR GARDEN, HOLLYHOCK TIME. c. 1910. Oil on canvas, 30 x 36 in. Private collection
In 1908, Vawter came to Brown County where he made a locally famous cottage garden.

second house, which Adina de Zavala recalled from childhood, had a loggia, draped with a yellow Banksia rose and a crimson rambler, that overlooked the front garden. Here, surrounded by a picket fence, were moss and tea roses with violets, pansies, and Johnny-jump-ups outlining the beds. Pinks, verbenas, geraniums, lady's slippers, and larkspur grew along the fence. In one corner stood a Cape jasmine and just inside the gate, an althea. On the west side of the house, beyond a magnolia, were irises, cockscomb, bachelor's buttons, zinnias, hollyhocks, and more roses. Roses also lined a passageway on the east side of the house. Mrs. de Zavala's passion for roses had reportedly been encouraged by her son's tutor, historian George Bancroft, who years later made a famous rose garden at his home in Newport, Rhode Island.[14]

Texas in the nineteenth century was occupied not only by old Spanish families and planters

T. C. Steele. FLOWER GARDEN AT THE HERMITAGE, BROOKVILLE. 1901. Oil on canvas, 13 x 18 in. Private collection
*Steele and J. Otis Adams bought an old house in Brown County in 1897 where the Steele family summered
and Adams lived full time. Its garden had lilacs, a poppy bed, hollyhocks, and many native plants.*

and ranchers from southern states, but by German immigrants, who settled in the hill country. Here on small farms they cultivated many more vegetables than their fellow Texans and included in their gardens native plants such as bluebonnets, redbud, honeysuckle, cross vine, grapes, and flowering willow as well as old-fashioned flowers. By 1876, the town of New Braunfels, established in 1845 by Prince Carl zu Solms Braunfels, was home to two noted nurseries and to many dedicated gardeners.[15]

San Antonio itself had a German neighborhood of substantial houses on large lots that included extensive gardens. Edward Steves, who arrived in 1848, built a house in the 1860s that was surrounded by a picket fence and included box-edged flower beds on either side of a central walk. It also boasted a cast-iron fountain picked up by Steves at the Philadelphia Centennial Exposition. These German settlements are now prime hunting grounds for the Texas rose rustlers who search for old-fashioned roses like Lady Banks. One Texas Lady Banks rose, planted in 1884, has even made it to the *Guinness Book of World Records.* It seems that the Texas heat and lack of humidity inimicable to delicate hybrid tea roses encourages such hardy old roses to grow to an astonishing size.[16]

Mrs. Saunders in the garden, Pasadena, California. Photograph, c. 1908. Huntington Library, San Marino, California
The Saunderses made an old-fashioned garden on a terraced slope behind their house in Pasadena.

Grandmother's Garden on the Pacific Coast

The garden beds are prim and square,
Box-bordered, scenting all the air,
And fruit trees on espaliers crawl
Around the high, old-fashioned wall.

Some little mistress, long ago,
Set out each straightly ordered row;
She watched the spicy pinks unfold,
The hollyhocks and marigolds;

And standing in the poppy bed
Is the old dial, where she read;
"Life is a Shadowe; soon 'tis Night,
Looke thou to God, thy Sun of Light."

Charles Buxton Going, "In an Old Garden"

GARDENS IN OREGON AND WASHINGTON STATE As in the Midwest, the literal roots of many old-fashioned gardens on the Pacific Coast could be found in the East, brought by the earliest settlers. One of these, Lewelling Henderson, credited with founding the orchard industry of the Northwest as well as an early nursery, is perhaps more noteworthy for his propagation of towns. Henderson, born in the Moravian community of Salem, North Carolina, headed west, settling first in Ohio where he began a new Salem. Restlessly moving further west he founded in succession Salem, Indiana; Salem, Illinois; and Salem, Iowa. Henderson finally came to rest in Oregon, where he began yet another Salem. In all of his moves, he had taken his favorite apple trees with him, both in remembrance of home and as a means of livelihood.[1]

Donna Schuster. MORNING SUNSHINE. 1917. Oil on canvas, 29 ½ x 29 ½ in. Courtesy The Redfern Gallery, Laguna Beach
Schuster in 1914 had joined William Merritt Chase's summer painting class at Carmel. She later owned a cottage at the Laguna Beach art colony.

Opposite: Frederick Frieseke. HOLLYHOCKS. 1914. Oil on canvas, 25 ½ x 32 in. The National Academy of Design, New York
Frieseke was able to find in California the same floral motifs he had painted in France.

Cherished seeds and cuttings of flowers and shrubs as well as fruit trees and vegetables accompanied most early settlers of the far West. Charlotte Matheny Kirkwood in 1905 recalled her mother's pioneer flower garden in Oregon's Willamette Valley, which was begun in 1844 from the contents of a seed sack that had occupied the most protected spot in the wagon going west. "The results exceeded her expectations; her garden became a dream of beauty. All the sweet old-fashioned favorites vied with each other in the blending of brilliant hues; throngs of gaily tinted butterflies reveled in the perfume-laden breath of pinks and roses."[2] Seeds, roots, and cuttings from her garden began many others in the valley.

An early settler of Olympia, Washington, Daniel R. Bigelow (1824–1905) had headed west after attending college in his native New York State and receiving a law degree from Harvard College. Several years after his arrival in 1851, he built himself an up-to-the-minute Gothic Revival house in Olympia, on the occasion of his marriage. His wife, Ann Elizabeth White, from Wisconsin,

Katherine Rogers's house, Beaux Arts Village, Washington. Photograph c. 1912. Collection Geraldine Armbruster
Window boxes made of bark ornamented Rogers's cottage.

Opposite: Bigelow house, Olympia, Washington. Photograph c. 1880. Bigelow House Collection, Olympia
Mrs. Bigelow's old-fashioned flower garden became a consuming interest second only to her work for women's suffrage.

had been one of the first schoolteachers in Washington Territory. She was also an early supporter of women's suffrage as was Bigelow himself, who in 1871 introduced an unsuccessful bill in the state legislature to give women the vote. Bigelow retired from politics shortly thereafter and he and Mrs. Bigelow cultivated their garden. In spring their front yard was a mass of daffodils followed by a succession of bloom from old perennials. When Mrs. Bigelow died in 1926, among the last of the original pioneers, her obituary noted that "her orchard and garden were her pet hobbies, and she developed her home into one of the beauty spots in the capital city."[3]

Along the Pacific Coast in Oregon and Washington, conditions for flower gardens were ideal. Temperatures hovered in the seventies in summer and remained above freezing in the winter, with abundant rain. Nonetheless, at the turn of the century, the artists who founded Beaux Arts village eschewed flower gardens, if not flowers. At this Arts and Crafts community on the shore of Lake Washington, across from Seattle, the purpose was to disturb the landscape as little as possible, leaving the firs, cedars, and other mature evergreens as the setting for rustic log houses and timber cottages. As an artists' cooperative, the village was a failure, with only fifteen houses built by 1916. Among these was the charming small cottage ornamented with bark window boxes, wisteria, old-

fashioned flowers, and flowering shrubs, built by Katherine Rogers, a schoolteacher, who rowed her-self to work each morning.[4]

EARLY GARDENS IN CALIFORNIA California's climate was more demanding than that of coastal Washington. In California, spring began in January with the coming of the rainy season; summer was rainless. It was an axiom at the turn of the century that "water in abundance must be provided for a garden," at least for an old-fashioned perennial one.[5] The exuberance of California life, both natural and cultural, the sense of unlimited possibilities, the fact that nearly anything from anywhere in the world seemed to grow given enough water, gave a startling luxuriance and often unsettling eclecticism to California gardens. Early settlers drawn to northern California during the gold rush of 1849 and those farther south, attracted by the blissfully warm climate and promise of agricultural abundance given sufficient water, at first attempted to reproduce the surroundings they had known elsewhere in the country.

Modest vine-covered cabins like the one in the hills of Marin County built by pioneer and

Thaddeus Welch. A Cottage in the Marin County Hills. c. 1895. Oil on canvas, 26 x 20 in. The Oakland Museum

painter Thaddeus Welch (1844–1919) in 1893 were not unusual. Here the flower garden, with sun-flowers towering conspicuously, was a tangle of hardy perennials and annuals left to fend for them-selves near the house. Even at military encampments like Fort Mason in San Francisco, officers and their families reproduced the informal abundance of the old-fashioned garden, although they pre-ferred cannonballs rather than stones to edge their flower beds.[6]

The landscape of southern California seen by the early homesteaders would have been unrec-ognizable to visitors in the 1890s such as Kate Sanborn, who viewed with skepticism the extravagant claims for the region in her sprightly *A Truthful Woman in Southern California* (1893). Then, what trees there were grew along the few watercourses, with most of the land covered in chaparral. Settlers in a climate inimical to water-loving eastern shrubs and perennials nonetheless attempted to have old-fashioned gardens.

William Alston Hayne, who arrived in Santa Barbara from South Carolina in 1868, built a two-story adobe house that he covered with clapboard. A center hall opened on a garden full of roses and fragrant shrubs that would have been at home in any southern town on the East Coast. Small door-yard gardens such as this could be watered easily. Other settlers were more ambitious. In nearby Montecito, Elsie Whitton Buell, who followed her husband from Vermont in 1884, planted a cottage garden of perennials and hardy annuals behind the two-story Queen Anne–style clapboard house

Joseph Raphael. THE GARDEN. n.d. Oil on canvas, 28 x 30 in. Collection Garzoli Gallery, San Rafael, California

they built in the 1890s. Not visible in a photograph of the house, but conspicuous in photographs of other homes in the area, was the ubiquitous windmill with water tower necessary to sustain such a garden. A lawn was seldom attempted, but luxuriant vines and roses, which loved the climate, were encouraged to wreath porches and fill yards.[7]

By 1890, three powerful influences began to shape California gardens. First, and most pervasive, was a new appreciation for the Spanish origins of California, exemplified in part by the decaying missions and adobe ranchos lining the Camino Real from San Francisco to San Diego. The second was the Arts and Crafts Movement, with its focus on the simple, outdoor life and the use of indige-

Mrs. Hervey J. Buell in her garden, Montecito, California. Photograph, c. 1900. Collection Susan Buell Simpson
Mrs. Buell made an old-fashioned flower garden beside her new house built in the mid-1890s.

Below: Buell house and yard, Montecito, California. Photograph, c. 1900. Collection Susan Buell Simpson

"Inner court of Ramona's Home, San Diego." Postcard, c. 1915. Private collection
The Estudillo rancho in San Diego, putative location of Ramona's marriage to Alessandro in the romance Ramona *(1884),*
was given a Mission Revival courtyard garden by architect Hazel Wood Waterman and became an instant tourist attraction.

nous materials and vernacular construction. The third was an appreciation of the climate and land-scape that was fostered by the growing ecological awareness on the part of a few influential writers and garden-makers.

HELEN HUNT JACKSON AND MISSION REVIVAL GARDENS

The Colonial Revival, which in the East engen-dered thousands of old-fashioned gardens based on New England or southern prototypes, spurred in California a new interest in the state's own distinctive Spanish colonial past. An early apologist for the Spanish occupation was Elizabeth Hughes, who in her *California of the Padres* (1875) held up the preindustrial, communal life of the Franciscan missions as a model for a materialistic present.

The Colonial Revival in California took off in the late 1880s when fueled by the wild popu-larity of the novel *Ramona* (1884) by poet Helen Hunt Jackson (1831–1885), who had grown up in Amherst, Massachusetts, and was a friend of Emily Dickinson. Jackson, who had earlier written *A Century of Dishonor* (1881) documenting the perfidy of the United States government in its treatment of Indian tribes, intended the novel as a western *Uncle Tom's Cabin*. Her aim was to spur public out-

Theodore Wores. THE ARTIST'S HOME, SARATOGA, CALIFORNIA. c. 1920. Oil on canvas, 16 x 20 in.
Collection Drs. Ben and A. Jess Shenson
Wores made a home and patio garden in an old adobe church.

rage at the plight of Indians previously attached to the missions who were being forced off their lands by settlers from elsewhere in the country. *Ramona* recounted the romantic and gripping story of the love and marriage between the eponymous heroine, brought up by an old, landed Spanish family, and Alessandro, the son of a chief, an altogether worthy young man who nonetheless was hounded from one remote village to the next by land-hungry Anglo interlopers. Ironically, it was the stately way of life on the ancient Spanish rancho, soon to disappear under American rule, rather than the plight of the Indians, that proved most memorable to contemporary readers.

Among the ranchos that Jackson had visited while gathering material for a series of articles in *Century Magazine* (1883; republished in *Glimpses of Three Coasts,* 1886) had been that of her chief informant, Don Antonio Coronel, in Los Angeles. She was enchanted by the Coronels' adobe house, "built after the ancient style on three sides of a square, surrounded by orchards, vineyards, orange

Benjamin C. Brown. THE JOYOUS GARDEN. c. 1900. Oil on canvas, 30 x 40 in. The Irvine Museum, Irvine, California
California gardens, like this one in Pasadena, often adopted the box borders and old-fashioned flowers of grandmother's garden.

groves, and looking out on an old-fashioned garden in which southernwood, rue, lavender, mint, marigolds and gilly flowers hold their own bravely, growing in straight and angular beds among the newer splendors of verbenas, roses, carnations, and geraniums."[8]

The Coronels recommended she visit the more rural rancho of the del Valles at Camulos, sixty miles northwest of the city, where life still went on as it had in old California. It was this adobe and its garden that became in *Ramona* "the representative house of the half barbaric, half elegant, wholly generous and free-handed life led there by Mexican men and women of degree." The patio garden, created by Don Ygnacio and Doña Isabel del Valle in the 1860s, enclosed on three sides by the house, was centered on a fountain surrounded by clipped Monterey cypress and four flower beds. Through a passage in the south wing was another flower garden, also centered on a fountain, planted with roses, carnations, myrtle, and fruit trees.[9]

In this real place, the fictional Moreno family of *Ramona* conducted much of their leisurely domestic life in the shelter of the veranda, where "there were many sorts of climbing vines—some coming from the ground, and twining around the pillars; some growing in great bowls." Here there were also "geraniums, carnations and yellow flowered musk," and just beyond the veranda "all was garden, orange grove, and almond orchard." The path through the garden was sheltered under a trellis of grapevines, where "the grapes filled and hardened, like opaque emeralds hung thick under the canopied vines. . . . the roses had fallen but there were lilies, and orange-blossoms, and poppies and carnations."[10]

Such romantic evocations of bucolic surroundings, where dignified Californians of European ancestry had conducted full lives in touch with the natural world, were found in serious histories, such as Herbert Howe Bancroft's tellingly titled *California Pastoral 1769–1848* (1888) as well as in accounts by descendants of old families, such as Guadalupe Vallejo, whose nostalgic "Ranch and Mission Days in Alta California" appeared in *Century Magazine* (1890). This mythical California past was eagerly appropriated by incoming Anglos as a way of establishing a regional identity and a collective history in a part of the country where their roots were very shallow indeed.

The transcontinental railroad had reached San Francisco in 1869, opening California to an influx of tourists as well as settlers. In that year alone seventy thousand people arrived by rail. The land boom in southern California of the 1880s was facilitated by the completion of the Sante Fe railroad from Chicago to Los Angeles. The railroad, as the largest private landowner in the state, had a vested interest in attracting ever more visitors. Publicity opportunities offered by the popularity of *Ramona* and the fascination with the mission era were quickly exploited with *Ramona* tours offered to the missions as well as to the Camulos rancho.[11]

In 1885, only three missions were still in use, and only one of them, at Santa Barbara, had a courtyard garden, which dated not to the eighteenth century but to the 1830s, after secularization of the missions by Mexico. Eighteen others were in ruinous condition and gardenless. Charles Fletcher Lummis, Harvard-educated ethnologist and writer, who had come to Los Angeles in 1885, led the movement for their responsible preservation. In his study, *The Spanish Pioneers* (1893), from the pages of his magazine *Land of Sunshine* (which he edited from 1895 to 1903), and in the Landmarks Club, which he helped found in 1895, he stressed the heroic and austere side of the mission era. Others involved in the restoration of missions and ranchos were not so rigorous.

At the turn of the century, the San Juan de Capistrano mission was given a Spanish Colonial Revival patio garden planted informally in stone-bordered beds with masses of old-fashioned perennials and vines as part of its restoration.[12] The early-nineteenth-century Estudillo family adobe and courtyard garden in San Diego were restored by architect Hazel Wood Waterman in 1908 for John D. Spreckels, owner of the grand Hotel del Coronado. It had been identified as the site of

Orrin Peck. THE BLESSING OF
THE FLOWERS, SANTA BARBARA
MISSION. Oil on canvas, 91 x 72 3/8
in. The Oakland Museum,
California

*The Santa Barbara Mission was the only
early Franciscan mission to have an extant
patio garden, one that dated to the 1830s.*

Ramona's marriage to Alessandro, and Spreckels soon opened it as a tourist attraction, building a special trolley line into Old Town to facilitate visits. Mrs. Hugh Lowther, owner of an adobe in the precinct
of the Mission of San Gabriel in Pasadena, hired landscape designer Florence Yoch to create a patio
garden "in the early manner" that seemed to demand a picket fence, climbing roses, and vines.[13]
Even San Francisco painter Theodore Wores (1860–1939), after study in Munich and a three-year
stay in Japan, chose to remodel an old adobe church in Saratoga, California, into a Mission
Revival–style house with enclosed patio garden.

Mission Revival by 1890 had become the official style of California, where it was enshrined
in train stations and on college campuses as well as in private homes. California's building for the
1893 World's Columbian Exposition in Chicago was an astonishing amalgam of facades and flanking
towers from three separate missions. Nonetheless, it was the democratic bungalow with its low,
ground-hugging lines, its overhanging eaves, its open plan, and enveloping garden that for contemporary observers seemed to exemplify California life.

THE ARTS AND CRAFTS INFLUENCE Gustav Stickley, doyen of the Arts and Crafts Movement, visited California in 1904 and was impressed by all he saw. He stayed first at the famous Mission Inn in Riverside. The inn, begun as a simple adobe, had expanded into a potent fantasy of bell towers, arcaded verandas, and tile-roofed additions that evoked for Stickley the romance of the mission era. Continuing south, Stickley was bowled over by the simple, vernacular architecture and the outdoor life possible there. Articles on California and bungalow life came to dominate his *Craftsman* magazine, all extolling a place where "the house, the garden, the terrace, the patio, the open porch are all one domain, one shelter from the outside world."[14]

For architectural critic Montgomery Schuyler writing in 1908, the bungalow was a truly democratic home, enabling people of modest means "in their abodes and their surroundings to give evidence of culture and refinement, to avoid the vulgarity of crudity on the one hand and the vulgarity of ostentation on the other."[15] Innovative architects, from Bernard Maybeck in Berkeley to Charles Sumner and Henry Mather Greene in Pasadena, began to build houses in local materials with simple lines and an integral relationship with the out-of-doors that were an apotheosis of the bungalow.

The planting of the patio or bungalow garden could be wildly eclectic, ranging from the completely exotic to a semitropical version of grandmother's garden. The patio of a house designed by Irving Gill in San Diego, for example, had heliotropes, stock, sweet peas, verbenas, wisteria, clematis, pansies, violets, asters, foxgloves, and larkspur but also rhus, nemophila, plumbago, and mariposas.[16] A Pasadena garden recorded by painter Benjamin Brown (1865–1942) sported a prim hedge of dwarf box as well as masses of pink and white phlox. (Brown's own garden studio was covered in vines and entered through a rose arbor.) Impressionist Frederick Frieseke (1874–1939), an expatriate in Giverny and elsewhere in France for much of his career, visited California in 1911, where he painted gardens in Pasadena and Santa Barbara. With the outbreak of World War I, he settled in Pasadena and recorded a flourishing row of hollyhocks that would have been at home in any grandmother's garden.

Garden writer Charles Frances Saunders (1859–1941), another Pasadena resident, wrote of his first glimpse of gardens there on a winter visit from the East Coast. Quite obviously smitten by California flora, he noted: "There were geraniums of every hue, banked in some cases house-high; callas grew literally in hedges, serving as party-fences between city lots; fuchsias and heliotrope hid beneath their masses of exquisite bloom the cottage walls against which they grew and looked in at second story windows; climbing roses smothered some houses completely, or climbed trees and hung festoons of rare color from the crowns twenty or thirty feet up in the air."[17] Saunders's first book, *In a Poppy Garden* (1904), was of poems dedicated to his wife, and his second, *California Wild Flowers* (1905), was illustrated with his wife's watercolors.

The Saunders's own "small cottage garden planted by ourselves" was begun in 1906. The lot of only ninety by sixty feet was made into terraced beds with low walls of arroyo stone and filled with "what plants will produce the best continuity of effect the year 'round with the least outlay of time and money." Commenting that "practically everything that grows in the Eastern garden may be grown here, besides much else," Saunders recommended the old-fashioned flowers: roses, geraniums, nasturtiums, sweet alyssum, verbenas, mignonette, foxgloves, violets, pansies, stock, calendulas, and chrysanthemums—with cacti and gaillardias the only natives.[18]

By 1900, southern California gardens large and small were the subjects of scores of articles and hundreds of postcard views. Mission-style gardens like that of "Ramona's Home," as the Estudillo family adobe was identified, grand estates in Santa Barbara and Montecito, and more informal cottage gardens became tourist attractions. A visitor in 1904 to the three-acre garden of flower painter Paul de Longpré in the new Los Angeles suburb called Hollywood marveled at the more than three thousand roses planted in a "simple, natural manner."[19] The garden was enclosed in an evergreen hedge covered in climbing roses and vines, with fragrant shrubs and masses of flowers, among them heliotropes, carnations, and nicotiana, mingled with the roses. Also on the tourist route were the much simpler cottage gardens found in picturesque artists' colonies that had sprung up along the coast in Carmel, Laguna Beach, and La Jolla.

GARDENS FOR A LAND OF LITTLE RAIN   Most of these gardens, whether of great estates or cottages, depended on an extravagant use of water to support plants unsuited to the environment. By 1900, an undercurrent of ecological awareness began to make itself felt. An appreciation of California's climate and native flora had since the 1890s been fostered by writers associated with *Land of Sunshine* magazine. One of these, Mary Austin, who had moved with her family in 1888 to the San Joaquin Valley of southern California, became the champion of the stark and piercingly beautiful landscape in essays of the 1890s that were expanded into the influential and evocative portrait of the region, *The Land of Little Rain* (1903).

Austin could also mine the vein of nostalgia for the "Old Spanish Gardens" with their vine-covered trellises, rows of artichokes, figs and pomegranates, climbing roses and vines, and old-fashioned flowers. But above all, it was the California natives and the palpable spirit of the desert that elicited her most profound response. In her autobiography, a turning point in her spiritual life was identified with a particular season and its flowers. "It was a dry April, but not entirely barren; mirages multiplied on every hand, white borage came out and blue nemophila; where the run-off of the infrequent rain collected in hollows, blue lupine sprang up as though pieces of sky had fallen. . . . suddenly she was aware of poppies coming up singly through the tawny, crystal-sanded soil, thin, piercing orange-colored flames . . . and then the warm pervasive sweetness of ultimate reality."[20]

A few prescient amateurs, like Lummis with his wild-flower meadow, and professionals, most notably horticulturist Kate O. Sessions (1857–1940) in articles for *California Garden Magazine*, began to advocate the use of hardy, drought-tolerant plants in private gardens. Sessions's nursery in San Diego propagated and sold trees, shrubs, and flowers from all over the world, but in her plantings for local houses she made extensive use of plants, especially natives, suited to the exacting soil and climate. To one customer who wanted hollyhocks, she categorically stated, "They do not like us and I don't like them! We have plenty of plants that do like our climate so I don't have anything to do with holly-hocks." She was among the earliest to make available in the trade the matilija poppy, the golden yellow flannelbush, and the California lilac, among many other natives.[21] The drought-tolerant gardens she designed, as well as the new plants and California natives she propagated, became known outside the state through descriptions by influential writers like Mrs. Francis King and through her work with nationally known architects and landscape designers such as Eric Gill and Samuel Parsons, Jr.

THE LEGACY OF GRANDMOTHER'S GARDEN By 1915, the horticultural innovations embodied in grandmother's garden had become part of the working vocabulary of professional landscape designers as well as amateur gardeners all across the country. Gardening ideas we view as up-to-the-minute today, xeriscaping or the extensive use of native plants, for example, can be traced to innovative American gardeners before 1900 who had been freed from rigid ideas about what gardens ought to be by the gentle revolution of grandmother's garden. The enclosed garden room of today was actually grandmother's outdoor parlor. The decorative use of vegetables and fruits in the flower garden was encouraged in grandmother's garden, as was the use of striking native "weeds." Intensive gardening in raised beds had been practiced in America since colonial days and was continued in the plank or box-bordered beds of grandmother's garden. The idea of a garden of fragrant flowers was as eagerly embraced by late-nineteenth-century gardeners as it is today. Lady Jean Skipwith cultivated a wild garden long before William Robinson, as did American gardeners in the late nineteenth century.

Aesthetic ideas usually attributed to English writers can be found in American gardening literature before the English books were known here. The importance of a plant's foliage and structure as well as its flower color in making garden pictures and the value of planning for sequence of bloom throughout the season were recognized by Anna Bartlett Warner and other writers in the 1870s. Massing plants for greatest effect, planting intensively for continuous bloom in the same spot, and

The "Alisal" wild flower carpet in February. Photograph by Charles Fletcher Lummis, 1905.
The Huntington Library, San Marino, California
Lummis eschewed a conventional garden for a meadow of wild flowers at his Los Angeles home.

orchestrating color harmonies and modulations were concepts recognized and used by Candace Wheeler, Celia Thaxter, and other American gardeners in the 1880s and 1890s. Color as well as fragrance was central to grandmother's garden and ranged from the muted color harmonies of the 1870s to the bold color contrasts in the artists' gardens of the 1890s. Certainly American gardeners were not isolated from English and European gardening ideas, but we emphatically have a national gardening tradition as well as regional ones, seen best in personal, individually made and maintained gardens like grandmother's.

American garden literature in the fifty years between 1865 and 1915 is amazingly rich and nuanced, not just in what it tells about American gardening, but in what it reveals about the writers themselves and the period in which they lived. Much of it was written by women in a confessional, first-person voice that is both accessible and often very moving in a way an impartial, how-to manual can never be. These American garden writers were grounded in our native soil, and their love for American flora and American traditions warms and enriches their descriptions of their own and others' gardens. Later garden writers owe them an often unacknowledged debt.

NOTES

The Bibliography contains full information for the works cited in brief in these notes.
The Bibliography is divided in two parts: works published through 1915
(pages 220–225) and works published after 1915 (pages 226–31).

THE ROOTS OF GRANDMOTHER'S GARDEN

1. Ann Leighton's *Early American Gardens* (1970) is the standard and very readable account of these gardens.
2. Anne Grant, *Memoirs of an American Lady* (American ed., 1876), 46.
3. Ann Leighton, *American Gardens in the Eighteenth Century* (1976), 281. Leighton transcribes all of Lady Skipwith's lists, 283–90. See also Peter Martin, *The Pleasure Gardens of Virginia* (1991), 126–31. The Skipwith Papers are in the Swem Library, College of William and Mary, Williamsburg, Virginia.
4. John Adams's diary for 1786, quoted in Leighton, *American Gardens in the Eighteenth Century*, 359.
5. Ann Leighton, *American Gardens of the Nineteenth Century* (1987), 267–68.
6. On Wagener, see Rosalie Reid, "Historian Seeks Marker for Atlanta" (1966).
7. Discussed in John R. Stilgoe, *Borderland* (1988), 118.
8. Ralph Waldo Emerson, *Selected Essays, Lectures, and Poems* (1990), 99–100.
9. Emerson, *Selected Essays*, 217. Emily Dickinson, *The Complete Poems of Emily Dickinson* (1960), no. 214.
10. Dickinson, *Complete Poems*, no. 178. See Cynthia Griffin Wolff's compelling biography (1988) for an elaboration of the idea of circumference and an analysis of Dickinson's poems.
11. Martha Dickinson Bianchi, *Emily Dickinson Face to Face* (1932), 39.
12. Harriet Beecher Stowe, *Uncle Tom's Cabin* (1852), 30 (reprint).
13. David P. Handlin, *The American Home* (1979), 89.
14. Catherine Beecher and Harriet Beecher Stowe, *The American Woman's Home* (1869), 282.
15. Harriet Beecher Stowe, "The Woman Question" (1865), 676. Letter quoted in Annie Fields, *Authors and Friends* (1893), 184.
16. Quoted in William Dean Howells, *My Mark Twain* (1910), 37.
17. The most recent account of her life is Joan D. Hedrick's *Harriet Beecher Stowe* (1994).

GRANDMOTHER'S GARDEN REDISCOVERED

1. William Leach, *True Love and Perfect Union* (1980), 64.
2. Mrs. S. O. Johnson, *Every Woman Her Own Flower Gardener* (1871), 5, 18, 120.
3. Anna Bartlett Warner, *Gardening by Myself* (1872), 64–66.
4. Ibid., 80–81, 18.
5. Ibid., 30, 77, 127.
6. Ibid., 19, 141.
7. Warner's remarks to a friend are quoted in Olivia Phelps Stokes, *Letters and Memories* (1925), 104.
8. Clarence Cook, "Beds and Tables, Part IV" (1876), 813–14.
9. Ella Rodman Church, *The Home Garden* (1881), 13, 7.
10. Richard L. Bushman, *The Refinement of America* (1992), 260.
11. E. A. Randall, "The Artistic Impulses in Men and Women" (1900), 420.
12. Alice Sawtelle Randall, "Miss Fidelia Bridges" (1901), 584. See also May Brawley Hill, *Fidelia Bridges* (1981).
13. Anne H. Warton, "Some Philadelphia Studios" (1885), 78. Ruth Irwin Weidner, *George Cochran Lambdin* (1986), 45.
14. The article is reprinted in William H. Gerdts, *Painters of the Humble Truth* (1981), 125.
15. See Katy Tetlow and Ann Bienstock, *The Flowers of Julia Dillon* (1987).

AMERICAN SCENES AND COTTAGE GARDENS

1. Charles Dudley Warner, *My Summer in the Garden* (1870), 176.
2. Thomas Bailey Aldrich, *An Old Town by the Sea* (reprint, 1883), 122. Aldrich on "Unguarded Gates," quoted in Ferris Greenslet, *The Life of Thomas Bailey Aldrich* (1908), 168–69.
3. Thomas Bailey Aldrich, *The Story of a Bad Boy* (reprint, 1908), 34, 36.
4. O. B. Bunce, "Charleston and Its Suburbs" (1874),

199–200.

5. Thomas Worthington Whittredge, *Autobiography* (1942), 63.

6. Will Low, *A Chronicle of Friendships* (1908), 266.

7. Lizzie W. Champney, "The Summer Haunts" (1885), 849. The Champneys were residents of another colonial village, Deerfield, Massachusetts (see the chapter below, "Painting Grandmother's Garden").

8. See Rodris Roth, "The New England, or 'Olde Tyme,' Kitchen," in Alan Axelrod, ed., *The Colonial Revival in America* (1985), 159–83.

9. "This is an art": Edward King, "In the Good Old Colony Times"(1895), 135. Will Low, quoted in Elizabeth McCausland, *The Life and Work of Edward L. Henry* (1949), 65.

10. Aldrich, *Old Town by the Sea*, 122.

11. Sarah Orne Jewett, *Country By-ways* (1881), 127.

12. Sarah Orne Jewett, *The Country of the Pointed Firs and Other Stories* (1896), 3–4 (reprint). Sarah Way Sherman, in *Sarah Orne Jewett, an American Persephone* (1989), points out the use of myth in the book.

13. Thomas Wentworth Higginson, "The Greek Goddesses" (1869), 108.

14. Jewett, *Country of the Pointed Firs and Other Stories*, 259 (reprint).

15. "It was a miracle": Francis Otto Matthiessen, *Sarah Orne Jewett* (1929), 2. On Jewett's first composition, see John Eldridge Frost, *Sarah Orne Jewett* (1960), 10.

16. Frost, *Jewett*, 77.

17. Gwen L. Nagel, "Sarah Orne Jewett's New England Gardens" (1986), 44.

18. Jewett, *Country By-ways*, 120–21.

19. Charlotte Perkins Gilman, *The Yellow Wallpaper and Other Writings* (1989), 5.

RESCUING THE OLD PLACE

1. George H. Ellwanger, *The Garden's Story* (1889), 34, 35, 52, 53.

2. Ibid., 146. As a late introduction, bleeding-heart (*Dicentra spectabilis*) had no business in the old-fashioned garden.

3. Samuel Parsons, Jr., *Landscape Gardening* (1891), 156, 202–3.

4. Ibid., 205–6.

5. Ibid., 217.

6. Mary Caroline Robbins, *The Rescue of an Old Place* (1892), 167–68.

7. Ibid., 93.

8. Ibid., 67.

9. Ibid., 72–73.

10. J. P. Mowbray, *The Making of a Country Home* (1901), 41, 49, 249.

11. Kate Sanborn, *Adopting an Abandoned Farm* (1891), 127, 138.

12. Kate Sanborn, *My Favorite Lectures of Long Ago* (1898), 3.

13. Mariana Griswold Van Rensselaer, *Art Out-of-Doors* (1893), 58, 63.

14. New York State, *Report of the Board of General Managers* (1894), 287–88.

15. Rossiter Johnson, ed., *A History of the World's Columbian Exposition* (1898), vol. 2: 459. One of the visitors to the exposition was Sarah Orne Jewett, who wrote to a friend on May 2, 1893: "Nothing wins more praise and admiration at the World's Fair than the Hancock house . . . the day has come when to live in the Hancock house itself would be the most charming distinction." Carl J. Weber, *Letters of Sarah Orne Jewett Now in the Colby College Library* (1947), 27.

16. Frank Waugh, *The Landscape Beautiful* (1910), 186. See also Alan Axelrod, ed., *The Colonial Revival in America* (1985), 200–204.

17. Charles Sprague Sargent, "Old-Fashioned Gardens" (1895), 281–82.

18. See Joyce Butler, *Abbott Fuller Graves* (1979).

19. Margaret Deland, *Golden Yesterdays* (1940), 109.

20. Leonard Barron, "The Summer Home of Margaret Deland" (1909), 464–65.

21. Katherine Burnside, *Childe Hassam in Connecticut* (1988), 5.

22. See Lisa N. Peters, "Twachtman's Greenwich Garden" (1989), and Paul Hochman, "Impressions of a House" (1992), 96.

23. Both photograph and painting are illustrated in *The Memoirs of Elizabeth Hill Cram* (1992).

THE COLONIAL REVIVAL AND THE OLD-FASHIONED GARDEN

1. Alice Morse Earle, *Margaret Winthrop* (1895), 334–35. See also Susan Reynolds Williams, "In the Garden of New England" (1992). Earle was a member of the National Society of the Colonial Dames and of the Daughters of the American Revolution, both founded in 1890.

2. Alice Morse Earle, "Old Time Flower Gardens" (1896), 167, 176.

3. Earle's letter is in the Sophia Smith Collection, Smith College Library, Northampton, Massachusetts. Jekyll's

book, actually titled *West Surrey Life*, treated many of the kinds of domestic impedimenta featured in Earle.

4. Alice Morse Earle, *Old Time Gardens* (1901), 4.

5. Ibid., 91, 42–43, 48.

6. Ibid., 161, 321. See Williams, "In the Garden," 98, for a description of the Worcester garden.

7. Earle, *Old Time Gardens*, 181, 179.

8. Arthur A. Shurtleff, "Some Old New England Flower Gardens" (1899), 423, 424.

9. W. E. Pendleton, "Old Fashioned Gardens" (1907), 507–8. Liberty Hyde Bailey, "An Old-Time Home Garden" (1902), 18–21. Helen Everson Smith, "An Ancient Garden" (1906), 112.

10. Rose H. Howe, *Elizabeth Bishop Perkins of York* (1979). See Sarah L, Griffith and Kevin D. Murphy, eds., *A Noble and Dignified Stream* (1992), for an in-depth discussion of the Colonial Revival in the Piscataqua region of Maine and New Hampshire.

11. Hildegard Hawthorne, "A Garden of Romance" (1910), 781–83.

12. Ibid., 785.

13. See Martha A. Sandweiss, ed., *Photography in Nineteenth Century America* (1991), and Madelyn Moeller, *Nineteenth Century Women Photographers* (1992).

14. Vicki Giles, "C. Alice Baker" (1976), 33.

15. Margery Burnham Howe, *Deerfield Embroidery* (1976), 37.

16. Frances Johnston, "The Foremost Women Photographers in America" (1901), 13.

17. Lizzie W. Champney, "The Summer Haunts" (1885), 857.

18. *Wallace Nutting's Biography* (1936), 105, 25. Among the houses Nutting owned, now museums, are the "Wentworth-Gardner House" in Portsmouth, New Hampshire; the "Webb House" in Wethersfield, Connecticut; and, in Massachusetts, the "Hazen-Garrison House" in Haverhill and the "Cutler-Bartlett House" in Newburyport.

Painting Grandmother's Garden

1. L. L. P., "The Impressionists" (1898).

2. John I. H. Downes, *Mariquita Gill* (1915), 17–18. See William H. Gerdts, *Lasting Impressions* (1992) and *Monet's Giverny* (1993), on American painters in France at the end of the nineteenth century and the beginning of the twentieth.

3. See *En Plein Air: Art Colonies at East Hampton and Old Lyme* (1989).

4. H. S. Adams, "Lyme—A Country Life Community" (1914), 92.

5. Robert Vonnoh to Bessie Potter Vonnoh, May 3 and May 4, 1901. Courtesy Mrs. Robert Rowe Thompson.

6. Ibid., May 7 and May 9, 1901. Courtesy Mrs. Robert Rowe Thompson.

7. Joseph Everett Chandler, *The Colonial House* (1924), 202. Beatrix Jones, "The Garden as a Picture" (1907), 2.

8. Rose Standish Nichols, "A Hilltop Garden in New Hampshire" (1924), 237.

9. See Keith N. Morgan, "Charles A. Platt's Houses and Gardens in Cornish" (1982).

10. William Bishop, "Hunting an Abandoned Farm" (1894), 41. Jennifer Martin, "Portraits of Flowers" (1977), 118.

11. Frances Grimes, "Reminiscences," quoted in Barbara Ball Buff and John Dryfhout, *A Circle of Friends* (1985), 41. Frances Duncan, "The Gardens of Cornish" (1906), 13.

12. Martin, "Portraits of Flowers" (1977), 117.

13. The visitor's article, entitled "An Artist Colony" and originally published in the *New York Tribune*, is reprinted in Buff and Dryfhout, *Circle of Friends*, 58.

14. Herbert C. Wise, "A Day at Northcote" (1902), 249. Stephen Parrish's gardening diaries are in the Dartmouth College Library, Hanover, New Hampshire. For a thorough study, see William Noble, "Northcote: An Artist's New Hampshire Garden" (1992).

15. Hazel W. Henderson, "An Impression of Cornish" (1903), 191. Duncan, "Gardens of Cornish," 19.

Two American Cottage Gardens

1. Celia Thaxter, *Letters* (1895), 27.

2. Quoted in Susan Faxton et al., *A Stern and Lovely Scene* (1978), 52.

3. Quoted in Celia Thaxter et al., *The Heavenly Guest* (1935), 119.

4. Ibid., 126.

5. Candace Wheeler, *Content in a Garden* (1901), 56–57.

6. Celia Thaxter, *An Island Garden* (1894), 71.

7. Ella Rodman Church, *Money-Making for Ladies* (1882), 160, 121, 119.

8. Candace Wheeler, *Yesterdays in a Busy Life* (1918), 238.

9. Ibid., 209, 238.

10. Ibid., 290. For Onteora, see E. Davis Gaillard, *The Ladies*

of Early Onteora (1994).

11. Wheeler, *Content*, 86, 132.
12. Ibid., 115.
13. Ibid., 41–42.
14. Ibid., 45–46.
15. Ibid., 51, 61.

The Arts and Crafts Movement and the American Cottage Garden

1. Mary Gay Humphries, "Women Batchelors in New York" (1896), 626.
2. Wendy Kaplan, *"The Art That Is Life"* (1987), 68. See also Carol Macht et al., *The Ladies, God Bless 'Em* (1976).
3. Susan Frackelton, "Rookwood Pottery," in *Sketch Book* 5 (February 1906): 374, quoted in Kenneth R. Trapp, ed., *Celebrate Cincinnati Art* (1982), 81.
4. Quoted in Peg Weiss, ed., *Adelaide Alsop Robineau* (1981), 29.
5. Charles Courtney Curran, "The Outdoor Painting of Flowers" (1909), 217–18.
6. Charles Courtney Curran, "A Class in Oil Painting" (1908), 52.
7. I am indebted to Kaycee Benton for documentation of Cragsmoor artists and gardens.
8. "An Artist's Ideal Home," *New York Herald* (1908).
9. Poultney Bigelow, "The Byrdcliffe Colony of Arts and Crafts" (1909), 393. McCall is quoted in Robert Edwards, *The Byrdcliffe Arts and Crafts Colony* (1984), 4.
10. Birge Harrison, *Landscape Painting* (1909), 142.
11. Samuel Howe, "Suburban Homes" (1909), 112.
12. Gustav Stickley, "A Country Home for a Businessman" (1910), 56–57.
13. Arthur A. Shurtleff, "The Grounds of an English Villager's Cottage" (1903), 9. Joakin Reinhart, "Landscape Gardening" (1903), 26. Mary Rankin Cranston, "Converting Backyards" (1909), 70.
14. Vivian Burnett, "Craftsman Gardens for Craftsman Homes" (1910), 55–56.
15. "Pergolas" (1911), 575.
16. "I shall plant": Walter Dyer, "The Philosophy of Gardens" (1911), 5. "Maze of flowers": Hanna Rion, "Three Hundred Acres and Three" (1911), 47. Gustav Stickley, "The Growing Individuality" (1911), 56.
17. [Hanna Rion], "The Garden of the Many Little Paths," *Craftsman* 17 (March 1910): 622.

18. Hanna Rion, *The Garden in the Wilderness* (1903), 203.
19. Mrs. Theodore Thomas, *Our Mountain Garden* (1904), 15–16, 175.
20. Helen R. Albee, "The Modern Craftsman" (1902), 47, and "A New England Industry" (1902), 292.
21. Helen R. Albee, *Hardy Plants* (1910), 33, 150.
22. Helen R. Albee, *The Gleam* (1911), 237.
23. Helen R. Albee, *A Kingdom of Two* (1913), 184, 150.

Cottage Gardens for Laborers and Suburbanites

1. Paul S. Boyer, *Urban Masses and Moral Order* (1978), 122–27.
2. Quoted in Arnold R. Alanen, "Immigrant Gardens" (1990), 161.
3. Margaret M. Mulrooney, *A Legacy of Coal* (1989), 21. Frick Company directive of October 6, 1910, from the archives of the Patch/Work Voices Project, Penn State University, University Park, Pennsylvania. See also John K. Gates, *The Beehive Coke Years* (1990).
4. George Washington Cable, "Home Culture Clubs" (1888), 502.
5. "Social Experiment in Northampton" (1904). The papers of the Home Culture Club, later called the People's Institute, are in the Forbes Library, Northampton, Massachusetts.
6. Flower garden contest flyer, 1899. Home Culture Club, Forbes Library, Northampton, Massachusetts.
7. George Washington Cable, *The Amateur Garden* (1914), 63, 47, 50.
8. William Haynes, "George Cable Talks of Gardens" (1917), 29.
9. Quoted in Arlin Turner, *George Washington Cable* (1966), 331, 56. Frank P. Stewart, "Neighborhood Garden Clubs" (1906), 123.
10. Cable, *Amateur Garden*, 141.
11. Quoted in Phillip Butcher, *George Washington Cable* (1959), 235.
12. "The Garden in Your Town" (1909), 176.
13. Anna H. Condict, "The Fourth Prize Garden" (1910), 95.
14. Helena Rutherfurd Ely to George Brett, July 6, 1902. Macmillan Company Records, New York Public Library, New York, Astor, Lenox and Tilden Foundations, Rare Books and Manuscripts Division.
15. Edith M. Thomas, "A Woman's Two-Year-Old Hardy

Garden" (1911), 95.

16. Helena Rutherfurd Ely, *A Woman's Hardy Garden* (1903), 23.

17. Helena Rutherfurd Ely Meade, "A Garden and a Book" (typescript, October 1951), 9–10. I am indebted to Mr. and Mrs. Danforth Ely for this memoir and photographs of Helena Ely's garden.

18. Ely, *Woman's Hardy Garden*, 14.

19. Ibid., 99, 94, 52.

20. Mabel Osgood Wright, critique of Helena Rutherfurd Ely's manuscript of *A Woman's Hardy Garden;* and Ely to George Brett, September 9, 1902. Macmillan Company Records, New York Public Library, New York, Astor, Lenox and Tilden Foundations, Rare Books and Manuscripts Division.

21. Mabel Osgood Wright to George Brett, July 10, 1899. Macmillan Company Records; New York Public Library, New York, Astor, Lenox and Tilden Foundations, Rare Books and Manuscripts Division.

22. Neltje Blanchan, *The American Flower Garden* (1909), 75–76.

23. Mabel Osgood Wright, *My New York* (1926), 232, 204.

24. Mabel Osgood Wright, *The Garden of a Commuter's Wife* (1901), 84–85.

25. Mabel Osgood Wright, *The People of the Whirlpool* (1903), 339.

26. See Elizabeth Stillenger, *The Antiquers* (1980), 105–12, for a study of Blaney as a collector.

27. Nancy Hale, *The Life in the Studio* (1957), 198, 117–18. See also Erica Hirshler, "Lilian Westcott Hale" (1992).

Grandmother's Garden in the Middle Atlantic and South

1. Grace Tabor, *The Landscape Gardening Book* (1911), 29, 12.

2. Helen Ashe Hays, *A Little Maryland Garden* (1909), 7.

3. Horace J. Carpenter, "An Art School at Valley Forge" (1905), 8. See also Margaret Vogel, *The Paintings of Hugh Henry Breckenridge* (1967).

4. Carolyn Whitmer, ed., *Memories of Grandmother's Garden* (1991), 22–23. I am indebted to Mrs. Whitmer for putting me in touch with several of the women whose memories are included in her booklet.

5. See Jane Barber White, "Restoration of a Poet's Garden" (1987), and J. Lee Greene, *Time's Unfading Garden* (1977).

6. "The Boylston House and Gardens" (c. 1980), 4. I am indebted to Jennie Dreher Evins for information on the garden.

7. Helen Ashe Hays, "A Colonial Garden Down South" (1910), 288, 290.

8. Flora Bella Surles, *Anne King Gregorie* (1968), 288, 290.

9. Martha R. Severns, *Alice Ravenel Huger Smith* (1993), 12. Smith's watercolors of Elizabeth Allston Pringle's "Chicora Wood" plantation illustrated Pringle's *A Woman Rice Planter* (1913).

10. Hildegard Hawthorne, *The Lure of the Garden* (1911), 40. The illustration had first appeared in Frances Duncan, "Charleston Gardens" (1907).

11. Louise Jones DuBose, *Enigma* (1963), 49, 61, 68. Blondelle Malone's diary, papers, and photographs are in the collection of the Columbiana Library, Columbia, South Carolina.

12. Malone's diary for July 30, 1908. Columbiana Library, Columbia, South Carolina.

13. Archibald Henderson, *Old Homes and Gardens of North Carolina* (1939), 16–17, and T. K. Bruner, "Mrs. Boyden's Garden" (1868). I am indebted to Mary Jane Fowler for digging out this reference. The description of Salisbury is in Henderson.

14. E. T. H. Shaffer, *Carolina Gardens* (1932), 264.

15. Ibid., 219–20. For a discussion of gardening contests, see Mary G. Arial and Nancy J. Smith, *Weaver of Dreams* (1977), 10.

16. Roberta Sewall Brandau, *History of the Homes and Gardens of Tennessee* (1936), 156–57. Alice B. Lockwood, ed., *Gardens of Colony and State* (1931), vol. 2: 358.

17. Mrs. Elizabeth Patterson Thomas, *Old Kentucky Homes and Gardens* (1939), 29–31. "Liberty Hall" was willed to the National Society of the Colonial Dames.

18. Lockwood, *Gardens*, vol. 2: 273–76, and Florine Meeks Cooney, *Garden History of Georgia* (1933), 128–29.

19. Viola Harrison to the author, June 1994.

20. Leona Venettozzi to the author, July 1994.

21. I am indebted to Suzanne Turner for information on Martha Turnbull's garden diaries. The Notarial Archives in New Orleans preserve many nineteenth-century garden plans.

22. See Richard Westmacott, *African-American Gardens* (1992).

Grandmother's Garden on the Frontier

1. "Locomotives, like huge flat-irons": "Nantucket" (1866), 296. Mary Austin, *Earth Horizon* (1932), 107, 79, 99.
2. Alice B. Lockwood, ed., *Gardens of Colony and State* (1931), vol. 2: 419, 320.
3. The plan is reproduced in Patricia Tice, *Gardening in America* (1984), 64. Pioneer nurseries: Charles Van Ravenswaay, *A Nineteenth Century Garden* (1977), 11.
4. Henrietta P. Keith, "A Minnesota Flower Garden" (1908), 428–29.
5. I am indebted to Michael B. Dougan, who kindly sent me dozens of photographs taken by his grandmother and aunt.
6. Michael B. Dougan and Carol W. Dougan, eds., *By the Cypress Swamp* (1980), 1–15. I am grateful to Tom W. Dillard, Director of the Arkansas Archives, University of Central Arkansas, for telling me of "Thanford" and its garden. Issues of *Clover Bend Poke Root* are in the Alice French Papers, Newberry Library, Chicago.
7. See William H. Gerdts and Judith Vale Newton, *The Hoosier Group* (1994). I am indebted to Jane Eckert for photographs and much helpful information about this group. The five artist-members were: Forsyth, Stark, Steele, Adams, and Richard B. Gruelle.
8. Selma Steele, Theodore L. Steele, and Wilbur D. Peat, *House of the Singing Winds* (1966), 118, 123, 125.
9. William Forsyth, *Art in Indiana* (1916), 16.
10. Paul Evans, *Art Pottery* (1987), 297–99.
11. Millie Van Wyke, *The Town of South Denver* (1991), 48, 20.
12. Harriet Beecher Stowe, *Palmetto Leaves* (1873), 206.
13. Grace Tabor, *Old-Fashioned Gardening* (1913), 2.
14. Adina de Zavala, "Memories of Grandmother's Garden" (1934). Xerox copy courtesy of the Daughters of the Republic of Texas Library, San Antonio.
15. See Terry G. Jordan, *German Seed in Texas Soil* (1966).
16. Mac Griswold and Eleanor Weller, *The Golden Age of American Gardens* (1992), 247. Thomas Christopher, *In Search of Lost Roses* (1993), 58.

Grandmother's Garden on the Pacific Coast

1. Carl Totemeier, "The American Botanical Tradition" (1990).
2. Mary Osborn Douthit, ed., *The Souvenir of Western Women* (1905), 88.
3. Shanna Stevenson, "Daniel Bigelow" (1993–94), 35.
4. See Norman J. Johnston, "A Far Western Arts and Crafts Village" (1976). I am indebted to Catherine J. Johnson for photographs and information about Katherine Rogers.
5. John McLaren, *Gardening in California* (1909), 2.
6. See Helen V. Brockhoff, *Thad Welch* (1966).
7. See David F. Myrick, *Montecito and Santa Barbara* (1987). I am indebted to Susan Buell Simpson for information about her great-grandmother.
8. Helen Hunt Jackson, *Glimpses of Three Coasts* (1886), 119. Ruth Odell, *Helen Hunt Jackson* (1939), 177.
9. Odell, *Helen Hunt Jackson*, 177. Alice B. Lockwood, *Gardens of Colony and State* (1931) 2:397.
10. Helen Hunt Jackson, *Ramona* (1884), 18–19, 125.
11. David Hurst Thomas, "Harvesting Ramona's Garden" (1991). Jackson's burial place in Colorado Springs became so popular as a tourist destination that her husband was forced to move her body to a more remote location.
12. Lockwood, *Gardens*, vol. 2: 394.
13. See Sally Bullard Thornton, *Daring to Dream* (1987), and Winifred Dobyns, *California Gardens* (1931), plate 180.
14. "The California Bungalow" (1907), 13. See also Gustav Stickley, "Nature and Art in California" (1904), 370–90.
15. Quoted in Kevin Starr, *Americans and the California Dream* (1973), 410.
16. "A House with a Garden Room" (1915), 564.
17. Charles Francis Saunders, "The Small California Garden" (1911), 79.
18. Ibid., 81.
19. Louis N. Richards, "The King of the Flower Painters" (1904), 3.
20. Mary Austin, *Earth Horizon* (1932), 198.
21. Elizabeth MacPhail, *Kate Sessions* (1976), 84, 66.

Selected Bibliography

Books, Articles, and Manuscripts through 1915

Adams, H. S. "Lyme—a Country Life Community." *Country Life in America* 25 (April 1914): 46–50.

Albee, Helen R. *The Gleam.* New York: Henry Holt and Co., 1911.

———. *Hardy Plants for Cottage Gardens.* New York: Henry Holt and Co., 1910.

———. *A Kingdom of Two: A True Romance of Country Life.* New York: Macmillan and Co., 1913.

———. "The Modern Craftsman: The Question of His Livelihood." *Craftsman* 2 (March 1902): 42–47.

———. "A New England Industry." *Craftsman* 2 (September 1902): 291–95.

Aldrich, Lillian. *The Shadow of the Flowers.* Boston: Houghton, Mifflin, 1912.

Aldrich, Thomas Bailey. *An Old Town by the Sea.* 1874. Reprint, Boston: Houghton, Mifflin, 1883.

———. *The Story of a Bad Boy.* 1870. Reprint, Boston: Houghton, Mifflin, 1908.

Arnold, T. J. "A Story of Textile Greenville." *Cotton* 80 (October 1915): 501–18.

"An Artist's Ideal Home: Wildweed a Picturesque Spot." *New York Herald,* August 30, 1908.

"An Artist's Paradise—Easthampton." *American Art Journal* 33 (September 18, 1880): 329.

The Artsman: The Art That Is Life. Published 1903–7.

Austin, Mary. *California: The Land of The Sun.* London: A & C Stack, 1914.

———. *The Land of Little Rain.* Boston: Houghton, Mifflin, 1903.

Bailey, Liberty Hyde. *Garden Making.* New York: Macmillan and Co., 1898.

———. "An Old-Time Home Garden." *Country Life in America* 3 (November 1902): 18–21.

Baker, John Cordis. *American Country Homes and Their Gardens.* Philadelphia: John C. Winston and Co., 1906.

Barnard, Charles. *My Handkerchief Garden, Size 20 x 60 Feet; Results: A Garden, Fresh Vegetables, Exercise, Health and $20.49.* 1869. Revised ed., Boston: Garden Publishing Co., 1893.

Barron, Leonard. "The Summer Home of Margaret Deland." *Country Life in America* 15 (March 1909): 463–66.

Bartlett, Rose. "How George Washington Cable Made His Home Town Bloom." *Ladies Home Journal* 27 (March 1910): 26–27, 36.

Beecher, Catherine, and Harriet Beecher Stowe. *The American Woman's Home; or, Principles of Domestic Science.* New York: J. B. Ford, 1869.

Beecher, Henry Ward. *Plain and Pleasant Talk about Fruits, Flowers and Farming.* New York: Derby and Jackson, 1859.

Bennett, Ida. *The Flower Garden.* New York: McClure, Phillips, and Co., 1903.

Benson, Frances M. "The Moran Family." *Quarterly Illustrator* 1 (April–June 1893): 66–84.

Beringer, Pierre N. "Le Roi des Fleurs: A Citizen of the Republic." *Overland Monthly* 35 (March 1900): 234–36.

Bigelow, Poultney. "The Byrdcliffe Colony of Arts and Crafts." *American Homes and Gardens,* October 1909: 389–93.

Bishop, William. "Hunting an Abandoned Farm in Upper New England." *Century Magazine* 26 (May 1894): 30–43.

Blanchan, Neltje [Nellie Blanchan Doubleday]. *The American Flower Garden.* New York: Doubleday, Page, and Co., 1909.

———. *Nature's Garden.* New York: Doubleday, Page, and Co., 1900.

Bolton, Sarah K. *Successful Women.* Boston: D. Lathrop Co., 1888.

Bray, Mary Matthews. "My Grandmother's Garden." *Atlantic Monthly* 103 (June 1909): 810–16.

Bruce, Edward C. "American Landscape Gardening." *Lippincott's* 24 (October 1879): 484.

Bruner, T. K. "Mrs. Boyden's Garden." *Watchman and Old North State,* May 29, 1868.

Brush and Pencil. Published 1897–1905.

Bunce, O. B. "Charleston and Its Suburbs." In William Cullen Bryant, ed. *Picturesque America.* Vol. 1. New York: D. Appleton and Co., 1874.

Burnett, Vivian. "Craftsman Gardens for Craftsman Homes." *Craftsman* 18 (April 1910): 46–57.

Burrage, Mildred Giddings. "Arts and Artists at Giverny." *World Today* 20 (March 1911): 344–51.

Cable, George Washington. *The Amateur Garden.* New York: Charles Scribner's Sons, 1914.

———. "Home Culture Clubs." *Century Magazine* 36 (August 1888): 497–507.

———. "Neighborly Gardens." *Good Housekeeping* 38 (April–May 1904): 332–42, 419–21, 467–70.

———. "Where to Plant What." *Century Magazine* 72 (May 1906): 90–98.

"The California Bungalow." *Craftsman* 13 (October 1907): 68–80.

Calvert, Frank. *Homes and Gardens of the Pacific Coast.* 1913. Reprint, Seattle: Queen Anne Historical Society, 1988.

Capen, Oliver Bronson. *Country Homes of Famous Americans.* New York: Doubleday, Page, and Co., 1902.

Carpenter, Horace J. "An Art School at Valley Forge, Pennsylvania." *New York Herald*, September 3, 1905.

Champney, Lizzie W. "The Summer Haunts of American Artists." *Century Magazine* 30 (October 1885): 845–60.

Church, Ella Rodman. *The Home Garden.* New York: D. Appleton and Co., 1881.

———. *Money-Making for Ladies.* New York: Harper and Brothers, 1882.

Coburn, Frederick W. "Philip L. Hale: Artist and Critic." *World Today* 14 (October 1907): 59–67.

Coleman, Emma. *A Historic and Present Building Guide to Old Deerfield.* Boston: Plimpton Press, 1907.

Condict, Anna H. "The Fourth Prize Garden." *American Homes and Gardens*, March 1910: 95–98.

Cook, Clarence. "Beds and Tables, Part IV," *Scribner's Monthly* 11 (April 1876): 813–14.

———. *The House Beautiful* 1878. Reprint, North River Press, 1980.

Cook, Rose Terry. *The Old Garden.* Boston: Prang, 1888.

Craftsman. Published 1901–18.

Cranston, Mary Rankin. "Converting Backyards into Gardens." *Craftsman* 16 (April 1909): 70–79.

Crawford, Mary Caroline. "Homes and Gardens of Cornish." *The House Beautiful* 21 (March 1907): 12–14.

Curran, Charles Courtney. "A Class in Oil Painting." *Palette and Bench* 14 (December 1908): 52.

———. "The Outdoor Painting of Flowers." *Palette and Bench* 15 (May 1909): 217–18.

Deland, Margaret. *The Old Garden.* Boston and New York: Houghton, Mifflin, 1886.

de Martin, Ralph. "An Artist's Home in Rose Valley." *American Homes and Gardens*, March 1909: 95–98.

De Weese, Truman A. *The Bend in the Road and How a Man of the City Found It.* New York: Harper and Brothers, 1913.

Dewing, Maria Oakey. *Beauty in the Household.* New York: Harper and Brothers, 1882.

———. "Flower Painters and What the Flower Offers to Art."
Art and Progress 6 (June 1915): 255–62.

Dexter, Almon [F. S. Dickson]. *And the Wilderness Blossomed.* Philadelphia: H. W. Fisher and Co., 1901.

Dillon, Julia McEntee. *Old Gardens of Kingston.* Kingston: Ulster Garden Club, 1915.

Douthit, Mary Osborn, ed. *The Souvenir of Western Women.* Portland, Ore.: Anderson and Duniway, 1905.

Downes, John I. H. *Mariquita Gill.* New Haven: privately printed, 1915.

Downing, Andrew Jackson. *A Treatise on the Theory and Practice of Landscape Gardening Adapted to North America.* 1841. Reprint, New York: O. Judd and Co., 1875.

Drake, Samuel Adams. *Our Colonial Homes.* Boston: Lee and Shepard, 1894.

Duncan, Frances. "An Artist's New Hampshire Garden." *Country Life in America* 11 (March 1907): 516–20, 554, 556, 558.

———. "Charleston Gardens." *Century Magazine* 73 (March 1907): 705–19.

———. "The Gardens of Cornish." *Century Magazine* 72 (May 1906): 3–19.

———. "How to Make an Old Fashioned Garden." *Ladies Home Journal* 26 (April 1909).

———. "Magnolia Gardens." *Century Magazine* 74 (August 1907): 513–19.

———. "An Old-Time Carolina Garden." *Century Magazine* 80 (October 1910): 803–11.

Dyer, Walter A. "The Philosophy of Gardens." *Craftsman* 20 (April 1911): 3–7.

Earle, Alice Morse. *Home Life in Colonial Days.* New York: Macmillan and Co., 1898.

———. Letters. Smith College Library, Northampton, Massachusetts. Sophia Smith Collection.

———. *Margaret Winthrop.* New York: Charles Scribner's Sons, 1895.

———. "Old Time Flower Gardens." *Scribner's Magazine* 20 (August 1896): 161–78.

———. *Old Time Gardens.* New York: Macmillan and Co., 1901.

———. *Sundials and Roses of Yesterday.* New York: Macmillan and Co., 1902.

"East Hampton." *The Studio* 2 (September 8, 1883): 104–6.

Egleston, Nathaniel Hillyer. *The Home and Its Surroundings.* New York: Harper and Brothers, 1884.

———. *Villages and Village Life with Hints for Their Improvement.* New York: Harper and Brothers, 1878.

Elder, Walter. *The Cottage Garden of America.* Philadelphia: Moss and Brother, 1848.

Elliot, J. Wilkinson. *A Plea for Hardy Plants.* New York:

Doubleday, Page and Co., 1910.

Elliot, Maud Howe, ed. *Art and Handicraft in the Women's Building of the World's Columbian Exposition, Chicago.* Paris and New York: Bossoud, Valadon, and Co.,1893.

Ellwanger, George H. *The Garden's Story.* 1889. 4th ed., New York: D. Appleton and Co., 1891.

Ely, Helena Rutherfurd. *Another Hardy Garden Book.* New York: Macmillan and Co., 1905.

———. *The Practical Flower Garden.* New York: Macmillan and Co., 1911.

———. *A Woman's Hardy Garden.* New York: Macmillan and Co., 1903.

Fields, Annie. *Authors and Friends.* Boston and New York: Houghton, Mifflin, 1893.

Finder, Antony P. "Third Garden Prize of Twenty-Five Dollars." *American Homes and Gardens,* February 1910: 56–58.

Frothingham, Jessie P. *Success in Gardening.* New York: Duffield and Co., 1913.

Gallatin, Albert E. "Landscapes of Clark G. Voorhees." *Modern Art in Venice and Other Notes.* New York: John Lane Company, 1910.

"The Garden in Your Town." *American Homes and Gardens,* January 1909: 176.

Gibson, William Hamilton. "The Wild Garden." *Harper's New Monthly Magazine* 81 (September 1890): 622–31.

Goodwin, Alfred Henry. "An Artist's Inspirited Country House." *Country Life in America* 8 (October 1905): 625–30.

Grant, Anne. *Memoirs of an American Lady.* 1808. American ed., Albany: Joel Munsell, 1876.

Greenslet, Ferris. *The Life of Thomas Bailey Aldrich.* Boston and New York: Houghton, Mifflin, 1908.

Griffiths, William Elliot. "George H. Boughton, Painter of New England Puritanism." *New England Magazine* 15 (December 1896): 481–501.

"A Group of Photographic Studies of Frances and Mary Allen." *Craftsman* 9 (May 1905): 221–22.

Hale Family Papers. Smith College Library, Northampton, Massachusetts. Sophia Smith Collection.

Harland, Marion. *Some Colonial Homesteads and Their Stories.* New York: G. P. Putnam's Sons, 1897.

Harrison, Birge. *Landscape Painting.* New York: Charles Scribner's Sons, 1909.

Hart, Mary Johnson. "Women and the Art of Landscape Gardening." *Outlook,* March 28, 1908: 694–704.

Hawthorne, Hildegard. "A Garden of Romance: Mrs. Tyson's at Hamilton House, South Berwick, Maine." *Century Magazine* 80 (September 1910): 778–86.

———. *The Lure of the Garden.* New York: Century Co., 1911.

Hayes, John Russel. *The Old-Fashioned Garden and Other Verses.* Philadelphia: John C. Winston and Co., 1895.

Hays, Helen Ashe. "A Colonial Garden Down South." *Country Life in America* 17 (January 1910): 288.

———. *A Little Maryland Garden.* New York: G. P. Putnam's Sons, 1909.

Hemenway, H. D. "Prize Garden Competition." *Art and Progress* 1 (November 1909): 38.

Henderson, Charles. *Henderson's Picturesque Gardens and Ornamental Gardening Illustrated.* New York: P. Henderson and Co., 1908.

Henderson, Hazel W. "An Impression of Cornish." *The Lamp* 27 (October 1903): 185–96.

Henderson, Peter. *Gardening For Pleasure.* New York: O. Judd and Co., 1887.

———. *Practical Floriculture.* New York: O. Judd and Co., 1869.

Higginson, Thomas Wentworth. "The Greek Goddesses." *Atlantic Monthly* 24 (July 1869): 97–108.

Hindermyer, Gilbert. "'Wyck,' an Old House and Garden at Germantown." *House and Garden* 2 (November 1902): 549–59.

Holder, Charles Frederick. "The Gardens of the Missions." *House and Garden* 15 (January 1909): 5–8.

Home Culture Club. Forbes Library, Northampton, Massachusetts. People's Institute Papers.

"A House with a Garden Room." *Craftsman* 27 (February 1915): 564.

Howe, Samuel. "Suburban Homes." *Craftsman* 17 (November 1909): 112–19.

Howells, William Dean. *My Mark Twain.* New York: Harper and Brothers, 1910.

Humphries, Mary Gay. "Women Batchelors in New York." *Scribner's Monthly* 20 (August 1896): 626–36.

Hutchinson, Francis Kingsley. *Our Country Home: How We Transformed a Wisconsin Woodland.* Chicago: A. C. McClurg and Co., 1908.

———. *Our Country Life.* Chicago: A. C. McClurg and Co., 1912.

"In the Old-Fashioned Gardens of New England." *Ladies Home Journal* 17 (February 1900): 24–26.

Ives, A. E. "The Old-Fashioned Garden." *Harper's Weekly* 56 (July 20, 1912): 20.

Jackson, Helen Hunt. *Glimpses of California and the Missions.* Boston: Little, Brown and Co., 1902.

———. *Glimpses of Three Coasts.* Boston: Roberts Brothers, 1886.

———. *Ramona.* Boston: Roberts Brothers, 1884.

James, George Warton. *Through Ramona's Country.* Boston: Little, Brown and Co., 1912.

Jarvis, M. R. "Old-Fashioned Garden." *Littel's Living Age,* September 8, 1900: 632.

Jellett, Edwin C. *Gardens and Gardeners of Germantown.* Germantown, Pa.: Site and Relic Society, 1914.

Jenkins, M. W. "Gardening as a Means of Recreation for Women." *Craftsman* 24 (April 1913): 111–14.

Jewett, Sarah Orne. *Country By-ways.* Boston: Houghton, Mifflin, 1881.

———. *The Country of the Pointed Firs and Other Stories.* 1896. Reprint, New York: W. W. Norton and Co., 1981.

———. *Letters of Sarah Orne Jewett.* Edited by Annie Fields. Boston: Houghton, Mifflin, 1911.

Johnson, Louisa. *Every Lady Her Own Flower Gardener.* 1832. American ed., Charleston, S.C.: S. Babcock and Co., 1842.

Johnson, Rossiter, ed. *A History of the World's Columbian Exposition.* 4 vols. New York: D. Appleton and Co., 1898.

Johnson, Mrs. S. O. *Every Woman Her Own Flower Gardener.* New York: Henry T. Williams, 1871.

Johnston, Frances. "The Foremost Women Photographers in America: Frances and Mary Allen." *Ladies Home Journal* 18 (July 1901): 13.

Jones, Beatrix. "The Garden as a Picture." *Scribner's Magazine* 42 (July 1907): 2–11.

Keeler, Charles. *The Simple House.* 1904. Reprint, Santa Barbara, Calif.: Peregrine Smith, 1979.

Keeler, Harriet L. *Our Garden Flowers.* New York: Charles Scribner's Sons, 1910.

Keith, Henrietta P. "A Minnesota Flower Garden." *American Homes and Gardens,* November 1908: 427–29.

King, Edward. "In the Good Old Colony Times." *Monthly Illustrator,* May 1895: 135.

Kirkland, Caroline. "Illinois in Springtime with a Look at Chicago." *Atlantic Monthly* 82 (September 1898): 479–88.

Lamb, Martha J. *The Homes of America.* New York: D. Appleton and Co., 1879.

L. L. P. "The Impressionists." *Boston Evening Transcript,* February 26, 1898.

Locke, Kate Greenleaf. "The Gardens of Southern California." *Century Magazine* 76 (September 1908): 716–24.

Locke, Seymour E. "Bungalows, What They Really Are." *House and Garden* (August 1907): 44–53.

Lodge, Henry Cabot. "The Restrictions of Immigration." *North American Review* 152 (January 1891): 27–36.

Long, Elias. *Ornamental Gardens for Americans.* New York: O. Judd and Co., 1885.

Low, Will. *A Chronicle of Friendships.* New York: Charles Scribner's Sons, 1908.

———. "In an Old French Garden." *Scribner's Magazine* 32 (July 1902): 3–19.

Lowell, Guy. *American Gardens.* Boston: Bates and Guild Co., 1902.

Lummis, Charles Fletcher. "The Carpet of God's Country." *Out West* 22 (1905): 306–17.

"Lyme, a Chapter of American Genealogy." *Harper's New Monthly Magazine* 52 (February 1876): 313–28.

Matthews, F. Schuyler. "The Wild Garden." *Littel's Living Age,* April 21, 1900: 137–49.

McAdam, Thomas. "The Gentle Art of Wild Gardening." *Country Life in America* 7 (March 1905): 470–73.

McCabe, James D. *The Illustrated History of the Centennial Exhibition.* Philadelphia: Jones Brothers, 1876.

McFarland, J. Horace. *My Growing Garden.* New York: Macmillan and Co., 1915.

McLaren, John. *Gardening in California: Landscape and Flower.* San Francisco: A. M. Robertson, 1909.

McLaughlin, Mary Louise. *China Painting.* Cincinnati: R. Clark and Co., 1877.

Macmillan Company Records. New York Public Library, New York. Astor, Lenox and Tilden Foundations, Rare Books and Manuscripts Division.

Merrick, L. "Artists' Summer Retreats." *American Art News,* June 17, 1911: 3.

Miller, Margaret. "The Deerfield Story." *Modern Priscilla,* July 1901: 1–2.

Moffat, Adelene. "The Story of a Club." *Cosmopolitan* 17 (August 1894): 435–39.

Monroe, Harriet. "Eagle's Nest Camp, a Colony of Artists and Writers." *The House Beautiful* 16 (August 1904): 5–10.

Mount, Mary Wilkinson. "The Gardens of Cornish." *Suburban Life* 18 (March 1914): 133–36, 184.

Mowbray, J. P. *The Making of a Country Home.* New York: Doubleday, Page, and Co., 1901.

Murphy, J. Francis. Archives of American Art, Smithsonian Institution, Washington, D.C. Emerson Crosby Kelly Materials.

"Nantucket." *Atlantic Monthly* 17 (March 1866): 296–302.

New York State. *Report of the Board of General Managers of the Exhibit of the State of New York at the World's Columbian Exposition.* Albany: James B. Lyon, 1894.

Northend, Mary H. *Remodeled Farmhouses.* Boston: Little, Brown and Co., 1915.

"Old-Fashioned Flowers." *Littel's Living Age,* April 6, 1907: 59–63.

"Old-Fashioned Garden Flowers." *Harper's Weekly* 46 (August

23, 1902): 1140–41, 1167.

Osborne, Charles Francis. *Historic Houses and Their Gardens.* Philadelphia: John C. Winston and Co., 1908.

———, ed. *Country Homes and Gardens of Moderate Cost.* Philadelphia: John C. Winston and Co., 1907.

Palette and Bench. Published 1908–10 (vols. 1, 2).

Parker, Constance. "The Garden of Forgotten Flowers." *Good Housekeeping* 44 (April 1907): 390–96.

Parsons, Samuel, Jr. *How to Plan the Home Grounds.* New York: Doubleday and McClure, 1899.

———. *Landscape Gardening.* New York: G. P. Putnam's Sons, 1891.

"Paul de Longpré, Flower Painter." *Craftsman* 8 (July 1905): 497–510.

Payson, Edward. "The Fifth Prize Garden." *American Homes and Gardens,* May 1910: 176–77.

Peixotto, Ernest Clifford. *Romantic California.* New York: Charles Scribner's Sons, 1910.

Pendleton, W. E. "Old Fashioned Gardens." *Country Life in America* 11 (March 1907): 507–8.

"Pergolas: The Most Picturesque and Practical Feature of the Modern Out-Door Life." *Craftsman* 19 (March 1911): 575–80.

Powell, E. P. *The Country Home.* New York: McClure, Phillips, and Co., 1904.

Powers, R. M. "Grandmother's Garden." *Woman's Home Companion* 38 (May 1911): 8.

Priestman, Mabel Tuke. "Rose Valley, a Community of Disciples of Ruskin and Morris." *House and Garden* 10 (October 1906): 159–65.

Pringle, Elizabeth Allston. *A Woman Rice Planter.* 1913. Reprint, Columbia: University of South Carolina Press, 1992.

Randall, Alice Sawtelle. "Miss Fidelia Bridges in Her Studio at Canaan." *Connecticut Magazine* 7 (1901): 583–88.

Randall, E. A. "The Artistic Impulses in Men and Women." *Arena* 24 (October 1900): 420.

Reinhart, Joakin. "Landscape Gardening." *Craftsman* 4 (April 1903): 26–34.

Richards, Louis N. "The King of the Flower Painters in His California Home." *Overland Monthly* 43 (May 1904): 395–402.

Riding, William H. "Working Women in New York." *Harper's New Monthly Magazine* 61 (June 1880): 25–37.

Rion, Hanna [Mrs. H. R. Ver Beck]. *The Garden in the Wilderness, by a Hermit.* New York: Baker and Taylor Co., 1903.

———. *Let's Make a Flower Garden.* New York: McBride, Nast, and Co., 1912.

———. "Three Hundred Acres and Three." *Craftsman* 20 (July 1911): 47–53.

Rion, Mary C. *Ladies' Southern Florist.* Columbia, S.C.: P. B. Glass, 1860.

Robbins, Mary Caroline. *The Rescue of an Old Place.* Boston: privately printed, 1892.

Root, R. R., and G. R. Forbes. "Notes upon a Colonial Garden in Salem, Massachusetts." *Landscape Architecture* 2 (October 1891): 16–20.

Saint-Gaudens, Homer. "Charles Courtney Curran." *Critic* 48 (January 1906): 38–39.

Sanborn, Kate. *Abandoning an Adopted Farm.* New York: D. Appleton and Co., 1894.

———. *Adopting an Abandoned Farm.* New York: D. Appleton and Co., 1891.

———. *Memories and Anecdotes.* New York: G. P. Putnam's Sons, 1915.

———. *My Favorite Lectures of Long Ago.* Boston: privately printed, 1898.

Sargent, Charles Sprague. "Old-Fashioned Gardens." *Garden and Forest,* July 17, 1895: 281–82.

Saunders, Charles Francis. "The Small California Garden." *House and Garden* 19 (February 1911): 70–81, 120–22.

Sedgwick, Mabel Cabot. *The Garden Month by Month.* New York: F. A. Stokes Co., 1907.

Shelton, Louise. *Beautiful Gardens in America.* New York: Charles Scribner's Sons, 1915.

———. *Continuous Bloom in America.* 1915. New York: Charles Scribner's Sons, 1915.

———. "The Garden at Hamilton House." *American Homes and Gardens,* November 1909: 422–25.

———. *The Seasons in a Flower Garden.* New York: Charles Scribner's Sons, 1906.

Shurtleff, Arthur A. "The Grounds of an English Villager's Cottage." *Craftsman* 4 (April 1903): 8–15.

———. "Some Old New England Flower Gardens." *New England Magazine* 30 (December 1899): 422–26.

Slade, Daniel Dennison. *The Evolution of Horticulture in New England.* New York: G. P. Putnam's Sons, 1895.

Slocum, Grace L. "An American Barbizon." *New England Magazine* 34 (July 1906): 563–71.

Smith, Helen Everson. "An Ancient Garden." *Century Magazine* 72 (May 1906): 112–19.

"Social Experiment in Northampton." *Boston Sunday Globe,* December 4, 1904.

Sorelle, Eugene. "An Old Fashioned Garden and What Grows in It." *Indoors and Out* 3 (March 1907): 278–80.

Stewart, Frank P. "Neighborhood Garden Clubs: What They Are Doing for a Massachusetts Town." *Suburban Life,*

September 1906: 123–24.

Stickley, Gustav. "A Country Home for a Businessman." *Craftsman* 19 (October 1910): 55–62.

———. "The Growing Individuality of the American Garden." *Craftsman* 20 (July 1911): 54–62.

———. "Nature and Art in California." *Craftsman* 6 (July 1904): 370–90.

Stoll, H. F. "Picturesque California Gardens." *The House Beautiful* 32 (June 1912): 24–26.

Stowe, Charles Edward. *The Life of Harriet Beecher Stowe.* Boston: Houghton, Mifflin, 1889.

Stowe, Harriet Beecher. *Palmetto Leaves.* Boston: James R. Osgood and Co., 1873.

———. *Uncle Tom's Cabin.* 1852. Reprint, New York: New American Library, 1981.

———. "The Woman Question; or, What Will You Do with Her?" *Atlantic Monthly* 16 (December 1865): 672–83.

Tabor, Grace. *The Garden Primer: A Practical Handbook on the Elements of Gardening for Beginners.* New York: McBride, Winston, and Co., 1911.

———. *The Landscape Gardening Book.* New York: McBride, Winston, and Co., 1911.

———. *Old-Fashioned Gardening: A History and Reconstruction.* New York: McBride, Nast, and Co., 1913.

Thanet, Octave [Alice French]. *An Adventure in Photography.* New York: Charles Scribner's Sons, 1893.

Thaxter, Celia. *Among the Isles of Shoals.* Boston: James R. Osgood and Co., 1873.

———. *An Island Garden.* Boston and New York: Houghton, Mifflin, 1894.

———. *Letters of Celia Thaxter.* Edited by Annie Fields and Rose Lamb. Boston and New York: Houghton, Mifflin, 1895.

Thomas, Edith M. "Notes from the Wild Garden." *Atlantic Monthly* 68 (August 1891): 172–78.

———. "A Woman's Two-Year-Old Hardy Garden from Seed." *American Homes and Gardens,* March 1911: 95–96.

Thomas, Mrs. Theodore. *Our Mountain Garden.* New York: Macmillan and Co., 1904.

Trask, Katrina. *In My Lady's Garden.* New York: Houghton, Mifflin, 1902.

Vallejo, Guadalupe. "Ranch and Mission Days in Alta California." *Century Magazine* 41 (December 1890): 183–92.

Van Rensselaer, Mariana. *Art Out-of-Doors: Hints on Good Taste in Gardening.* New York: Charles Scribner's Sons, 1893.

Verplanck, Virginia. *Every Day in My Garden.* New York: William R. Jenkins, 1913.

———. *A Year in My Garden.* New York: Williams Printing Co., 1909.

Wainwright, Susan S. "Plea for the Enclosed Garden." *Atlantic Monthly* 97 (April 1906): 509–13.

Warner, Anna Bartlett. *Gardening by Myself.* New York: Anson D. F. Randolph and Co., 1872.

———. *Miss Tiller's Vegetable Garden and the Money She Made by It.* New York: Anson D. F. Randolph and Co., 1873.

Warner, Charles Dudley. *My Summer in the Garden.* Boston: Field, Osgood, and Co., 1870.

———. *On Horseback, a Tour in Virginia, North Carolina, and Tennessee.* Boston: Houghton, Mifflin, 1889.

———. *Our Italy.* New York: Harper and Brothers, 1891.

Warton, Anne H. "Some Philadelphia Studios." *The Decorator and Furnisher,* December 1885: 78.

Waugh, Frank. *The Landscape Beautiful.* New York: O. Judd and Co., 1910.

———. *Landscape Gardening.* New York: O. Judd and Co., 1899.

Welsh, Herbert. *The Artists of Germantown.* Germantown, Pa.: Site and Relic Society, 1913.

Wheeler, Candace. *Annals of Onteora 1887–1914.* New York: E. W. Whitfield, 1914.

———. *Content in a Garden.* Boston and New York: Houghton, Mifflin, 1901.

———. "The Decorative Use of Wildflowers." *Atlantic Monthly* 95 (May 1905): 630–34

———. *Household Art.* New York: Harper and Brothers, 1893.

Wheeler, Dora. "The Vacation Home on the Mountain." *Christian Union Supplement* 41 (May 29, 1890): 785.

White, Goddard M. "Where the Garden Is the Center of the House." *Craftsman* 25 (March 1914): 567–73.

Wild, H. "Perennial or Old-Fashioned Garden." *American Homes and Gardens,* October 1914: 338–41.

Wilkins, Mary E. *Evalina's Garden.* New York: Harper and Brothers, 1899.

———. *Understudies.* New York: Harper and Brothers, 1901.

Wise, Herbert C. "A Day at Northcote, New Hampshire." *House and Garden* 2 (June 1902): 240–51.

Wood, E. D. "Grandmother's Garden." *Overland Monthly,* n.s., 61 (June 1913): 548.

Wright, Mabel Osgood. *Flowers and Ferns in Their Haunts.* New York: Macmillan and Co., 1901.

———. *The Garden of a Commuter's Wife.* New York: Macmillan and Co., 1901.

———. *The Garden, You and I.* New York: Macmillan and Co., 1906.

———. *The People of the Whirlpool.* New York: Macmillan and Co., 1903.

Books, Articles, and Manuscripts after 1915

Alanen, Arnold R. "Immigrant Gardens on a Mining Frontier." In Mark Francis, ed., *The Meaning of Gardens.* Cambridge, Mass.: MIT Press, 1990.

American Society of Landscape Architects. *Illustrations of the Work of Members.* 4 vols. New York: J. Hayden Twiss, 1931–34.

Andersen, Jeffrey W. "The Art Colony at Old Lyme." In *Connecticut and American Impressionism.* Storrs, Conn.: William Benton Museum of Art, 1980.

Arial, Mary G., and Nancy J. Smith. *Weaver of Dreams: A History of the Parker District.* Columbia, S.C.: R. L. Bryan Co., 1977.

Aslin, Elizabeth. *The Aesthetic Movement.* New York: Excalibur Books, 1969.

Austin, Mary. *Earth Horizon: An Autobiography.* Boston: Houghton, Mifflin, 1932.

Axelrod, Alan, ed. *The Colonial Revival in America.* New York: W. W. Norton and Co., 1985.

Azers, William, ed. *A Poor Sort of Heaven, A Good Sort of Earth: The Rose Valley Arts and Crafts Experiment.* Chadds Ford, Pa.: Brandywine River Museum, 1983.

Barendsen, Joyce P. "William Nutting, An American Tastemaker: The Pictures and Legend." *Winterthur Portfolio* 18 (Summer–Autumn 1983): 187–91.

Barrington, Amy L. "A Field of Delite: The Country Home of Two Well-Known Artists, Mr. and Mrs. Albert Herter." *The House Beautiful* 45 (April 1919): 189–91, 241.

Barter, Judith. *Currents of Expansion: Painting in the Midwest 1820–1940.* St. Louis: Saint Louis Art Museum, 1977.

Bartinique, A. Patricia. *Gustav Stickley: His Craft.* Parsippany, N. J.: Craftsmen Farms Foundation, 1993.

Berry, Rose V. S. "Lilian Westcott Hale—Her Art," *American Magazine of Art* 18 (February 1927): 67.

Bianchi, Martha Dickinson. *Emily Dickinson Face to Face.* Boston: Houghton, Mifflin, 1932.

Birnbaum, Charles A., and Lisa E. Crowder, eds. *Pioneers of American Landscape Design: An Annotated Bibliography.* Washington, D.C.: National Park Service, 1993.

Bissell, Ervanno Bower. *Glimpses of Santa Barbara and Montecito Gardens.* Santa Barbara, Calif.: privately printed, 1926.

Blair, O. Karen. *The Clubswoman as Feminist: True Womanhood Redefined 1868–1914.* New York: Holmes and Meier, 1980.

Borris, Eileen. *Art and Labor: Ruskin, Morris and the Craftsman Ideal in America.* Philadelphia: Temple University Press, 1986.

Boydston, Jeanne, et al. *The Limits of Sisterhood: The Beecher Sisters on Women's Rights and Women's Sphere.* Chapel Hill: University of North Carolina Press, 1987.

Boyer, Paul S. *Urban Masses and Moral Order in America 1820–1920.* Cambridge, Mass.: Harvard University Press, 1978.

"The Boylston House and Gardens." Typescript. Archives of American Gardens, Washington, D.C. c. 1980.

Brandau, Roberta Sewall. *History of the Homes and Gardens of Tennessee.* Nashville: Parthenon Press, 1936.

Brandimarte, Cynthia A. "Somebody's Aunt and Nobody's Mother: The American China Painter and Her Work 1870–1920." *Winterthur Portfolio* 23 (Winter 1988): 203–24.

Brawley, James S. *The Rowan Story 1753–1953.* Salisbury, N.C.: Rowan Printing Co., 1953.

Briggs, Loutrell. "Amateur Gardens." *Country Life in America* 57 (March 1930): 49–50.

Brockhoff, Helen V. *Thad Welch, Pioneer and Painter.* Oakland, Calif.: Oakland Art Museum, 1966.

Brown, Gillian. *Domestic Individualism: Imaging Self in Nineteenth Century America.* Berkeley: University of California Press, 1990.

Buder, Stanley. *Pullman, an Experiment in Industrial Order and City Planning.* New York: Oxford University Press, 1967.

Buff, Barbara Ball. "Cragsmoor, an Early American Art Colony." *Antiques,* November 1978: 1055–67.

———. "Dublin, New Hampshire." *Antiques,* April 1982: 942–51.

Buff, Barbara Ball, and John Dryfhout. *A Circle of Friends: Art Colonies of Cornish and Dublin.* Durham: University of New Hampshire Art Galleries, 1985.

Burke, Doreen Bolger, et al. *In Pursuit of Beauty: Americans and the Aesthetic Movement.* New York: Metropolitan Museum of Art, 1986.

Burnside, Katherine. *Childe Hassam in Connecticut.* Old Lyme, Conn.: Florence Griswold Museum, 1988.

Bushman, Richard L. *The Refinement of America.* New York: Alfred A. Knopf, 1992.

Butcher, Phillip. *George Washington Cable: The Northampton Years.* New York: Columbia University Press, 1959.

Butler, Joyce. *Abbott Fuller Graves 1859–1936.* Kennebunk, Maine: Brick Store Museum, 1979.

———. "The Genre Paintings of Abbott Graves." *Antiques,* August 1982: 308–13.

Callen, Anthea. *Women Artists of the Arts and Crafts Movement.* New York: Pantheon, 1979.

Carr, Gerald L. "Hugh Henry Breckenridge, a Philadelphia Modernist." *American Art Review,* May 1978: 92–99, 119–22.

Chandler, Joseph Everett. *The Colonial House.* New York: Robert M. McBride and Co., 1924.

Chotner, Deborah, et al. *John Twachtman: Connecticut Landscapes.* Washington, D.C.: National Gallery of Art, 1989.

Christian, Francis Archer, and Susan Williams Massie. *Homes and Gardens in Old Virginia.* Richmond: Garrett and Massie, 1931.

Christopher, Thomas. *In Search of Lost Roses.* New York: Avon Books, 1993.

Clark, Patricia Gardner. "Arts and Crafts in Santa Barbara: The Tale of Two Studios." *Noticias* 38 (Winter 1992): 61–76.

Clark, Robert Judson. *The Arts and Crafts Movement in America 1876–1916.* Princeton, N.J.: Princeton Art Museum, 1976.

Clayton, V. T. "Reminiscence and Revival, the Old-Fashioned Garden 1890–1910." *Antiques,* April 1990: 892–905.

Colby, Virginia Reed. "Stephen and Maxfield Parrish in New Hampshire." *Antiques,* June 1979: 1290–98.

Cooney, Florine Meeks. *Garden History of Georgia 1733–1933.* Atlanta: Peach Tree Garden Club, 1933.

Cortissoz, Royal. "Ruger Donoho." *New York Tribune,* November 16, 1916.

Cragsmoor Free Public Library. *E. L. Henry's Country Life.* Cragsmoor, N.Y.: 1981.

———. *Helen M. Turner (1858–1958), a Retrospective.* Cragsmoor, N.Y.: 1983.

Cram, Elizabeth Hill. *Memoirs of Elizabeth Hill Cram.* Boston: privately printed, 1992.

Curry, David Park. *Childe Hassam: An Island Garden Revisited.* Denver: Denver Art Museum, 1990.

Daniel, Pete, and Raymond Smock. *A Talent for Detail: The Photographs of Miss Francis Benjamin Johnston 1889–1910.* New York: Harmony Books, 1974.

Deland, Margaret. *Golden Yesterdays.* New York: Harper and Brothers, 1940.

de Zavala, Adina. "Memories of Grandmother's Garden." *Dallas Morning News,* December 16, 1934.

Dickinson, Emily. *The Complete Poems of Emily Dickinson.* Edited by Thomas H. Johnson. Boston: Little, Brown and Co., 1960.

Dobyns, Winifred. *California Gardens.* New York: Macmillan and Co., 1931.

Doell, M. Christine Klim. *Gardens of the Gilded Age: Nineteenth Century Gardens and Homegrounds in New York State.* Syracuse, N.Y.: Syracuse University Press, 1986.

———. "Verdant Frames: Plant Portraits from the Ellwanger and Barry Collection." *University of Rochester Library Bulletin* 39 (1986): 11–23.

Dominik, Janet Blake. *Early Artists in Laguna Beach: The Impressionists.* Laguna Beach, Calif.: Laguna Art Museum, 1986.

Donahue, Maris. "Sarah Orne Jewett's 'Dear Old House and Home.'" *Downeast Magazine,* August 1977: 62–67.

Dougan, Michael B., and Carol W. Dougan, eds. *By the Cypress Swamp: The Arkansas Stories of Octave Thanet.* Little Rock, Ark: Rose Publishing Co., 1980.

Douglas, Ann. *The Feminization of American Culture.* New York: Alfred A. Knopf, 1977.

DuBose, Louise Jones. *Enigma: The Career of Blondelle Malone in Art and Society 1879–1951.* Columbia: University of South Carolina Press, 1963.

Duncan, James. "Landscape Taste as a Symbol of Group Identity." *Geographical Review* 63 (July 1973): 334–55.

Eberwein, Jane Donahue. *Dickinson: Strategies of Limitation.* Amherst: University of Massachusetts Press, 1985.

Edwards, Robert. *The Byrdcliffe Arts and Crafts Colony: Life by Design.* Newark: Delaware Art Museum, 1984.

Emerson, Ralph Waldo. *Selected Essays, Lectures, and Poems.* New York: Bantam Books, 1990.

En Plein Air: Art Colonies at East Hampton and Old Lyme. East Hampton, N.Y.: Guild Hall Museum, 1989.

Evans, Paul. *Art Pottery of the United States.* New York: Feingold and Lewis, 1987.

Fairbrother, Trevor J., et al. *The Bostonians: Painters of an Elegant Age 1870–1930.* Boston: Museum of Fine Arts, 1986.

Faris, John T. *Old Gardens in and about Philadelphia.* Indianapolis: Bobbs-Merrill, 1932.

Faude, Wilson H. "Candace Wheeler, Textile Designer." *Antiques,* August 1977: 258–61.

Favretti, Rudy J. *Gardens and Landscapes of Virginia.* Little Compton, R.I.: Fort Church Publishers, 1993.

Favretti, Rudy J., and Joy Favretti. *For Every House a Garden.* Chester, Conn.: Pequot Press, 1977.

Faxton, Susan, et al. *A Stern and Lovely Scene: A Visual History of the Isles of Shoals.* Durham: University of New Hampshire Art Galleries, 1978.

Fell, Derek. *The Impressionist Garden.* New York: Crown, 1994.

Feltwell, John, and Neil Oldenwall. *Live Oak Splendor: Gardens along the Mississippi.* Dallas, Tex.: Taylor Publishing Co., 1992.

Fiske, Turbese Lummis, and Keith Lummis. *Charles F. Lummis, the Man and His Work.* Norman: University of Oklahoma Press, 1975.

Forsyth, William. *Art in Indiana.* Indianapolis: H. Lieber Co., 1916.

Foshay, Ella M. *Reflections of Nature: Flowers in American Art.* New York: Alfred A. Knopf, 1984.

Friedman, Jean E. *The Enclosed Garden: Women and Community in the Evangelical South 1830–1900.* Chapel Hill: University of North Carolina Press, 1985.

Frost, John Eldridge. *Sarah Orne Jewett.* Kittery Point, Maine: Gundalow Club, 1960.

Gaillard, E. Davis. *The Ladies of Early Onteora.* Onteora, N.Y.: privately printed, 1994.

Gates, John K. *The Beehive Coke Years.* Uniontown, Pa.: privately printed, 1990.

Gearhart, Edna. "Benjamin Brown of Pasadena." *Overland Monthly and Out West Magazine,* July 1924: 314–16.

Gerdts, William H. *American Impressionism.* New York: Abbeville Press, 1984.

———. *Art across America.* 3 vols. New York: Abbeville Press, 1990.

———. *Down Garden Paths: The Floral Environment in American Art.* Cranbury, N.J.: Associated University Presses, 1983.

———. *Lasting Impressions: American Painters in Giverny 1865–1915.* Evanston, Ill.: Terra Foundation for the Arts, 1992.

———. *Monet's Giverny: An Impressionist Colony.* New York: Abbeville Press, 1993.

———. *Painters of the Humble Truth: Masterpieces of American Still Life 1801–1939.* Columbia, Mo.: University of Missouri Press, 1981.

Gerdts, William H., and Peter Frank. *Indiana Influence: The Golden Age of Indiana Landscape Painting.* Fort Wayne, Ind.: Fort Wayne Art Museum, 1984.

Gerdts, William H., and Judith Vale Newton. *The Hoosier Group: Five American Painters.* Indianapolis: Eckert Publications, 1994.

Giles, Vicki. "C. Alice Baker." Historic Deerfield Summer Fellowship Program Paper, 1976. Henry N. Flynt Library, Deerfield, Mass.

Gilman, Charlotte Perkins. *The Yellow Wallpaper and Other Writings.* New York: Bantam Books, 1989.

Giroud, Mark. *Sweetness and Light: the "Queen Anne" Movement 1860–1900.* New Haven: Yale University Press, 1984.

Grauber, Ernest Leslie. *T. C. Steele: Indiana Painter 1847–1926.* Fort Wayne, Ind.: Fort Wayne Museum of Art, 1967.

Green, Harvey. *The Light of the Home: An Intimate View of the Lives of Women in Victorian America.* New York: Pantheon, 1983.

Greene, J. Lee. *Time's Unfading Garden: Anne Spencer's Life and Poetry.* Baton Rouge: Louisiana State University Press, 1977.

Griffith, Sarah L., and Kevin D. Murphy, eds. *A Noble and Dignified Stream: The Piscataqua Region in the Colonial Revival.* York, Maine: Old York Historical Society, 1992.

Griswold, Mac, and Eleanor Weller. *The Golden Age of American Gardens.* New York: Harry N. Abrams, 1992.

Hale, Nancy. *The Life in the Studio.* New York: Avon Books, 1957.

Handlin, David P. *The American Home: Architecture and Society 1815–1915.* Boston: Little, Brown and Co., 1979.

Haynes, William. "George Cable Talks of Gardens." *House and Garden* 32 (December 1917): 28–29.

Hedrick, Joan D. *Harriet Beecher Stowe: A Life.* New York: Oxford University Press, 1994.

Hedrick, U. P. *A History of Horticulture in America to 1860.* 1950. Reprint, Portland, Oreg.: Timber Press, 1988.

Henderson, Archibald. *Old Homes and Gardens of North Carolina.* Chapel Hill: University of North Carolina Press, 1939.

Higham, John. *Strangers in the Land: Patterns of American Nativism 1889–1929.* New York: Atheneum, 1985.

Hill, Anna Gilman. *Forty Years of Gardening.* New York: Frederick Stokes Co., 1938.

Hill, May Brawley. *Fidelia Bridges: An American Pre-Raphaelite.* New Britain, Conn.: New Britain Museum of American Art, 1981.

———. "Gardening by Myself." *Hortus* 19 (Autumn 1991): 44–50.

———. "Grandmother's Garden." *Antiques,* November 1992: 726–35.

———. *Grez Days: Robert Vonnoh in France.* New York: Berry-Hill Galleries, 1987.

Hills, Patricia. *Eastman Johnson.* New York: Clarkson A. Potter, 1972.

Hirshler, Erica. "Lilian Westcott Hale (1880–1963): A Woman Painter of the Boston School." Ph.D. diss., Boston University, 1992.

Historical Society of Talbot County. *The Art of Gardening: Maryland Landscapes and the American Garden Aesthetic 1750–1930.* Easton: Maryland Historical Society, 1985.

Hochman, Paul. "Impressions of a House." *HG,* November 1992: 94–98.

Hollingsworth, Buckner. *Her Garden Was Her Delight.* New York: Macmillan and Co., 1962.

Hoppin, Martha J. *The Emmets.* Pittsfield, Mass.: Berkshire Museum, 1982.

Howard, Leland G. *Otto Stark 1859–1926.* Indianapolis:

Indianapolis Museum of Art, 1977.

Howe, Margery Burnham. *Deerfield Embroidery.* New York: Scribner's, 1976.

Howe, Rose H. *Elizabeth Bishop Perkins of York.* Brunswick, Maine: Harpswell Press, 1979.

Huntington, David C. *The Quest for Unity: American Art between World's Fairs 1876–1893.* Detroit: Detroit Institute of Arts, 1983.

Jackson, John Brinckerhoff. *American Space: The Centennial Years 1865–1876.* New York: W. W. Norton and Co., 1972.

Jacobs, Katherine L. "Celia Thaxter and Her Island Garden." *Landscape* 24, no. 3 (1980): 12–17.

James, Edward J., ed. *Notable American Women 1607–1950.* 3 vols. Cambridge, Mass.: Harvard University Press, 1971.

Johnston, Norman J. "A Far Western Arts and Crafts Village." *Journal of the Society of Architectural Historians* 35 (March 1976): 51–54.

Jones, Arthur F., and Bruce Weber. *The Kentucky Painter from the Frontier Era to the Great War.* Lexington: University of Kentucky Art Museum, 1981.

Jordan, Terry G. *German Seed in Texas Soil: Immigrant Farmers in Nineteenth Century Texas.* Austin: University of Texas Press, 1966.

Kaplan, Wendy. *"The Art That Is Life": The Arts and Crafts Movement in America 1875–1920.* Boston: Museum of Fine Arts, 1987.

Kardon, Janet, ed. *The Ideal Home 1900–1920.* New York: American Crafts Museum, 1993.

Kelly, Mary. *Private Woman, Public Stage: Literary Domesticity in Nineteenth Century America.* New York: Oxford University Press, 1984.

Kolodney, Annette. *The Lands before Her: Fantasy and Experience of the American Frontier.* Chapel Hill: University of North Carolina Press, 1984.

Leach, William. *True Love and Perfect Union: The Feminist Reform of Sex and Society.* New York: Basic Books, 1980.

Leighton, Ann. *American Gardens in the Eighteenth Century: "For Use or for Delight."* Boston: Houghton, Mifflin, 1976.

———. *American Gardens of the Nineteenth Century: "For Comfort and Affluence."* Amherst: University of Massachusetts Press, 1987.

———. *Early American Gardens: "For Meate or Medicine."* Boston: Houghton, Mifflin, 1970.

Lesko, Diane. *Gari Melchers.* Saint Petersburg, Fla.: Museum of Fine Arts of Saint Petersburg, 1990.

Lewis, Albert Addison. *Boxwood Gardens Old and New.* Richmond: William Byrd Press, 1924.

Lockwood, Alice B., ed. *Gardens of Colony and State.* 2 vols. New York: Charles Scribner's Sons for the Garden Club of America, 1931.

Ludwig, Cory L. *The Arts and Crafts Movement in New York State 1890–1920.* Hamilton, N.Y.: Gallery Associates of New York State, 1983.

MacAdam, Barbara. *Clark G. Voorhees 1871–1933.* Old Lyme, Conn.: Lyme Historical Society, 1981.

Macbeth Gallery. *Memorial Exhibition: Paintings of the Late Ruger Donoho.* New York, 1916.

McCausland, Elizabeth. *The Life and Work of Edward L. Henry 1841–1919.* Albany: State University of New York, 1949.

McClaugherty, Martha Crabill. "Household Art: Creating the Artistic Home 1863–93." *Winterthur Portfolio* 18 (Spring 1983): 1–26.

McCormick, Kathleen. "Spencer's Gifts." *Historic Preservation*, January–February 1994: 66–69, 92, 94.

Macht, Carol, et al. *The Ladies, God Bless 'Em: The Women's Art Movement in Cincinnati in the Nineteenth Century.* Cincinnati: Cincinnati Art Museum, 1976.

MacPhail, Elizabeth. *Kate Sessions, Pioneer Horticulturist.* San Diego, Calif.: San Diego Historical Society, 1976.

Marling, Karal Ann. *George Washington Slept Here: Colonial Revivals and American Culture 1876–1986.* Cambridge, Mass.: Harvard University Press, 1988.

———. *Woodstock: An American Art Colony 1902–1977.* Poughkeepsie, N.Y.: Vassar College Art Gallery, 1977.

Martin, Jennifer. "Portraits of Flowers: The Out-of-Door Still-Life Paintings of Maria Oakey Dewing." *American Art Review* 4 (December 1977): 48–55, 114–18.

Martin, Laura. *Grandma's Garden.* Marietta, Ga.: Long Street Press, 1990.

Martin, Peter. *The Pleasure Gardens of Virginia from Jamestown to Jefferson.* Princeton, N.J.: Princeton University Press, 1991.

Matthiessen, Francis Otto. *Sarah Orne Jewett.* Boston: Houghton, Mifflin, 1929.

Moeller, Madelyn. *Nineteenth Century Women Photographers: A New Dimension in Leisure.* Norwalk, Conn.: Lockwood-Matthews Mansion Museum, 1992.

Moore, Charles W., William J. Mitchell, and William Turnbull. *The Politics of Gardens.* Cambridge, Mass.: Harvard University Press, 1988.

Morgan, Keith N. "Charles A. Platt's Houses and Gardens in Cornish, New Hampshire." *Antiques*, July 1982: 117–29.

Mulrooney, Margaret M. *A Legacy of Coal: The Coal Company Towns of Southwestern Pennsylvania.* Washington, D.C.: U.S. Department of the Interior, 1989.

Myrick, David F. *Montecito and Santa Barbara: From Farms to Estates.* Glendale, Calif.: Trans Anglo Books, 1987.

Nagel, Gwen L. "Sarah Orne Jewett's New England Gardens."

Colby Library Quarterly 22 (March 1986): 43–62.

Nevins, Deborah. "Poet's Garden, Painter's Eye." *House and Garden* 156 (August 1964): 92–96, 154, 156.

———. "The Triumph of Flora: Women and the American Landscape, 1890–1935." *Antiques*, April 1965: 904–22.

Newton, Norman J. *Design in the Land: The Development of Landscape Architecture*. Cambridge, Mass.: Harvard University Press/Belknap Press, 1971.

Nichols, Rose Standish. "A Hilltop Garden in New Hampshire." *The House Beautiful* 55 (March 1924): 237–40.

Noble, William. "Northcote: An Artist's New Hampshire Garden." *Journal of the New England Garden History Society*, Fall 1992: 1–9.

Nutting, Wallace. *Wallace Nutting's Biography*. Framingham, Mass.: Old America Company, 1936.

Odell, Ruth. *Helen Hunt Jackson*. New York: D. Appleton and Co., 1939.

Padilla, Victoria. *Southern California Gardens: An Illustrated History*. Berkeley: University of California Press, 1961.

Parrish, Maxfield. *Stephen Parrish (1846–1938)*. Boston: Vose Galleries, 1982.

Peat, Wilbur D. *Pioneer Painters of Indiana*. Indianapolis: Art Association of Indianapolis, 1954.

Peters, Lisa N. "Twachtman's Greenwich Garden." In *In the Sunlight: The Floral and Figurative Art of J. H. Twachtman*. New York: Spanierman Gallery, 1989.

Phillips, Sandra S. *Charmed Places: Hudson River Artists and Their Houses, Studios, and Vistas*. New York: Harry N. Abrams, 1988.

Pisano, Ronald. *Long Island Landscape Painting*. Boston: Little, Brown and Co., 1985.

———. *Ruger Donoho (1857–1916), a Retrospective Exhibition*. New York: Hirschl and Adler Galleries, 1977.

Reid, Rosalie. "Historian Seeks Marker for Atlanta." *The Stockton Record*, July 27, 1966.

Rhoads, William B. *The Colonial Revival*. New York: Garland, 1977.

Romines, Ann. *The Home Plot: Women, Writing and the Domestic Ritual*. Amherst: University of Massachusetts Press, 1992.

Rosenberg, Rosalind. *Beyond Separate Spheres: Intellectual Roots of Modern Feminism*. New Haven: Yale University Press, 1982.

Rothman, Sheila M. *Woman's Proper Place: A History of Changing Ideas and Practices, 1870 to the Present*. New York: Basic Books, 1978.

Sale, Edith. *Historic Gardens of Virginia*. 1923. Reprint, Richmond: William Byrd Press, 1930.

Sandweiss, Martha A., ed. *Photography in Nineteenth Century America*. New York: Harry N. Abrams, 1991.

Scully, Vincent. *The Shingle Style and the Stick Style*. New Haven: Yale University Press, 1955.

Sears, John F. *Sacred Places: American Tourist Attractions in the Nineteenth Century*. New York: Oxford University Press, 1989.

Seeton, B. "Gardening Books for the Commuter's Wife." *Landscape* 28, no. 2 (1985): 41–47.

Severns, Martha R. *Alice Ravenel Huger Smith*. Charleston, S.C.: Carolina Art Association, 1993.

Shaffer, E. T. H. *Carolina Gardens*. Chapel Hill: University of North Carolina Press, 1932.

Sherman, Sarah Way. *Sarah Orne Jewett, an American Persephone*. Hanover, N.H.: University Press of New England, 1989.

Slocum, Grace. "Old Lyme." *American Magazine of Art* 15 (December 1924): 635–42.

Slosson, Elvenia, ed. *Pioneer American Gardening*. New York: Howard McCann, 1951.

Smith, Mary Ann. *Gustav Stickley: The Craftsman*. Syracuse, N.Y.: Syracuse University Press, 1983.

Smith-Rosenberg, Carroll. *Disorderly Conduct: Visions of Gender in Victorian America*. New York: Oxford University Press, 1968.

Starr, Kevin. *Americans and the California Dream*. New York: Oxford University Press, 1973.

Steele, Selma, Theodore L. Steele, and Wilbur D. Peat. *House of the Singing Winds: The Life and Work of T. C. Steele*. Indianapolis: Indianapolis Historical Society, 1966.

Stein, Roger B. *John Ruskin and Aesthetic Thought in America, 1840–1900*. Cambridge, Mass.: Harvard University Press, 1967.

Stern, Madeleine. *We the Women*. New York: Shulte, 1963.

Stevenson, Shanna. "Daniel Bigelow." *Columbia*, Winter 1993–94: 31–34.

Stilgoe, John R. *Borderland: Origins of the American Suburb, 1820–1939*. New Haven: Yale University Press, 1988.

Stillenger, Elizabeth. *The Antiquers*. New York: Alfred A. Knopf, 1980.

Stokes, Olivia Phelps. *Letters and Memoirs of Susan and Anna Warner*. New York: G. P. Putnam's Sons, 1925.

Surles, Flora Bella. *Anne King Gregorie*. Columbia, S.C.: R. L. Bryson Co., 1968.

Tetlow, Katy, and Ann Bienstock. *The Flowers of Julia Dillon*. Ulster County Historical Society, 1987.

Thaxter, Celia, et al. *The Heavenly Guest, with other Unpublished Writing*. Edited by Oscar Laighton. Andover, Mass.: Smith and Coutts, 1935.

Thaxter, Rosamond. *Sandpiper: The Life and Letters of Celia Thaxter.* Francestown, N.H.: M. Jones Co., 1963.

Thomas, David Hurst. "Harvesting Ramona's Garden: Life in California's Mythical Mission Past." In *Columbian Consequences*, edited by David Hurst Thomas. Washington, D.C.: Smithsonian Institution Press, 1991.

Thomas, Mrs. Elizabeth Patterson. *Old Kentucky Homes and Gardens.* Louisville: Standard Printing Co., 1939.

Thornton, Sally Bullard. *Daring to Dream: The Life of Hazel Wood Waterman.* San Diego, Calif.: San Diego Historical Society, 1987.

Thornton, Tamara Plathins. *Cultivating Gentlemen: The Meaning of Country Life among the Boston Elite 1785–1860.* New Haven: Yale University Press, 1990.

Tice, Patricia. *Gardening in America 1830–1910.* Rochester, N.Y.: Margaret Strong Museum, 1984.

Totemeier, Carl. "The American Botanical Tradition." *New York Times*, March 11, 1990.

Trapp, Kenneth R. *The Arts and Crafts Movement in California: Living the Good Life.* New York: Abbeville Press, 1993.

———, ed. *Celebrate Cincinnati Art.* Cincinnati: Cincinnati Art Museum, 1982.

Trenton, Patricia Jean. "The Evolution of Landscape Painting in Colorado: 1820–1900." Ph.D. diss., University of California, Los Angeles, 1980.

Trenton, Patricia Jean, and William Gerdts. *California Light 1900–30.* Laguna Beach, Calif.: Laguna Art Museum, 1990.

Turner, Arlin. *George Washington Cable.* Baton Rouge, La.: State University Press, 1966.

Turner, Suzanne McNeil. "The Skipwiths of Prestwould Plantation." *Virginia Cavalcade* 10 (Summer 1960): 42–47.

Van Ravenswaay, Charles. *A Nineteenth Century Garden.* New York: Main Street Press, 1977.

Van Wyke, Millie. *The Town of South Denver.* Boulder, Colo.: Pruett Publishing Co., 1991.

Vianus, Martha. *A Widening Sphere: Changing Roles of Victorian Women.* Bloomington: University of Indiana Press, 1977.

Vogel, Margaret. *The Paintings of Hugh Henry Breckenridge (1870–1937).* Dallas, Tex.: Valley House Gallery, 1967.

Walker, John Alan. *Benjamin Chambers Brown (1865–1942): A Chronological and Descriptive Bibliography.* Big Pine, Calif.: John Alan Walker, 1989.

Weber, Carl J., ed. *Letters of Sarah Orne Jewett Now in the Colby College Library.* Waterville, Maine: Colby College Press, 1947.

Weber, David J. *The Spanish Frontier in North America.* New Haven: Yale University Press, 1992.

Weidner, Ruth Irwin. *George Cochran Lambdin (1830–1896).* Chadds Ford, Pa.: Brandywine River Museum, 1986.

Weinberg, H. Barbara, Doreen Bolger, and David Park Curry. *American Impressionism and Realism: The Painting of Modern Life, 1885–1915.* New York: Metropolitan Museum of Art, 1994.

Weiss, Peg, ed. *Adelaide Alsop Robineau: Glory in Porcelain.* Syracuse, N.Y.: Syracuse University Press, 1981.

Weitzer, Karen G. *California's Mission Revival.* Los Angeles: Hennessy and Ingalls, 1984.

Welch, William C. *Antique Roses for the South.* Dallas, Tex.: Taylor Publishing Co., 1990.

Westmacott, Richard. *African-American Gardens in the Rural South.* Knoxville: University of Tennessee Press, 1992.

Westphal, Ruth Lilly. *Plein Air Painters of California: The Southland.* Irvine, Calif.: Westphal Publishing, 1982.

Wheeler, Candace. *The Development of Embroidery in America.* New York: Harper and Brothers, 1921.

———. *Yesterdays in a Busy Life.* New York: Harper and Brothers, 1918.

White, Jane Barber. "Restoration of a Poet's Garden." *American Horticulturist*, October 1987: 26–31.

Whitmer, Carolyn. *Memories of Grandmother's Garden.* Pensacola, Fla.: Lost Bay Press, 1991.

Whittredge, Thomas Worthington. *The Autobiography of Worthington Whittredge 1820–1910.* Edited by John I. H. Baur. Brooklyn: Brooklyn Museum, 1942.

Williams, Dorothy Hunt. *Historic Virginia Gardens: Preservations of the Garden Club of Virginia.* Charlottesville: University Press of Virginia, 1975.

Williams, George. "A Painter of Colorful Gardens." *International Studio* 76 (January 1923): 304–9.

Williams, Susan Reynolds. "In the Garden of New England: Alice Morse Earle and the History of Domestic Life." Ph.D. diss., University of Delaware, 1992.

Wilson, Richard Guy, et al. *The American Renaissance 1876–1917.* Brooklyn: Brooklyn Museum, 1979.

Wolfe, Judith. "Childe Hassam in East Hampton." In *Childe Hassam 1859–1935.* East Hampton, N.Y.: Guild Hall Museum, 1981.

Wolff, Cynthia Griffin. *Emily Dickinson.* Reading, Pa.: Addison-Wesley Co., 1988.

Wolschke-Bulmahn, Joachim. "From the War Garden to the Victory Garden: Political Aspects of Garden Culture in the United States during World War I." *Landscape Journal* 11 (Spring 1992): 51–57.

Wright, Mabel Osgood. *My New York.* New York: Macmillan and Co., 1926.

INDEX

Pages in *italics* refer to captions and illustrations.

Aaron, Leona Jones, 176; *177*
Adams, J. Otis, 188; *195*
   The Cottage Garden, 186
Adams, John, 14
Adams, William Howard, 8
Aesthetic Movement, 32–33, 40, 118
Ageratum, 99
Aiken (South Carolina), 169, 171, 173; *172*
Albee, Helen R., 140–41; *141*
Aldrich, Thomas Bailey, 43–45, 51; *44*
Allen, Frances and Mary, 88–90; *87, 91*
Almond, Flowering, 96, 175, 181
Althea, 14, 153, 176, 194
Amaryllis, 176
Ambrosia, 55, 184
Amherst (Massachusetts), 19, 23, 205
Anemone, 14, 95
Anshutz, Thomas, 165
Antiques, 49–50, 77, 160, 161
Apple, 40, 197; *37, 60, 139*
Appledore Island, 111–19, 123; *110, 112–17*
Arborvitae hedge, 106
Arbutus, 21
Arkansas, garden in, 185–86
Arkville (New York), 133–34; *133*
Artemisia, 119, 184
Arts and Crafts Movement, 8, 125–41, 146, 200, 203
Aster, 14, 21, 25, 56, 74, 107, 119, 138, 183, 210
Auricula, 67
Austin, Mary, 179–80, 211
Azalea, 74, 132

Bachelor's buttons, 61, 194
Bagley (Pennsylvania), *144*
Bailey, Liberty Hyde, 140
Baker, C. Alice, 88
Banana shrub, 176, 177

Bancroft, George, 194
Bancroft, Herbert Howe, 208
Bangor (Maine), *33*
Barberry, 153
Barnard, Charles, 28
Bartram, John, 82
Bauman, Gustave, 190
   Grandma Battin's Cottage, 193
Beale, Jessie Tarbox, *52–53*
Beardsley, Hezekiah, *10*
Beaux Arts Village (Washington), 200–201; *200–201*
Beckwith, James Carroll, *Onteora Landscape, 121*
Beecher, Catherine, 24
Beecher, Henry Ward, 43
Bellflowers, 61; *129*
Bennett, Ida, 151
Bethlehem (New Hampshire), 140; *141*
Bethlehem (Pennsylvania), 122
Betts, Anna Whelan, *171*
Bierstadt, Albert, 191–92
Bigelow, Daniel R., 199–200
Black-eyed Susan, 138
Blair, John, 16; *20*
Blanchan, Neltje (pseudonym), 156–57
Blaney, Dwight, 74, 160; *75*
Bleeding-heart, 215*n2*
Blomfield, Reginald, 165
Bloodroot, 14, 122
Bluebonnet, 195
Bolton, Sarah K., 126
Borage, 211
Boughton, George Henry, 49
Bouncing-betty, 143
Boyden, Frank, *87*
Boyden, Jane Henderson, 174
Boyden, May Shober, 175
Boylston, Sarah, 168
Brader, A. F., *Property of Andrew Crim, 178*
Bradford, William, on gardens, 11

Breck, John Leslie, 94, 160
   Garden, Ironbound Island, Maine, 74; 75
   In Monet's Garden, 92
Breckenridge, Hugh Henry, 165
   The Flower Garden, 166–67
   White Phlox, 166
"Breezy Meadows" (Massachusetts), 65; *3, 64*
Bremer, Anne Millay, *An Old Fashioned Garden, 2*
Bridal wreath, 175
Bridges, Fidelia, 34–36, 40; *36, 37, 39*
   Daisy, Larkspur, and Nasturtium, 34
Brooklyn (New York), 16, 80; *20*
Brown, Benjamin C., 210
   The Joyous Garden, 207
Brown, J. Appleton, 118
   Old Fashioned Garden, 115
   Poppies in a Garden, 113
Brown County (Indiana), 188–90; *186–87, 193–95*
Browne, Matilda, *In Vorhees' Garden, 7*
Bryant, William Cullen, 18, 43, 122; *19*
Buell, Elsie Whitton, 202; *204*
Bungalows, 209–10
"Bungle House" (New York), *139*
Burnham, Daniel, 66
Buttercup, 181
Byers, Elizabeth, 192; *188*
Byrdcliffe Colony (New York), 134–35

Cable, George Washington, 146–48
Cactus, 211
Calendula, 211
California, gardens in, 17, 134, 192, 201–12; *20, 196, 202–7, 209, 213*
Calycanthus, 14, 184
Cambridge (Massachusetts), 19; *22*
Camden (South Carolina), 169
Camellia, 175, 176

Campanula, 107
Camulos (California), 207, 208
Canaan (Connecticut), 34, 36, 40; *37*
Candytuft, 14, 139, 163
Canna, *185*
Canterbury bell, 21, 55, 67, 83, 93, 184; *79*
Cardinal flower, 153
Carlinville (Illinois), 179–80
Carmel (California), 211; *198*
Carnation, 163, 207, 208, 211
    Clove, 67
Carnegie, Andrew, 146
Catskill (New York), 17, 18; *18*
Cazenovia (New York), 82
Cedar Mere (Long Island), *19*
"Cedars, the" (Louisiana), 176
Celandine, 14
Chadwick, William, *On the Porch, 98–99*
Champion-McAlpine house (Georgia), 176
Champney, Elizabeth Williams, 48, 90
Champney, James Wells, 90
    Poppies and Hollyhocks, 89
Charleston (South Carolina), 169, 173; *170–71*
Chase, William Merritt, 95, 120, 173; *100, 198*
Chicago (Illinois), 181; *182–83*
Childs, Margaret, *87*
China, painting of, 119, 127, 129, 130
Chrysanthemum, 153, 166, 175, 211
Church, Ella Rodman, 32, 119
Church, Frederic Edwin, 43; *22*
Cincinnati (Ohio), 127–29; *126, 127*
Clayton, Virginia Tuttle, 6
Claytonia, 14
Clematis, 63, 67, 119, 153, 165, 210; *71, 107*
"Clover Bend" (Arkansas), 185–86
Cobaea scandens, 119, 184
Cockscomb, 194
Cole, Thomas, 17–18, 43; *18–19, 22*
Coleman, Emma Louise, 88
Colman, Samuel, 120
Colonial gardens, 11–14, 41, 59–60, 63–64, 74, 78, 138, 164, 212; *13, 15*
Colonial kitchen, reconstructed, 48
Colonial Revival, 77–83, 88, 105, 205

Colorado, gardens in, 191–92; *189*
Colorado Springs (Colorado), 192, 219*n11*; *189*
Columbia (South Carolina), 168, 171–73; *172*
Columbine, 14, 67, 107, 153, 184
Condict, Anna H., 148
Coneflower, *48–49*
Connecticut, gardens in, 25, 34, 40, 74, 82, 96–99, 154–60; *7, 15, 25, 37, 70–71, 98–100, 156*
Constitution Island (New York), 28; *28*
Cook, Clarence, 32
Coolidge, Baldwin, *16*
Cooper, James Fenimore, 18
Coralbell, 166
Coreopsis, 139, 163, 176
Cornflower, 30, 107, 139, 176
Cornish (New Hampshire), 101–8; *106–9*
Coronel, Don Antonio, 206–7
Cottage gardens, 16, 17, 83, 107, 111–19, 122–23, 134, 137, 166, 177; *85, 110, 111, 113–17, 186*
    in France, 93–95, 173; *92, 94*
    manual for, 140–41
    in Midwest, 180, 181, 187–88, 190; *193, 194*
    in South, 177
    in suburbs, 148–61; *149, 150, 152–53, 155–56, 158–59, 161*
    in West, 192, 200–203, 210–11; *189, 200–202*
    for workers, 143–48, 175; *144*
Cowslip, 163
Cozzens, Frederick S., 43
Craftsman homes and gardens, 136–41
Cragsmoor (New York), 50, 132–33; *52, 53, 57, 124, 135*
Crane, Walter, 120
Crawford, Allen, 185
Crocus, 63, 106
Cross vine, 195
Cucumber, wild, 118
Curran, Charles Courtney, 132
    A Corner of Grandmother's Garden, 132; *129*
    The Lanterns, 124
Currant, 165
    Flowering, 181

Cutting, Mrs., *16*
Cypress, Monterey, 207

Daffodil, 14, 55, 61, 200
Dahlia, 61, 99, 105, 148
Daisy, 132, 134, 165, 166; *34*
    Shasta, 138
Dana, Olive E., 111
Dandelion, 139
Datura, 183
Day lily, 14, 61, 67, 166
Decorative Arts Movement, 119–20
Dedham (Massachusetts), *158*, 160–61
Deerfield (Massachusetts), 88–90; *87, 89, 91*
de Forest, Lockwood, 120
Deland, Margaret, 59, 71, 185
Delaware, garden in, *130–31*
Delphinium, 83, 133, 138, 154, 161, 181
del Valle, Doña Isabel, 207
del Valle, Don Ygnacio, 207
Denver (Colorado), 192
Deutzia, 176
Dewing, Maria Oakey, 101, 105
    Bed of Poppies, 108–9
    The Garden in May, 109
Dewing, Thomas Wilmer, 101, 105
Dexter, Almon, 140
de Zavala, Adina, 193–94
Dianthus, 138; *109*
Dicentra spectabilis, 61, 215*n2*
Dickinson, Emily, 19–24, 51, 205; *23*
Dickson, F. S., 140
Dillon, Julia McEntee, 41
    Artist's Home and Studio, 41
Dodecatheon, 14
Dogwood, 175
Donoho, Gaines Ruger, 95; *97, 103*
    Auratum Lilies, 104
Doubleday, Mrs. Frank, 156–57
Dougan, Ida Woodside, 184–85; *185*
Dougan, Kathleen, 184; *185*
Downing, Andrew Jackson, 15–16, 24; *20*
Du Bois, W. E. B., 167
Duncan, Frances, 105, 108, 163; *171*
Dunn, Harvey T., 191
Durand-Ruel, Paul, 94
Dusty miller, 67

Dutchman's-pipe, 118

Earle, Alice Morse, 77–81, 90; *79*
Earle, Ralph, *Houses Fronting New Milford Green*, *15*
Early American gardens, 157, 160
East Aurora (New York), 135–36; *139*
East Hampton (Long Island), 48–49, 95; *48, 49, 73, 97, 103, 104*
Eberle, John, *22*
Elder, Walter, 16
Ellwanger, George H., 60–61; *60*
Ely, Helena Rutherfurd, 148–54; *149*
Emerson, Ralph Waldo, 19–21, 51
Emmet, Lydia, 95
    Grandmother's Garden, *100–101*
Emmet, Rosina, 120
Essex Falls (New Jersey), 148
Eustis, Celestin, 169, 171
Eyebright, Daisy, 27–28

Fairchild, Benjamin F., 154
Fairfield (Connecticut), 154–60; *156*
Farrand, Beatrix Jones, 99
Fawcett, Edwin A., *79*
Fennel, 179, 184
Feverfew, 138
Field, Amanda, 192
Fields, James, 114
Fig, 175, 193, 211
Fishkill (New York), 82; *82*
Flannelbush, 212
Florida, gardens in, 192, 193
Forget-me-not, 93
Forsyth, William, 190
    Garden Party, *190*
    Our Yard, *190*
Fort Washington (Pennsylvania), 165, *166*
Foss, A. H., *180–81*
Fournier, Alexis Jean, 136
    Hollyhocks in the Garden, The Bungle House, *139*
Four-o'clock, 138, 163, 176
"Four Winds" (New York), 130; *128–29*
Foxglove, 21, 66, 88, 133, 148, 166, 179, 181, 184, 210, 211; *129*
Frackelton, Susan, 129

Framingham (Massachusetts), 90; *76*
Frankfort (Kentucky), 176; *174*
"Frary House" (Massachusetts), 88
Fraxinella, 14; *82, 156*
French, Alice, 185
Frick, H. C., Coke Company, 146; *144*
Frier, Charles, *22*
Frieseke, Frederick, 210
    Hollyhocks, *198–99*
Fuchsia, 67, 210
Fullerton, Edith, 151
Fumitory, 14

Gaillardia, 176, 211
Gallup, Avery, 192
Gallup, Charlotte, 192
Galveston (Texas), 193
Gardening contests, 145–48, 175; *144*
Gardening manuals
    colonial, 12; *13*
    post–Civil War, 24, 27–30, 32, 60–61, 138, 140–41, 147–51, 154, 156–57, 164, 213
    pre–Civil War, 14–16, 27, 138
Gates, Howard, *189*
Gates Mills (Ohio), *180*
Gentian, 21
Georgia, gardens in, 176
Geranium, 30, 67, 147, 187, 194, 207, 208, 210, 211
Gerdts, William H., 6
Germantown (Pennsylvania), 40–41, 165; *38*
Gill, Eric, 212
Gill, Irving, 210
Gill, Mariquita, 95
Gillyflower, 9, 21, 23, 25, 163, 207
Gilman, Charlotte Perkins, 56
Giverny (France), 94, 95, 161, 173, 210; *92*
Gladiolus, 29, 132
Going, Thomas Buxton, 197
Goldenrod, 74, 134, 138; *53*
Grant, Anne, 12
Graves, Abbott Fuller, 68–74
    Grandmother's Doorway, *68–69*
    In a Kennebunkport Garden, 70; *69*
Gray, Asa, 140
Greacen, Edmund, *The Old Garden*, *98*

Greatorex, Eliza Pratt, 49–50, 169, 192
Green, Elizabeth Shippen, 165
Greenaway, Kate, 165
Greene, Henry Mather, 210
Greenfield (Massachusetts), *150*
Green Hills (New Hampshire), 105; *109*
Greenville (South Carolina), 175
Greenwich (Connecticut), 74, 154; *70–71*
Gregorie, Anne Porcher, 169
"Grey Gardens" (Long Island), 165
Grez-sur-Loing (France), 95, 96; *94*
Grimes, Frances, 105
Griswold, Florence, 96; *98–99*
Griswold, Mac, 6

Hale, Lilian Westcott, 160–61; *158*
Hale, Philip Leslie, 160–61
    The Crimson Rambler, *155*
    The Red Barn, *142*
    Wisteria, *158*
Hale, Susan, 161
Hamilton, Edward, 95
Hamilton, Hamilton, *Girl with Hollyhocks*, *26*
Hamilton, William, 14
"Hamilton House" (Maine), 83, 86; *50–51, 85–87*
"Hampton-Preston" (South Carolina), 168, 173
Handy, Jeremiah, *The Artist's Rose Garden*, 33; *33*
Harrison, Birge, 169
Hartford (Connecticut), 44; *25*
Hassam, Childe, 74, 99, 118
    Celia Thaxter's Garden, Appledore, Isle of Shoals, *116–17*
    The Garden in Its Glory, *116*
    In the Garden, *110*
    July Night, 95; *97*
    Old House and Garden, East Hampton, *73*
    A Room of Flowers, 118; *112*
Hawthorne, Hildegard, 83, 169
Hayes, John Russel, 163
Hayne, William Alston, 202
Hays, Helen Ashe, 164, 168
Heartsease, 9, 21, 67; *23*
Hecla (Pennsylvania), *144*

Helianthus, 107
Heliotrope, 29, 67, 83, 93, 163, 210, 211
Hemenway, H. D., 148
Hemlock, 23, 107
Henderson, Hazel W., 108
Henderson, Lewelling, 197
Henderson, Sarah Alexander, 174
Henry, Edward Lamson, 49–50; *52–53*
   Garden at Cragsmoor, 53
   News of the War of 1812, 50; *57*
Hepatica, 14, 138
"Hermitage" (Indiana), 188; *195*
"Hermitage, The" (Tennessee), 175–76
Herter, Alfred and Adele, 95; *103*
Hewett, Emma, 56
Hibiscus, 14, 185
Higginson, Thomas Wentworth, 21, 51, 54
Hill, Alice Stewart, 192
Hill, Anna Gilman, 165
Hill, John Henry, *Sunnyside with Picknickers, 58*
Hingham (Massachusetts), 62–63; *63*
Holly, 177
Hollyhock, 14, 46, 54, 56, 61, 63, 66, 83, 107, 108, 132–34, 138, 148, 154, 161, 163, 166, 173, 176, 180, 181, 184, 193, 197, 210, 212; *26, 34–35, 37, 47–49, 84–85, 89, 116–17, 194, 195, 198–99*
"Hollyhocking," 74
Homer, Winslow, 33, 54
   In the Garden, 31
Honeysuckle, 14, 24, 54, 55, 56, 59, 61, 63, 67, 71, 119, 175, 182, 184, 195; *71*
Hooked rugs, 140
Hooper, Charles Edward, 164
Hoosier Group, 190, 219*n7; 190*
Horsford, Cornelia, *85*
Hound's-tongue, 14
"House of the Singing Winds" (Indiana), 188–89; *186–87*
Howells, William Dean, 51
Hubbard, Elbert G., 135–36
Hudson River School, 18, 43, 120; *19*
Hughes, Elizabeth, 205
Hunt, William Morris, 88
Hyacinth, 14, 106, 138
   Grape, 61

Hydrangea, 185; *102, 185*

Illinois, gardens in, 179–81
Immigrants, 44–45, 143–46
Impatiens, 180
Impressionism, 93–99, 118, 187; *155*
Indiana, gardens in, 187–90; *186–87, 190, 193, 195*
Interplanting, 122–23
Iris, 14, 61, 74, 83, 105, 107, 122, 132, 134, 135, 139, 161, 165, 166, 173, 175, 181, 188, 194; *37*
   Fleur-de-lis, 67
   Japanese, 95
   Pseudacorus, 40
Ironbound Island (Maine), 74, 160; *75*
Irving, Washington, 62; *58*
Irvington (Indiana), 190; *190*
Italian gardens, 102–5
Ives, Alice E., 143

Jack-in-the-pulpit, 133
Jackson, Andrew, 175
Jackson, Helen Hunt, 192, 205–6, 219*n11*
Jacksonville (Illinois), 181
Jacob's ladder, 66
Japanese decorative arts, 32, 40, 129
Japanese lanterns, *97, 124, 190–91*
Jasmine, 14, 175, 176
   Cape, 177, 194; *177*
   Winter, 176
Jefferson, Thomas, 14
Jekyll, Gertrude, 8, 78, 123
Jessamine, Carolina, 169, 184
Jewett, Sarah Orne, 51–56, 83, 88, 118, 185, 215n.; *50, 51*
"John Cotton Smith House" (Connecticut), 82
Johnny-jump-up, 9, 181, 194
Johnson, Eastman, 46
   Catching the Bee, 46
   Hollyhocks, 46; *47*
   Old Mount Vernon, 44–45
Johnson, Louisa, 27–28
Johnson, Mrs. S. O., 27
Johnston, Frances Benjamin, 90
Jones, Frances Coates, 132

   At the Garden Gate, 130–31
   A Midsummer Garden, 130
Joseph's coat, 67
Josselyn, John, 11

Kansas, garden in, *180–81*
Keeler, Harriet L., *180*
Keith, Dora Wheeler, 120, 122
Kennebunkport (Maine), 68–71; *69*
Kentucky, gardens in, 176
King, Mrs. Francis, 212
Kingston (New York), 41; *41*
Kirby, Julia Duncan, 181
Kirkwood, Charlotte Matheny, 199
Kiss-me-quick, 180

Ladies' delight, 55, 63; *79*
Ladylocks, 179
Lady slipper, 88, 194
Laguna Beach (California), 211; *198*
La Jolla (California), 211
Lambdin, George Cochran, 40–41
   Among the Roses, 38
   Roses on a Wall, 41; *39*
Larkspur, 30, 40, 54–56, 59, 61, 66, 71, 93, 105, 107, 108, 148, 163, 165, 181, 194, 210; *34*
Laurel, Cherry, 177
Lavender, 184, 207
Lawson, William, 12; *13*
Lexington (Massachusetts), 148
Lilac, 14, 50, 93, 96, 165, 175, 176, 181, 188; *195*
   California, 212
Lily, 21, 54, 77, 95, 134, 135, 139, 141, 153, 175, 179, 208; *71, 84–85, 106*
   Auratum, *104*
   Blackberry, 14
   Japanese, 173
   Lemon, 122; *82*
   Madonna, 61, 107, 184
   Martagon, 14
   Plantain, 67
   St. Bruno's, 67
   Spider, 176
   Spotted, 83
   Tiger, 61, 67, 148, 183, 188
   Turk's-cap, 74; *72*

White, 14
Yellow, 105, 107
See also Day lily
Lily of the valley, 14, 61, 67
Limner, Beardsley, *Mrs. Hezekiah Beardsley,* 10
Live-forever, 181
Lobelia, 25, 122
London-pride, 54, 55
Longfellow, Henry Wadsworth, 18–19, 180; *22*
Long Island, gardens in, 48–49, 78, 95, 165; *16–17, 19, 48, 49, 73, 84–85, 97, 103, 104*
Longworth, John, 127
Longworth, Nicholas, 127
"Lorenzo" (New York), 82
Los Angeles (California), 206–7, 208, 211
Loudon, John Claudius, 15
Loudon, Mrs., 27
Louisiana, gardens in, 146, 176–77; *162*
Love-in-a-mist, 180
Low, Will, 46
Lowell, Amy, 93
Lowell, Elizabeth, *Judge A. Aiken's Garden, Greenfield, Massachusetts,* *150*
Lowther, Mrs. Hugh, 209
Lummis, Charles Fletcher, 208, 212; *213*
Lupine, 14, 211
Lychnis, 181
Lynchburg (Texas), 193–94
Lynchburg (Virginia), 165–67; *168*

McCall, Jane Byrd, 134
McFarland, J. Horace, 157
McLain, A. H., *180–81*
McLaughlin, Mary Louise, 127
McMahon, Bernard, 14–15, 164
Magnolia, 96, 194
"Magnolia Gardens" (South Carolina), 173
Maine, gardens in, 68–71, 74, 111–19, 140; *33, 50, 69, 75, 110, 112–17*
Mallow, 14
Malone, Blondell, 171–73; *172*
Maltese Cross, *48–49*

Marigold, 25, 107, 122, 143, 181, 197
Marin County (California), 201–2; *202*
Mariposa, 210
Marjoram, 179, 184
Maryland, garden in, 164–65
Massachusetts
    Columbian Exposition garden of, 67
    gardens in, 19, 46, 62–63, 65, 78, 80–82, 88–90, 146–48, 160–61; *3, 22, 47, 55, 63, 64, 76, 87, 89, 91, 115, 150, 158, 159, 161*
Matrimony vine, 180
Matunuck (Rhode Island), 161; *142*
Maybeck, Bernard, 210
"Meadowburn Farm" (New Jersey), 151–54; *149*
Meadowsweet, *48–49*
Mecklenburg County (Virginia), 14
Metcalf, Willard, *Purple, White, and Gold,* 96, 132; *100*
Metcalf (Massachusetts), *3*
Michigan, gardens in, 184
"Middleton Place" (South Carolina), 14, 169
Mignonette, 14, 21, 29, 56, 66, 105, 211
"Miles Brewton House" (South Carolina), 169; *170–71*
Miller, Ellen, 88
Miller, Wilhelm, 164
Millet, Francis David, 48
Minneapolis Craftshouse, 136
Minnesota, gardens in, 183–84
Mint, 179, 207
Minturn (Arkansas), 185
Mission Revival, 208–9; *205*
Mississippi, garden in, 176; *177*
Missouri, garden in, 184–85; *185*
Moccasin flower, 14
Mock orange, 14, 177
Moffat, Adelene, 146, 148
"Moffatt-Ladd House" (New Hampshire), 82
Monarda, 122
Monet, Claude, 93–94, 173; *92*
Moneywort, 181
Monkshood, 14, 61, 66
Montecito (California), 202, 211; *204*
"Monticello" (Virginia), 14

Moonflower, 138, 184
Moore, Charles Herbert, 18
    Thomas Cole's House, 18–19
Moran, Mary Nimmo, 48
Moran, Thomas, 48; *48, 49*
Morning glory, 21, 59, 90, 105, 180, 183, 193; *116*
    Mexican, 119
Morris, William, 120, 125, 135, 136
Morse, Frances Clary, 78; *79*
"Mount Gulian" (New York), 82; *82*
"Mount Vernon" (Virginia), 14, 46, 96; *44–45*
Mowbray, J. P., 64
Murdock, Mrs. William, 174
Murphy, Adah Smith, 133–34; *133*
Murphy, J. Francis, 133–34; *133*
Musk, 208
Myrtle, 177, 207
    Crepe, 175, 176

Nantucket Island, 46
Narcissus, 14, 63, 176
Nasturtium, 67, 119, 122–23, 138, 163, 211; *34–35, 48–49, 53, 116*
Native American plants, 17, 63, 66, 83, 107, 120–23, 133, 140, 153, 165, 190, 212; *195*
    in West, 192, 195, 211, 212; *195, 213*
Nemophila, 210, 211
Nesho (Missouri), 184–85; *185*
"Nestledown" (Long Island), 123
New Braunfels (Texas), 195
Newburyport (Massachusetts), 81–82, 216n18; *115*
New Hampshire, gardens in, 44–45, 82, 101–8, 140; *16, 44, 106–9*
New Hope (Pennsylvania), 165
New Iberia (Louisiana), *162*
New Jersey, gardens in, 46, 148, 151–54, 163; *42, 149*
New Milford (Connecticut), *15*
New Orleans (Louisiana), 146, 177
Newport (Rhode Island), 46, 194
Newton (Kansas), *180–81*
New York City, 49, 61
New York State
    Columbian Exposition garden of,

66–67
gardens in, 16–18, 28, 41, 50, 62, 78, 82, 96–99, 122–23, 130, 132–36, 138–39, 148; *18–19, 20, 28, 41, 52, 53, 57, 58, 60, 80–82, 102, 121, 124, 128–29, 133, 135, 139*
See also Long Island
Nichols, Maria Longworth, 127–29, 192; *126*
Nichols, Rose Standish, 102
Nicotiana, 138, 184, 185, 211; *185*
None-so-pretty, 88
"Nook Farm" (Connecticut), 25, 44; *25*
Northampton (Massachusetts), 146–48
North Carolina, gardens in, 173–75
"Northcote" (New Hampshire), 106–8; *106, 107*
Nutting, Wallace, 90, 216*n18*; *76*

"Oakland" (South Carolina), 169
Oakley, Violet, 165
Ohio, gardens in, 181–83; *126, 180*
"Olana" (New York), *22*
Old Lyme (Connecticut), 95–99; *7, 98–100*
Olmsted, Frederick Law, Jr., 66
Olympia (Washington), 199–200; *200–201*
Onteora (New York), 122–23; *121*
Orange, 193, 208
Orchis, fringed, 122
Oregon, gardens in, 199
Ornithogalum, 14
Osgood, Samuel, 154
Osgood, Susan, 160; *161*
"Osgood-Brockway House" (Massachusetts), 81–82
Oyster Bay (Long Island), 95

Paenoia, 96
Palmer, Pauline, 181
Palmer, William Jackson, 192
Pansy, 21, 83, 119, 153, 194, 210, 211; *23*
Parker, Lawton S., 181
Woman in a Garden, 182–83
Parker, Thomas, 175
Parrish, Maxfield, *106, 107*

Parrish, Stephen, 106–8; *106, 107*
Parsons, Samuel, Jr., 61, 65, 212
Pasadena (California), 209, 210; *196, 207*
Passionflower, 118, 173
Peck, Orrin, *The Blessing of the Flowers, Santa Barbara, 209*
Pennsylvania, gardens in, 14, 40–41, 82, 134, 163, 165; *34–35, 38*
"Penny Royal" (New York), 122–23
Peony, 21, 23, 24, 54, 56, 61, 74, 80, 93, 105, 107, 133, 153, 165, 166, 175, 181, 183–85; *82*
Chinese, *60*
Pequaket (New Hampshire), 140
Perennials, 80, 138, 154, 201; *22, 156*
Pergolas, 102, 138, 151, 166, 192; *103, 107*
Periodicals on gardening
post–Civil War, 62, 71, 82, 108, 148, 163–64, 183
pre–Civil War, 15–17
Periwinkle, 181
Perkins, Elizabeth, 83; *84–85*
Persac, Adam, *Shadows-on-the-Teche, New Iberia, Louisiana, 162*
Petunia, 25, 56, 67, 99, 147, 187
Philadelphia (Pennsylvania), 40, 82; *34–35*
Phlox, 14, 29, 40, 59, 61, 66, 74, 105, 107, 132, 133, 138, 143, 148, 165, 166, 176, 210; *37, 48–49, 70–71, 79, 84–85, 129, 166–67*
Drummond, 119, 183
"Phloxdale" (Pennsylvania), 165; *166*
Photography by women, 86–90, 134, 184; *152–53, 156, 185*
Pink, 14, 61, 107, 143, 183, 194, 197, 199; *79, 129*
Clove, 181
Country, 83
Grass, 181
Indian, 67
Mullen, 179
Pitman, Benn, 127, 129; *127*
Platt, Charles Adams, 105
Plum, 96, 193
Plumbago, 210
Pollock, Frank Lillie, 125
Polyanthus, 67

Pomegranate, 211
Poppy, 59, 61, 67, 71, 74, 94, 134, 143, 163, 165, 166, 184, 197, 208, 212; *75, 89, 113, 195*
California, 119, 138
Matilija, 212
Oriental, 107
Shirley, 105, 107, 119, 139; *109, 116*
Portsmouth (New Hampshire), 44–45, 82, 216*n18*; *44*
Portulaca, 81, 180
Potter, Bessie, 96; *102*
Pottery, 127–30, 192
Powers, Rose Mill, 179
Prang, Louis, and Company, 36
"Prestwould" (Virginia), 14
Price, William L., 134
Primrose, 21, 59, 67, 148
Evening, *79*
Prince's-feathers, 63
Pringle, Elizabeth, 168
Privet, 165, 177, 187
Pullman (Illinois), 145

Ramona, 205–6, 208–9, 211; *205*
Raphael, Joseph, *The Garden, 203*
Redbud, 195
Redfield, Edward, 165
Repton, Humphrey, 15
"Reveille" (Virginia), 167; *170–71*
Rexford, Eben E., 27
Rhode Island, gardens in, 46, 161, 194
Rhododendron, 153
Ribbon grass, 61, 181
Richards, William Trost, 35; *39*
A Summer Afternoon in a Garden in Philadelphia, 34–35
Richardson house (Georgia), 176
Richmond (Virginia), 167; *170–71*
Rion, Hannah, 138–40
Ritman, Louis, 181
Riverside (California), 210
Robbins, Mary Caroline, 62–63; *63*
Robineau, Adelaide Alsop, 130–32; *129*
Robineau, Elizabeth, *128–29*
Robinson, William, 8, 140, 164
Rochester (New York), 60–61; *60*
Rocket, 14, 61; *79*
Rockland Lake (New York), 96–99; *102*

Rogers, Fairman, 40
Rogers, Katherine, 200–201; *200–201*
Rookwood Pottery, 129–30, 192; *126*
Rose, 21, 24, 29, 30, 40–41, 55, 56,
        63–64, 106, 132, 134, 138, 141,
        153, 168, 174–77, 185, 188,
        193, 194, 199, 202, 203, 207,
        210, 211; *33, 38, 39, 70–71,
        80–81, 84–87, 177*
        American Pillar, 166
        'Baltimore Belle', 64
        Banksia, 176, 177, 194
        Blush, 181
        Bridal, 63
        Brier, 61
        Button, 143
        Cabbage, 14
        Cherokee, 177
        Cinnamon, 71, 176
        'Clara Barton', 96
        Climbing, 67, 169, 176, 209, 211;
        166–67
        Damask, 64, 96
        Dorothy Perkins, 139, 187
        Gloire de Dijon, 105
        'Lady Banks', 171, 173, 195
        'La France', 40
        Madame Plantier, 107
        Marbled, 14
        Moss, 181, 194
        Multiflora, 187
        Old, 61, 133, 166; *82*
        Rambler, 107, 139, 153, 165, 184,
        187, 194; *155*
        Seven Sisters, 165
        Shrub, 175; *109*
        Souvenir de la Malmaison, 105
        Tea, 40, 194, 195
        Yellow, 14, 161, 181, 192
"Rose-Dale" (Brooklyn, New York), *20*
Rosedale (Colorado), 192
"Rosedown" (Louisiana), 177
Rose-of-Sharon, 166, 184
Rose Valley (Pennsylvania), 134
Roycroft (New York), 135–36
Rudbeckia, 148
Rue, 179, 184, 207
Ruskin, John, 18, 35, 125, 134, 135

St. Augustine (Florida), 193
St. Francisville (Louisiana), 177
Saint-Gaudens, Augustus, 101, 102
Salem (Massachusetts), 160; *159, 161*
Salem (Oregon), 197
Salisbury (North Carolina), 173–75
Salvia, 99, 183
San Antonio (Texas), 193–94, 195
Sanborn, Kate, 65, 202; *3, 64*
San Diego (California), 208–10, 212;
        205
Sandson, T. C., *62*
San Francisco (California), 202, 208
San Joaquin County (California), 17,
        211; *20*
San Juan de Capistrano (California), 208
Santa Barbara (California), 134, 202,
        208, 210, 211; *209*
Santa Fe (New Mexico), 193
Saratoga (California), 209; *206*
Sargent, Charles Sprague, 67
Saunders, Charles Francis, 210–11
Savannah (Georgia), 176
Sawier, Paul, *Liberty Hall Garden, 174*
Scabious, Sweet, 14, 30
Scarlet runner, 180
Schuster, Donna, *Morning Sunshine, 198*
Schuyler, Montgomery, 210
Scotch broom, 175
Scott, Mary Mason, 176
Senna, wild, 14
Sessions, Kate O., 212
Share, Hortense, 183
Sharon (Connecticut), 82
Sheldon, George, 88
Shelter Island (Long Island), 78; *84–85*
Shelton, Louise, 151
Shurtleff, Arthur A., 81, 137
Sion Hill (Mississippi), 176; *177*
Skipwith, Lady Jean, 14, 212; *13*
Smith, Alice Ravenel Huger, 169; *171*
Smith, J. B., *The Residence and Property of
        Mr. John Blair, "Rose-Dale," 20*
Smith, Jessie Willcox, 165
Smyth, Ellison, 175
Snakeroot, 40
Snapdragon, 66, 143
Snowball, 175, 181
Snowberry bushes, 56
Snowdrop, 14, 61

Snow-pink, 61
Solms Braunfels, Prince Carl zu, 195
Solomon's seal, 14
Southampton (Long Island), 95, 165
South Berwick (Maine), 51, 83; *50,
        86–87*
South Carolina, gardens in, 14, 61,
        168–72; *170–72*
Southernwood, 88, 181, 207
Spencer, Anne, 165–67; *168*
Spiderwort, 14
Spirea, 175
Spreckels, John D., 208
Spring Hill (Tennessee), 175
Stark, Otto, 190
        Suzanne in the Garden, 182
Star-of-Bethlehem, 63, 122
Steele, Selma, 188–89; *186–87*
Steele, Theodore C., 187–88
        *Flower Garden at the Hermitage,
        Brookville, 195*
        Peony Garden, 186–87
Steele, Zulma, 135
Stephens, Anna Sophia, 43
Steves, Edward, 195
Stickley, Gustav, 136, 146, 210; *137*
Stock, 14, 107, 183, 210, 211; *79*
Stokesia, 107
Stowe, Harriet Beecher, 24–25, 27, 43,
        193; *25*
Summit (New Jersey), 46; *42*
Sumner, Charles, 210
Sunflower, 14, 61, 65, 67, 80, 134, 139,
        202; *53, 202*
Sussex County (New Jersey), 151–54;
        149
Sweet alyssum, 21, 29, 71, 83, 143, 211
Sweetbriar, 59
Sweet clover, 61
Sweet olive, 176
Sweet pea, 21, 25, 29, 61, 107, 119, 138,
        165, 176, 210
Sweet-rocket, 163
Sweet Sultan, 30
Sweet William, 14, 21, 59, 61, 67, 105,
        107, 148, 181, 184; *79*
"Sylvester Manor" (Long Island), 78;
        84–85
Syracuse (New York), 130, 136
Syringa, 181

Tabor, Grace, 164, 192
Tappen, Christopher, 41
Tarrytown (New York), 62; *58*
Tennessee, gardens in, 175
Texas, gardens in, 192, 193–95
Thanet, Octave (pseudonym), 185
Thaxter, Celia Laighton, 111–19, 122, 123, 140, 213; *110, 112–17*
Thomas, Edith, 77
Thomas, Mrs. Theodore, 140
Thompson, F. A., 175
Tiffany, Louis Comfort, 95, 120
Touch-me-not, 180
Tradescantia, 61
Trillium, 14, 88, 133
Tropaeolum cultivar 'Lucifer', 119
Troy (New York), 148
Trumpet creeper, 61
Tulip, 61, 63, 106, 139
Turnbull, Martha, 177
Turner, Helen, 132–33
    Morning, 135
Turner, Ross, 74, 118, 160
    Salem Garden, 159
Twachtman, John Henry, 74, 173
    The Cabbage Patch, 74; *72*
    On the Terrace, 70–71
Twain, Mark, 25
Tyson, Emily, 83; *50–51*

Valerian, 61, 154
Vallejo, Guadalupe, 208
Van Briggle, Artus, 192; *189*
"Van Cortlandt Manor" (New York), 78, 160; *80–81*
Van Rensselaer, Mariana Griswold, 65–66
Vaughn, Elizabeth Tyson (Elise Tyson Vaughn), 83, 86; *87*
Vawter, Will, 189–90
    Our Garden, Hollyhock Time, 194
"Veasy Plantation" (Georgia), 176
Vegetable gardens, 23, 28, 50, 137–38, 148, 151, 164, 211; *53*
    colonial, 11–12; *13*
    in Midwest, 180, 188
    in South, 169, 174, 176, 185; *162*
    of workers, 145–46, 175; *144*
Ver Beck, Mrs. H. R., 138–40

Verbena, 67, 119, 147, 187, 194, 207, 210, 211
Veronica, 25
Verplanck, Virginia, *82*
Viburnum, 185
Violet, 14, 122, 194, 210, 211
    Dogtooth, 14
    English, 63, 107
Virginia, gardens in, 14, 46, 165–67; *13, 44–45, 168*
Virginia creeper, 71, 153, 180; *48–49, 107*
Vonnoh, Robert, 96, 132; *102*
    Jardin de Paysanne, 95; *94*
Vorhees, Clark, 96, 100; *7*

Wagener, Ernst, 17; *20*
"Waldstein" (Connecticut), 154–60; *156*
Walker, Edna, 135
Waller, Benjamin, *13*
Wallflower, 14, 67
Warner, Anna Bartlett, 28–30, 32, 61, 212; *28*
Warner, Charles Dudley, 44, 140
Warner, Susan, 28–29
Warren, Andrew, *Long Island Homestead, Study from Nature, 16–17*
Washington, George, 14, 19, 46, 96
Washington State, gardens in, 199–201; *200–201*
Waterman, Hazel Wood, 208; *205*
Waugh, Frank, 67
Weir, Dorothy, 74; *71*
Welch, Thaddeus, 202
    A Cottage in the Marin County Hills, 202
Weller, Eleanor, 6
Westboro (Massachusetts), *55*
Weston (Massachusetts), 160
Wheaton (Illinois), 180–81
Wheeler, Candace Thurber, 118, 120–23, 125, 126, 213
White, Ann Elizabeth, 199–200
Whitehead, Ralph Radcliffe, 134–35
"White Pines" (New York), 134–35
Whiting, Margaret, 88
Whittredge, Worthington, 46, 192
    In the Garden, 42
Wickham, Grace, 132

Wild plants. *See* Native American plants
"Wildweed" (New York), 133–34; *133*
Wilkins, Mary E., 52, 56, 185; *55*
Willamette Valley (Oregon), 199
Williamsburg (Virginia), *13*
Willow, flowering, 195
Windham (New Hampshire), *16*
Windmills with water towers, 203
Wisconsin, gardens in, 184
Wise, Herbert C., 107–8
Wisteria, 61, 119, 166, 168, 169, 173, 175, 210; *158*
Women
    decorative arts by, 119–20, 125–32
    domestic confinement of, 56, 146, 148
    gardening costume for, 151
    gardening manuals for, 12, 24, 27–30, 138, 140–41, 154, 213
    in Jewett's fiction, 54
    not by nature weak, 27
    outdoor painter's costume for, *36*
    painted in gardens, 46, 132; *26, 47, 155, 182, 183, 186, 198–99*
    photography by, 86–90, 134, 184; *152–53, 156, 185*
    Stowe's manual for, 24
Worcester (Massachusetts), 78, 80; *79*
Wores, Theodore, 209
    The Artist's Home, Saratoga, California, 206
    Thomas Moran's House, East Hampton, Long Island, 48–49
Workers, cottage gardens for, 143–48, 175; *144*
World's Columbian Exposition (1893), 60, 66–67, 120, 209, 215*n15*
Wright, Mabel Osgood, 154–60; *22, 152, 153, 156*
Wyant, Alexander, 133

Yoch, Florence, 209
York (Maine), 83, 88; *84–85*
Yucca, 181, 184

Zinnia, 25, 67, 108, 194

Photograph Credits

The author and publisher wish to thank the individuals, galleries, and institutions for permitting the reproduction of works in their collections. Those credits not listed in the captions are provided below. All references are to page numbers.

H. V. Allison Galleries, New York: 130; Berry-Hill Galleries: 34, 97, 104, 124; Chicago Historical Society: 66; Christie's, New York: 139; Collection Craftsman Farms Foundation: 137; Denver Public Library, Western History Department: 188; Eckert Fine Art, Indianapolis: 182, 186 (both), 190, 194, 195; The Fairfield Historical Society, Connecticut: 152, 153; Henry Art Gallery, University of Washington, Seattle. Horace C. Henry Collection (Steven J. Yound, photo, 1984): 73; Courtesy Hirschl and Adler Galleries, New York: 35; Historic Hudson Valley, Tarrytown, New York: 80 (both), Gift in memory of Mrs. John D. Rockefeller, Jr., by her children, 58; Liberty Hall Historic Site, Frankfort, Kentucky: 174; R. H. Love Galleries, Chicago: 158, 166, 182; National Museum of American Art, Washington, D.C./Art Resource, New York: 109, 110, 116; National Parks Service, Weir Farm National Historic Site, Branchville, Connecticut: 71; New Britain Museum, Connecticut. Harriet Russel Stanley Fund (E. Irving Blomstrann, photo): 47; New York State Office of Parks, Recreation and Historic Preservation, Olana State Historic Site, Hudson, New York: 22; Patch/Work Voices Project, Penn State University, Uniontown, Pennsylvania: 144 (both); Photograph courtesy Gerald Peters Gallery, New York: 121; Pocumtuck Valley Memorial Association Library, Deerfield, Massachusetts: 87 (both), 91; Lyman V. Rutledge Isles of Shoals Collection, Portsmouth Public Library: 110; David

A. Schorsch Company, New York: 20 (both), 177; Spanierman Gallery, New York: 26, 69, 72; Skinner, Inc., Boston: 142; Smithsonian Institution, Archives of American Gardens, Garden Club of America Collections (Edward van Altena): 19, 171 (Joseph Hawkins) 103; Courtesy the Society for the Preservation of New England Antiquities, Boston: 16, 51, 63, 161, (N. L. Stebbins, photo): 55, 85; Sotheby's, New York: 100; South Caroliniana Library, Columbia: 172 (both); The Stowe-Day Foundation, Hartford, Connecticut: 25; Joseph Szaszfai: 10; Photographs © 1994 courtesy Terra Museum of American Art, Chicago: 92, 94, 166; Photographic Services, University of New Hampshire, Durham: 50, 180; Vose Galleries, Boston: 129; Wadsworth Atheneum, Hartford. The Dorothy Clark Archibald and Thomas L. Archibald Fund. The Ella Gallup Sumner and Mary Catlin Sumner Collection Fund. The Krieble Family Fund for American Art. The Gift of James Junius Goodwin and the Douglas Tracy Smith and Dorothy Porter Smith Fund: 15; Courtesy Richard York Gallery, New York: 39, 130.

The poem on page 23 from *The Complete Poems of Emily Dickinson,* edited by Thomas H. Johnson. Copyright 1929, 1935 by Martha Dickinson Bianchi; copyright © renewed 1957, 1963 by Mary L. Hampson, by permission Little, Brown and Company.